OXFORD POLITIC~~AL~~

Series editors: Will Kymlicka, David Miller and Alan Ryan

———

DELIBERATIVE DEMOCRACY
AND BEYOND

OXFORD POLITICAL THEORY

Oxford Political Theory presents the best new work in contemporary political theory. It is intended to be broad in scope, including original contributions to political philosophy, and also work in applied political theory. The series will contain works of outstanding quality with no restriction as to approach or subject matter.

DELIBERATIVE DEMOCRACY AND BEYOND

LIBERALS, CRITICS, CONTESTATIONS

JOHN S. DRYZEK

OXFORD
UNIVERSITY PRESS

OXFORD
UNIVERSITY PRESS

Great Clarendon Street, Oxford OX2 6DP

Oxford University Press is a department of the University of Oxford.
It furthers the University's objective of excellence in research, scholarship,
and education by publishing worldwide in

Oxford New York

Athens Auckland Bangkok Bogotá Buenos Aires Cape Town
Chennai Dar es Salaam Delhi Florence Hong Kong Istanbul Karachi
Kolkata Kuala Lumpur Madrid Melbourne Mexico City Mumbai Nairobi
Paris São Paulo Shanghai Singapore Taipei Tokyo Toronto Warsaw
with associated companies in Berlin Ibadan

Oxford is a registered trade mark of Oxford University Press
in the UK and in certain other countries

Published in the United States
by Oxford University Press Inc., New York

First published 2000
New as Paperback edition 2002

British Library Cataloguing in Publication Data
Data available

Library of Congress Cataloging in Publication Data
Data available
ISBN 0-19-829507-3
ISBN 0-19-925043-X (Pbk.)

1 3 5 7 9 10 8 6 4 2

Typeset by Hope Services (Abingdon) Ltd.
Printed in Great Britain
on acid-free paper by
Biddles Ltd., Guildford & King's Lynn

PREFACE

Around 1990 the theory of democracy took a definite deliberative turn. Prior to that turn, the democratic ideal was seen mainly in terms of aggregation of preferences or interests into collective decisions through devices such as voting and representation. Under deliberative democracy, the essence of democratic legitimacy should be sought instead in the ability of all individuals subject to a collective decision to engage in authentic deliberation about that decision. These individuals should accept the decision only if it could be justified to them in convincing terms.

In this book I try to determine what the theory of democracy should look like in the wake of the deliberative turn. The field of democratic theory is today both large and lively. I take a critical tour through the major contemporary theories of democracy, including those that are hostile to deliberation (for the deliberative turn did not sweep quite everyone before it). I begin and end as a proponent of deliberative democracy who nevertheless rejects some of the directions in which deliberative democracy has been taken. I believe that it is important to distinguish between two tendencies that are now generally mixed under the deliberative heading. The first has reached an easy accommodation with liberal and constitutional thinking. The second is more insistently critical of liberal constitutionalism and its surrounding political economy. Thus I take issue with those I consider dubious friends of the deliberative approach. In light of the distinctions I have made, I deal with critics of deliberative democracy, and consider some extensions made necessary by key features of today's world and made possible by this sort of emphasis on discourse and communication.

In 1990 I published a book called *Discursive Democracy* which turned out to be one of the early works in this area. Indeed, at the time I was unaware of the work being done by others on these issues, and I did not use the terms deliberation or deliberative democracy at all in that book (only a part of which is actually about democratic theory). I actually still prefer the term 'discursive democracy' to 'deliberative democracy', even though they now seem to be used interchangeably, and deliberative democracy more often. Yet discursive democracy is actually the better term for three reasons. First, deliberation can be a personal decision process, in which the individual mulls things over in his or her mind, not necessarily a collective social process at all. (As will be shown in Chapter 1, this causes substantial problems for those who take their deliberative bearings from John Rawls's political philosophy.) A discursive process, in contrast, is necessarily social and intersubjective. It has to involve communication, whereas deliberation does not. Second, deliberation has connotations of calm, reasoned, argument. This is unnecessarily constraining and renders the model vulnerable to those who point out that this sort of gentlemanly discussion is not a good paradigm for democracy. A discursive process connotes something much more expansive in the kinds of communication it allows, including unruly and contentious communication from the margins. Third, the term 'discourse' draws attention to two traditions of political theory that, though attaching different connotations to the term, are central when it comes to making sense of deliberation. To one school of thought, followers of Michel Foucault, a discourse is like a prison; it conditions the way people think. To another school of thought, influenced by Jürgen Habermas, discourse means precisely the opposite: it is pure freedom in the ability to raise and challenge arguments. The approach I take here emphasizes contestation across discourses in the public sphere as a key component of democracy, so discourses are not prisons. On the other hand, discourses in the Foucauldian sense do exist, so discourse in the Habermasian sense cannot wish them away.

The issues at stake here are not merely terminological, concerning the name to give a common approach. It is probably too late to establish a distinction *between* deliberative and discursive democracy, setting them up as alternatives—too many people have used these terms interchangeably (including myself on some occasions). Nor would such a distinction be productive, because many key tenets are shared. In this light, the best way to proceed is to treat deliberative democracy as the more inclusive category, with liberal constitutionalist deliberative democracy as one major strand. In Chapter 1 I will show that most theorists of deliberative democracy, including those who once took a more critical stance, have made their peace with liberal constitutionalism. I reserve the term discursive democracy for the other major strand, which is both more critical and more expansive in its orientation to the liberal state. In advocating discursive democracy, there is a sense in which I too am a critic of deliberative democracy—or at least of its liberal constitutionalist tendency—even though I subscribe to many of its tenets.

My previous book on democracy was *Democracy in Capitalist*

Times (1996). That book was concerned with the prospects for democratic innovation in a world of growing constraints imposed by the capitalist political economy. This present book operates in different terrain: that of democratic theory, rather than the real-world political economy. I do not think that any of the conclusions of the two books are inconsistent. However, this book moves beyond the previous one in developing a more sophisticated dynamic analysis of the relationship between the state and the public sphere or civil society. In addition, I now highlight discourses as sources of order, and so the contestation of discourses as central to democracy.

Three of these chapters are extensively revised versions of journal articles. Chapter 4 was originally published as 'Political Inclusion and the Dynamics of Democratization', *American Political Science Review*, 90 (1996): 475–87. Chapter 5 was originally published as 'Transnational Democracy', *Journal of Political Philosophy*, 7 (1999): 30–51. Chapter 6 was originally published as 'Political and Ecological Communication', *Environmental Politics*, 4 (1995): 13–30.

I have benefited from the opportunity to present parts of this project to the Northern Arizona University Department of Political Science, the School of Public and International Affairs at Virginia Polytechnic Institute and State University, the Conference on Environmental Justice at the University of Melbourne in 1997, the Political Theory Workshop at Nuffield College, the Centre for the Study of Environmental Change and Philosophy Department at the University of Lancaster, the Southwest Political Theory Network at Reading University, and the Department of Politics at Keele University. At these venues and elsewhere, I learned much from comments from and conversations with Terence Ball, Richard Bellamy, Susan Bickford, Margaret Clark, Molly Cochran, Andrew Dobson, Robyn Eckersley, Mark Edmundson, Erik Engstrom, James Farr, Frank Fischer, James Fishkin, Robert Goodin, Maarten Hajer, Barry Hindess, Robert Keohane, Christian List, Gerry Mackie, Freya Mathews, David Miller, Greg Myers, Claus Offe, John O'Neill, Val Plumwood, Michael Saward, David Schlosberg, Mimi Sheller, Bron Szerszynski, Douglas Torgerson, Paul Wapner, Iris Young, and three anonymous reviewers. Much of the writing was done while I was a visitor at Nuffield College, Oxford, and I thank the Warden, Fellows, and students for their hospitality and provision of an excellent working environment. I also thank Dominic Byatt, my editor at Oxford University Press, for his insights and encouragement.

CONTENTS

Introduction: The Deliberative Turn in Democratic Theory

The final decade of the second millennium saw the theory of democracy take a strong deliberative turn. Increasingly, democratic legitimacy came to be seen in terms of the ability or opportunity to participate in effective deliberation on the part of those subject to collective decisions. (Note that only the ability or opportunity to participate is at issue; people can choose not to deliberate.) Thus claims on behalf of or against such decisions have to be justified to these people in terms that, on reflection, they are capable of accepting. The reflective aspect is critical, because preferences can be transformed in the process of deliberation. Deliberation as a social process is distinguished from other kinds of communication in that deliberators are amenable to changing their judgements, preferences, and views during the course of their interactions, which involve persuasion rather than coercion, manipulation, or deception. The essence of democracy itself is now widely taken to be deliberation, as opposed to voting, interest aggregation, constitutional rights, or even self-government. The deliberative turn represents a renewed concern with the authenticity of democracy: the degree to which democratic control is substantive rather than symbolic, and engaged by competent citizens.

This interest in authenticity means that deliberative democracy's welcome for forms of communication is conditional. The exact content of these conditions is a matter of some dispute. Some deliberative democrats, especially those who traffic in 'public reason', want to impose narrow limits on what constitutes authentic deliberation, restricting it to arguments in particular kinds of terms (see Chapter 1). A more tolerant position, which I favour, would allow argument, rhetoric, humour, emotion, testimony or storytelling, and gossip. The only condition for authentic *deliberation* is then the requirement that communication induce reflection upon preferences in non-coercive fashion. This requirement in turn rules out domination via the exercise of power, manipulation, indoctrination, propaganda, deception, expressions of mere self-interest, threats (of the sort that characterize bargaining), and attempts to impose ideological conformity. Such agents of distortion can be counteracted to the degree of equality in deliberative competence across political actors (for an earlier and more exhaustive statement of what constitutes authentic deliberation, see Dryzek, 1990*a*, esp. pp. 14–19). Authentic *democracy* can then be said to exist to the degree that reflective preferences influence collective outcomes. In subsequent chapters I will try to shed further light on these issues through encounters with critics of deliberation and those friends who I believe have taken deliberative democracy in wrong directions, as well as with some key features of the contemporary world.

Now, an emphasis on deliberation is not entirely new. Antecedents can be found in the *polis* of ancient Greece, in the political theory of contributors to the Western canon such as Edmund Burke and John Stuart Mill (see Elster, 1998, pp. 4–5), and in theorists from the early twentieth century such as John Dewey (1927). (For more detail on the history of deliberative democracy, see the Introduction to Bohman and Rehg, 1997.) Still, prior to 1990 the term deliberative democracy was used but rarely; the term was invented by Joseph Bessette (1980), and given impetus by Bernard Manin (1987) and Joshua Cohen (1989). By the late 1990s, deliberative democracy provided the focal point for much if not most democratic theory. John Rawls and Jürgen Habermas, respectively the most important liberal theorist and critical theorist of the late twentieth century, lent their prestige to the deliberative turn by publishing major works in which they identified themselves as deliberative democrats (Rawls, 1993; Habermas, 1996*a*).

I seek to establish what a defensible theory of democracy must look like in the wake of the deliberative turn. Thus my purview extends beyond deliberative democracy to contemporary democratic theory as a whole, and so I visit all the major contemporary models of democracy. I share many of the basic tenets of the deliberative turn (and indeed I can claim a small part in its inception; see Dryzek, 1987*a*, Dryzek, 1990*a*). However, unlike many of those who now sail under the deliberative banner, I will argue that a defensible theory of deliberative democracy must be critical in its orientation to established power structures, including those that operate beneath the constitutional surface of the liberal state, and so insurgent in relation to established institutions.

I refer to this more critical strand of deliberative democracy as discursive democracy, which (contrary to much current usage, which tends to use 'deliberative' and 'discursive' interchangeably) I distinguish from a model confined to politics in the vicinity of liberal constitutionalism. The project of this book is to build upon this distinction, and via encounters with friends and critics of deliberation, determine what a theory of discursive democracy should look like. I will then argue that discursive democracy should be pluralistic in embracing the necessity to communicate across difference without erasing difference, reflexive in its questioning orientation to established traditions (including the tradition of deliberative democracy itself), transnational in its capacity to extend across state boundaries into settings where there is no constitutional framework, ecological in terms of openness to communication with non-human nature, and dynamic in its openness to ever-changing constraints upon and opportunities for democratization.

In distinguishing between liberal constitutionalist deliberative democracy, and discursive democracy, I do not mean to imply that these two categories are mutually exclusive and collectively exhaustive. They share some key features, including a rejection of aggregative models of democracy. Not everything in the field falls neatly into these two categories. They are best thought of as two tendencies, that in many works are often scrambled. Part of my task is to establish what is at stake in making this distinction more clearly.

Chapter 1 begins with critique of those who see the institutional structure of liberal democracy as the uniquely proper home for deliberation. Indeed, liberal deliberative enthusiasts see constitution-making itself as being an especially appropriate venue for deliberation. While there is nothing intrinsically wrong in seeking deliberation in such venues, it is unnecessarily constraining so long as one believes that the representative institutions and legal system of liberal democratic state should be the exclusive or even just primary home of political deliberation. I argue that any such exclusive focus ties deliberation to a needlessly thin conception of democracy, growing ever thinner in light of the constraints that the capitalist market economy imposes upon effective state democracy. Thus there are some important dimensions along which I believe that deliberative democracy is losing its way, depleted of the resources it needs to reply to its critics more effectively.

Deliberative democracy's other theoretical root lies in critical theory. Unfortunately, critical theory has itself become far too compromised by an ever-closer association with liberalism and its state. The critical edge needs to be resharpened. One way to do this is to ground deliberative democracy in a strong critical theory of communicative action, and to re-emphasize oppositional civil society and public spheres as sources of democratic critique and renewal. In the latter part of Chapter 1 I lay the foundations for an account of discursive democracy that refuses confinement to the constitutional surface of the liberal state.

In subsequent chapters I will take on the most important critics of deliberative democracy, and examine also the extensions of the discursive approach that have to be made in response to these critics. The first set of critics of deliberative democracy appears in Chapter 2. These are found among social choice theorists, liberal extremists who turn a science of politics against deliberative democracy. Suspicious of the arbitrariness and instability inherent in any notion of democracy, they claim that the kind of unconstrained communication favoured by deliberative democrats will only make matters worse. I argue that there are mechanisms endogenous to deliberation that resolve the problems highlighted by social choice theory. However, a strong response must be grounded in a conception of democracy that emphasizes the construction of public opinion through the contestation of discourses and its transmission to the state via communicative means, including rhetoric. This notion of democracy parallels the aggregative liberal model in which elections are the main transmission mechanism from public opinion to governmental action. The advantage of this alternative account is that it is invulnerable to the social choice attack on democracy-as-voting, and it resonates with the idea of the public sphere as a reservoir of democratic authenticity developed in Chapter 1. The introduction of rhetoric goes against deliberative democrats who believe that the only kind of valid communication is rational argument.

Chapter 3 takes on critics who arrive from the opposite direction. Whereas social choice theorists fear that deliberation is too unstructured and therefore chaotic, the difference democrats who arrive in Chapter 3 believe that deliberation is exclusive and constraining in the kinds of voices and kinds of people that it can hear. Where social choice sceptics see unmanageable variety, difference democrats see only stifling uniformity. Any emphasis on rational argument in particular is said by them to be coercive because it means that many oppressed individuals and groups will find it hard to communicate effectively, even if admitted to the deliberative forum. I argue that deliberation across difference is indeed possible, and that the various kinds of communication highlighted by difference democrats should be admitted. However, they should not be admitted uncritically, and their own coercive potential should be recognized and countered by holding them to critical standards. These additional modes of communication should not be seen as alternatives to rational argument, but as supplements to it. Deliberation across difference is best conceptualized in terms of the contestation of discourses rather than the (postmodern) play of identity and difference. This conceptualization allows an explicit place for oppressive discourses (if they did not exist it might be necessary to invent them). One way of subjecting that contestation to dispersed and so democratic control is through the network form of organization in civil society, which I discuss at length.

The first three chapters highlight the contestation of discourses in civil society, but that does not mean we should give up on the possibility of authentic democracy within the confines of the state, of the kind sought by liberal constitutionalist deliberative democrats. When it comes to the choice between civil society and the state, the only answers that make sense are those developed in historical and comparative terms. Sometimes it makes sense to highlight the state, sometimes civil society, and sometimes both. It all depends on the configuration of state imperatives and social movement interests, as well as the kind of inclusion that the state can offer to groups. If state imperatives and defining movement interests cannot be reconciled, then entry into the state means co-optation and being bought off cheaply, a poor exchange for the loss of democratic vitality of the public sphere. If the two can be reconciled, entry into the state is a much better bargain, from the point of view of democracy as a whole as well as the instrumental interests of the actors involved. Chapter 4 develops a historical account of democratization, and applies it to the strategic choices facing social movements. Within this history, exclusive states can sometimes prove to be surprisingly positive in their influence on democracy; democratization means inclusion, but that inclusion can be in the polity beyond the state.

In today's world, however, control over issues increasingly eludes the state and its associated civil society. For ours is the age of globalization as well as democracy, and the locus of political control has increasingly moved into the international arena. Can democracy, and deliberative democracy in particular, follow suit? Chapter 5 argues that they can. Against those who want to introduce more government of a more democratic kind into the international system, I argue in this chapter for democratization of the discursive sources of order that already exist within the international system. Again, the network form of organization plays a crucial role in bringing the contestation of these discourses under dispersed and so democratic control. This time the networks in question are transnational.

More well-guarded than boundaries between states is that between humanity and nature. Democratic theorists of all stripes have, for all their differences, been adamant that democracy is only for human subjects. In Chapter 6 I argue that ecological crisis requires us to rethink such anthropocentric arrogance. Nature cannot vote, or have its interests aggregated alongside those of humans. But in nature we will find communication, which can be connected to communication within the human world. An expanded notion of discursive democracy is better-placed than more conventional models of democracy to think about such extension. Green democracy seeks effectiveness in communication that transcends the boundary of the human and non-human worlds.

In the final chapter I attempt to link these various developments, and to show that they have tight connections to each other, especially in a world where traditions lose their grip and reflexive choice across discourses becomes increasingly possible.

As a supplement to my main argument, I will also try to speak to some of the main intramural points of contention among deliberative democrats that are not necessarily captured by the distinction between liberal constitutionalist deliberative democracy and discursive democracy. Following is a list of these intramural points. I should stress that they do not orient the structure of the analysis in the chapters that follow, and so I do not refer to this list explicitly, until I provide explicit answers to all of these points in the conclusion, based on the analysis of the intervening chapters. Some do receive sustained treatment because they are crucial in establishing the distinction between liberal constitutionalist and discursive variants of deliberative democracy (for example, the first point is the main topic of Chapter 3), others receive only passing attention.

- Should deliberation be restricted to rational argument, or admit other kinds of communication (emotional, or rhetorical, for example)?
- If it does admit these other kinds, how should their relation to argument be conceptualized; should rational argument remain sovereign, or can these alternatives contribute equally to the outcome of deliberation?
- Does deliberation's emphasis on reasoned argument constitute a restraining and possibly even anaesthetizing force that neutralizes justified dissent?
- Are there some kinds of communication (perhaps prejudiced, racist, or sectarian) that should be ruled out in advance?

- Are there particular process values (such as impartiality, civility, or reciprocity) to which deliberators must be committed before they can be admitted to the forum?
- Must acceptable argument be couched in terms of the public interest, common to all, or are more particular and partial interests admissible? If the latter can enter, do we allow deliberation to coexist with bargaining?
- Should deliberation be oriented to consensus, or is it just a prelude to voting?
- Is the proper location of deliberation the existing representative institutions and legal system of liberal democracy, or should deliberation extend more broadly throughout society?
- Might existing representative institutions prove inhospitable to effective deliberation, such that alternative locations should be sought?
- Should deliberation be constrained by constitutional specifications that rule out in advance particular outcomes of deliberation?
- Is political equality central to the deliberative ideal, and if so how much deviation from that ideal should be tolerated? What if anything is to be done about unequal individual capacities to deliberate?
- Is deliberation a means for arriving at decisions that solve social problems more effectively, or is it just an intrinsically desirable procedure, irrespective of the problem-solving substance of its outcomes?
- Should we try to subject all decisions to extensive deliberation, or just particular important ones, such as constitutional matters?
- Is deliberation to be confined to members of a predefined community, or can it occur effectively across community boundaries, or when no established community is present?

These points of contention provide grist to the burgeoning literature on deliberative democracy. However, it is not exactly my intent here to provide a full summary accounting of where the model and field of deliberative democracy has been and where it stands today (for useful such exercises, see Blaug, 1996; Bohman and Rehg, 1997; Bohman, 1998*b*). So while I do revisit the list explicitly in the final chapter, it does not provide a framework for the intervening chapters. My main task is to determine the overall shape that ought to be taken by the theory of democracy in the wake of the deliberative turn, especially in the light of the contrast between liberal constitutionalist deliberative democracy and discursive democracy, and to this I now turn.

CHAPTER 1

Liberal Democracy and the Critical Alternative

My exploration of how the theory of democracy might look in the wake of the deliberative turn begins with an examination of the sources of that turn. The story has two starting points: in liberal constitutionalism (which turns out to be mostly from and about the United States), and critical theory. While these two frameworks once represented sharply different outlooks on the world of politics and democracy, they have recently met—on mostly liberal terms. I argue that there are good reasons to lament this convergence, especially given that its terms connote a blunting of the critical edge of deliberative democracy. I try to retrieve this critical edge by renewing the distinction between liberal constitutionalist and discursive strands of deliberative democracy. Deliberative democracy should involve a continued quest for democratic authenticity, rather than easy accommodation with the prevailing liberal political economy.

By authenticity I mean the degree to which democratic control is engaged through communication that encourages reflection upon preferences without coercion. As I pointed out in the Introduction, this condition is met to the degree that domination via the exercise of power, manipulation, indoctrination, propaganda, deception, expressions of mere self-interest, threats, and the imposition of ideological conformity are all absent. These distorting agents will diminish to the extent of equality in deliberative competence across political actors. Towards the end of this chapter I will link these authenticity conditions to the critical theory of democracy, and so discursive democracy, demonstrating the need to resist the embrace of liberal constitutionalism.

Deliberative Democracy in Liberal Constitutionalism

As befits the most pervasive political force of the modern era, liberalism comes in many varieties. But at its core is a common doctrine based on the assumption that individuals are mostly motivated by self-interest rather than any conception of the common good, and that they themselves are the best judges of what this self-interest entails. When the interests of different individuals cannot be reconciled to their mutual benefit through operation of the market economy, politics comes into play. Liberal politics is therefore mostly and properly about the reconciliation and aggregation of predetermined interests under the auspices of a neutral set of rules: that is, a constitution. A fear that self-interested individuals, even if they are in the majority, may turn public power to private advantage then necessitates a set of constitutional rights to protect individuals against government, and against each other. These rights come with corresponding obligations to respect the rights of others and duties toward the government that secures rights.

Liberalism so defined is actually silent on the issue of democracy. Some liberals, especially those with unlimited faith in the market and unlimited scepticism about government, are not democrats of any sort, stressing the protection of freedom against oppressive democratic majorities. Such protection can be achieved through legal means; it does not have to matter whether or not the laws in question are democratically determined. Historically, the rise of liberalism preceded the rise of modern democracy. Liberals until the early twentieth century generally regarded democracy with unease, fearing that untutored and unrestrained masses would show little respect for liberal rights and constitutional niceties. The *most* democratic of nineteenth-century liberals, John Stuart Mill, is also associated with the overwhelming need to protect individuals against the 'tyranny of the majority'. In fact, Mill anticipated an uneasy relationship between liberalism and deliberative democracy: he sought to promote more expanded and informed public debate, but at the same time wanted to contain it and prevent it from upsetting the rationality of government (Mill, 1962 [1835]). Mill can be interpreted as the grandfather of contemporary liberal constitutionalist deliberative democracy, the contradictions of which can already be discerned in his writings.

It is only in the twentieth century that liberalism and democracy really reached an accommodation, such that 'liberal democracy' could fall easily from the lips, and indeed become by century's end the world's dominant political ideology. Yet still liberal democracy remained only a rough compromise between two different sets of principles. Political theorists still have trouble deducing a set of liberal democratic principles from a common set of premises, even as liberal democracy in practice flourishes as never before. (Elsewhere—Dryzek 1996*a*—I have argued that there is little point in trying to finalize the details of any model of democracy; but many liberal political theorists believe deductions from philosophical foundations to models of democracy are important.)

At first sight, a deliberative conception of democracy would seem by definition irreconcilable to a liberal version of democracy. For deliberative democracy by definition is open to preference transformation within political interaction, while liberal democracy by definition deals only in the reconciliation and aggregation of preferences defined prior to political interaction (Miller, 1992, and Warren, 1992, are among those who emphasize this distinction). Yet liberalism is a flexible doctrine, and as we will see some liberals now allow that there are circumstances in which individuals can be open to deliberative persuasion, even if this does involve considerable softening of what was long thought to be a part of liberalism's hard core. Thus a deliberative conception of democracy turns out to facilitate a more effective reconciliation of liberal and democratic principles—in connection, moreover, with the specifically constitutional aspects of liberalism long thought most resistant to democracy. Of course, the mere fact that deliberative democracy helps solve some problems for liberals would be insufficient reason to endorse it. But liberal deliberative democrats argue that the resultant political theory is both intrinsically attractive and attuned to key features of this liberal, democratic, and culturally plural age.

There are three analytically distinct, but practically reinforcing, ways in which the idea of deliberation can be deployed to develop a tight connection between liberalism and democracy; and so three ways in which deliberative democracy can be assimilated to liberalism. They are as follows.

1. Deliberative Principles Justify Liberal Rights

Liberal democrats by definition believe in popular control *and* individual rights. Of course, these two principles are often in tension, because democratic majorities can easily decide not to respect particular rights, especially those of unpopular minorities. Liberal deliberative democrats can help resolve this tension by arguing that there are some basic rights that must be respected, namely those necessary for the effective exercise of democratic citizenship, and so for deliberative democracy itself. These rights would include those to free expression and association, and to a basic education, perhaps even a certain level of material well-being.

Deliberation by definition specifies that individuals must communicate about collective decisions in terms that are capable of reflective acceptance on the part of those subject to the decision. At first sight this characteristic might suggest that deliberation is incompatible with the liberal account of politics as the pursuit, interaction, and aggregation of interests defined in advance and privately by individuals. However, this politics of private interests requires some kind of institutional framework. When it comes to making decisions about this framework itself, some liberals, notably Rawls (1993), argue that 'public reason' should filter political arguments, which can be couched only in terms of interests based on the common humanity of free and equal citizens. Rawls himself promotes public reason only in the context of a specified range of issues—concerning the content of the constitution and questions of 'basic justice'.

Other deliberative democrats, notably Joshua Cohen (1996), seek broader application of this kind of reasoning. Claus Offe (1997) would classify this more expansive view as a species of 'left-liberalism' that departs from the assumption of liberalism proper (or what Offe calls, departing a bit from standard usage, 'libertarianism') that preferences are rightly determined prior to political interaction, and do not change in the context of interaction. Cohen attempts to derive the main rights and equalities central to liberalism through reference to the idea of 'free public reasoning among equals' (p. 99), under which 'participants regard one another as equals; they aim to defend and criticize institutions and programs in terms of considerations that others have reason to accept' (p. 100). Cohen, like Rawls, accepts that 'reasonable pluralism' means that arguments that persuade like-minded individuals (for example, members of the same religion) will not be persuasive to all members of society, which gives force to the need to couch arguments in terms differently-minded individuals (such as members of a different religion) can accept.

The direct implications of public reasoning so conceived begin with freedom of expression, simply as a matter of respect for 'reasonable pluralism' and the equal deliberative standing of those with whom one disagrees (Cohen, 1996, p. 105). Religious freedom follows because religious reasons cannot count as public reasons. These commitments are therefore immune to public reason, and so properly off-limits when it comes to public policy (p. 103). Political equality, in the form of equal political rights, follows because it is impossible to argue in terms compelling to *all* that some should have fewer political rights (pp. 106–7). In short, Cohen argues that deliberative democracy requires commitments to a set of substantive political principles, many of which turn out to be those traditionally valued by liberals. Yet his broad view of deliberation's domain fits uneasily with liberalism's core tenet that ordinary (as opposed to constitutional) politics is mostly about the pursuit and aggregation of predefined interests. Cohen's argument does not begin from liberalism's hard core of principles; rather, his achievement is to derive some (but not all) liberal principles from a starting point in democracy. Thus it is perhaps not surprising that some liberal principles—notably the idea that politics is mostly about the aggregation of predefined interests—are not reached by his argument.

2. *Liberal Constitutions Promote Deliberation*

A basic liberal argument is that constitutions are necessary first and foremost to enable individuals to enjoy a private life immune from public invasion, though of course constitutions also set up the institutions of government. A deliberative interpretation of the liberal constitution emphasizes instead its role in the creation of a public realm for deliberation. This realm is composed in part of institutions of government, notably courts and legislatures, which are treated as effective, rational, and legitimate only to the extent they incorporate authentic deliberation. But this realm also encompasses informal processes of public debate to which larger publics can be admitted.

To begin with legislatures, Rawls (1997, p. 772) specifies 'a framework of constitutional democratic institutions that specifies the setting for deliberative legislative bodies' as one of the 'three essential elements of deliberative democracy' (the other two are public reason and 'the knowledge and desire on the part of citizens generally to follow public reason'). The term deliberative democracy was first used by Joseph Bessette (1980) in the context of an interpretation of the United States constitution as a set of principles to ensure effective public deliberation, especially within Congress. For the most part Bessette believes that Congress measures up to the deliberative task, though he also recognizes and laments departures from the ideal. Obviously this is not the only way this particular liberal constitution can be interpreted. Other interpretations highlight particular specifications of political authority, obligations, and, as I have noted, individual rights for the sake of protecting private life. Bessette expands his argument about Congress in his book *The Mild Voice of Reason* (Bessette, 1994). (This title should start alarm bells ringing among those who think that mild reason is necessarily conservative, such that we should seek more unruly alternatives to it. I will address this issue at length in Chapter 3.) In a rare non-American contribution to this genre, John Uhr (1998) too emphasizes the legislature, applying deliberative principles to reform of the Australian parliament.

Deliberation within liberal institutions has also been highlighted by deliberative scholars of a legal bent. In this light, decision making under constitutional law is not merely the application of categorical judgement in applying general rules and rights to particular cases, or deciding what to do when rules and rights conflict. Instead, deliberation about the meaning and applicability of rules is central. What rights mean in particular cases has to be the subject of deliberation, be it in a parliamentary assembly, a court, or in more wide-ranging political debate. For rights only have real force if they are given reflective acceptance by the citizens who both take advantage of these rights for themselves and respect these rights as held by others.

Such deliberation can occur within panels of judges, such as the United States Supreme Court (which Rawls, 1993, p. 231, among others, regards as the exemplary deliberative institution), and within juries. It can even be found in adversarial encounters of lawyers, in the courtroom or outside. Adversarial encounters are largely strategic in that the goal is to out-manoeuvre one's opponent within the constraints of formal rules (as opposed to principles of free discourse) in the interests of a pre-established position. However, those with an interest in presenting the truth about a case also have an incentive to prove it and convince judge, jury, and onlookers.

Constitutional promotion of deliberation within a larger public realm is highlighted by a leading deliberative democrat among constitutional lawyers, Cass Sunstein, who goes so far as to define deliberative democracy in terms of constitutionalism (Sunstein, 1997, pp. 94–5). Sunstein interprets the United States Constitution in its entirety, rather than its legal order in particular, as a device for the protection and promotion of generalized political deliberation across the polity as a whole, not only (or even primarily) the court system (Sunstein, 1993a). Michael Walzer (1991) argues in similar spirit that the deliberative function of the United States Constitution lies not in the opportunities it specifies for deliberation within governmental structures (be it courts or Congress), but rather the broader public realm which it protects. For Walzer, the Bill of Rights is the crucial document that makes possible a vibrant civil society of associational life where debate can proceed on public issues of all sorts. Neither Sunstein nor Walzer is a liberal; but it is easy to see how their arguments could be adopted by liberal deliberative democrats.

3. Constitution-Making is Itself a Deliberative Process

Some liberal deliberative democrats believe that deliberation should orient and pervade all institutions at all times. Other liberal scholars believe that deliberation is essential, but wish to restrict it to particular kinds of occasions: especially constitution-making ones (see Estlund, 1993). Here liberal *democrats* differ from their less democratic liberal kin, who have treated constitutions and (in particular) their embodied rights as a matter for specification informed only by moral and legal philosophy, not the popular will. Among constitutionalist liberal democrats, Bruce Ackerman (1991) in *We the People* treats debates such as those attending the writing and adoption of the United States Constitution as exemplars of deliberative democracy in action. But he also believes that the capacity to deliberate is a scarce resource, so reasons of economy dictate that most issues and occasions cannot and should not receive this sort of treatment. Only great crises of the state such as the Constitutional Founding, the Great Depression and the Civil War (in particular its associated constitutional amendments) could and did bring forth deliberation by the American people, as opposed to their government. One might question here what Ackerman means by 'the people'—he certainly does not mean all the people, or perhaps even very many of them. (I hope he doesn't mean 'people like me'.)

Deliberative democracy's place at the heart of liberal constitutional thinking has been confirmed by the announcement of liberalism's leading thinker, John Rawls, that his idea of 'a well-ordered constitutional democracy' should be 'understood also as a deliberative democracy' (Rawls, 1997, pp. 771–2). For Rawls (1993), as for Ackerman, deliberation is not to be the normal mode of governmental decision-making. To Rawls, deliberation guided by public reason should only be about constitutional affairs, and about legislation inasmuch as it affects matters of the constitution and what he calls 'basic justice'. Basic justice refers to equality of opportunity and the distribution of material goods. Applying public reason, 'citizens are to conduct their fundamental discussions within a framework of what each regards as a political conception of justice based on values that the others can reasonably be expected to endorse' (Rawls, 1993, p. 226). The product is 'a constitution, the essentials of which all citizens as free and equal citizens may be reasonably expected to endorse in light of principles and ideals acceptable to their common human reason' (1993, p. 137).

Benhabib (1996*b*, p. 75) among others points out that public reason is for Rawls first and foremost an ideal for the content of arguments made by individual citizens or their representatives. Arguments must be couched in terms capable of acceptance by all members of the polity, ruling out both material self-interest and partial worldviews as reasons and motives. Rawls downplays the *social* or interactive aspect of deliberation, meaning that public reason can be undertaken by the solitary thinker. This is deliberation of a sort—but only in terms of the weighing of arguments in the mind, not testing them in real political interaction. Moreover, there is in Rawls no particular reason to extend deliberation from personal reflection to political interaction. For in specifying that public reason adduces only arguments in terms that all individuals can be expected to accept, Rawls implies that all individuals will reason in the same way, and must ultimately reach the same conclusions. Rawlsian public reason is singular, and produces consensus. Given that reason is singular, no interactive process is necessary to enable it to produce its conclusions.

Now, Rawls does believe that one of the three essentials of deliberative democracy (beyond public reason itself and a constitutional framework) is 'knowledge and desire on the part of citizens generally to follow public reason and to realize its ideals in their political conduct', which in turn requires 'public occasions of orderly and serious discussion of fundamental questions and issues of public policy' (1997, p. 772). Yet these occasions provide only expressive opportunities; for Rawls, there is nothing endogenous to interactions that induces individuals to reason and behave according to the precepts of public reason. Public reason is a set of commitments that individuals must adopt before they enter the public arena, not what they will be induced to discover once they are there.

The right conclusions can, then, be discovered by any reflective individual; and who better to reflect, and to set aside material self-interest and sectarian argument, than the professional political philosopher or legal theorist? Rawls himself does not shrink from specifying in great detail the constitutional arrangements to which he believes the exercise of public reason must point. And he regards the United States Supreme Court as an exemplary deliberative body, the best and proper home for public reason in the US polity (Rawls, 1993, p. 231). The Court is hardly a democratic body (it is accountable to nobody), nor is it really a deliberative one in the interactive sense. But its members are professional experts in the exercise of public reason, which they follow in personal reflection. In short, and his self-description notwithstanding, Rawls is a deliberative democrat in a very thin sense. This is not to gainsay the important influence that Rawlsian notions of public reason have in thinking about deliberative democracy, even if they must be detached from Rawls's own anti-social— and so anti-political—approach to deliberation.

Having surveyed three ways to link deliberative democracy and liberal constitutionalism, it should be stressed that these links are not mutually exclusive alternatives. There is at first sight a slight inconsistency between the first and the third: for if the very idea of deliberation requires a specific set of liberal rights, as the first linkage suggests, how can we subject the content of these rights to deliberation, as the third linkage mandates? This apparent problem may be less severe in practice than it appears in theory, for constitution-makers could deliberate about what (say) freedom of expression means, and the best way of protecting it, even though they could not contemplate dispensing with rights to protect freedom of expression altogether. If Cohen is correct that the very idea of deliberation requires such rights, then any participant in constitution-making could only argue against them by engaging in a performative contradiction.

This minor difficulty aside, there is nothing to prevent liberal deliberative democrats combining all three of these linkages. For example, the liberal schools of thought that emphasize, respectively, deliberation within constitutional structure and deliberation about constitutional structure (links 2 and 3) are united in the hands of Amy Gutmann and Dennis Thompson (1996), who also believe that particular liberal principles can be derived from deliberative precepts (link 1). Gutmann and Thompson explicitly call for deliberation to proceed under constitutional arrangements that are themselves constructed by deliberative means (1996, p. 200). When it comes to the first kind of link, Gutmann and Thompson specify the degree of liberty necessary for individuals to be effective deliberators—echoing Cohen's derivation of particular freedoms from the idea of deliberation. More controversially from the liberal point of view, they argue for welfare state arrangements that would guarantee the basic material needs that individuals must have met before they can participate effectively in deliberative politics. The welfare state can also equalize material conditions for deliberators.

Gutmann and Thompson also believe in a set of ideals that resemble Rawlsian public reason. These are the foundational principles of deliberative democracy: reciprocity, or 'the capacity to seek fair terms of social cooperation for their own sake' (pp. 52–3); publicity; and accountability, to constituents and other citizens, to citizens of other political systems, and to future generations. The principle of reciprocity rules out sectarian arguments; also banned are arguments that violate principles of human integrity and political equality. However, Gutmann and Thompson depart from Rawlsian public reason in that they do not believe that argument should be confined to what is in the common interest of all. Rather, deliberators should endeavour to make arguments that are intelligible in the terms of partial views (such as religious doctrines) which they do not themselves share. The product will not generally be consensus, but it may be mutual respect and a *modus vivendi* (thus providing an effective response to critics such as Femia, 1996, pp. 378–80 who mistakenly believe that deliberation must culminate in a 'unified public will').

Gutmann and Thompson have a particularly expansive view of deliberation's liberal domain, believing that all political issues that feature deep moral disagreement should be treated through deliberation. They do not expect deliberation to produce consensus, but they do expect it to yield understanding and mutual respect, thus making even deep moral conflicts on issues such as abortion more tractable. In the hands of Gutmann and Thompson, deliberative democracy begins to look like a complete political theory.

The Limits of Liberalism

At one level it is hard to object to these liberal deployments of deliberative democracy, as they promise to make democracy within (and occasionally about) constitutional structure more authentic. However, there are a number of hard questions that can be pressed against the liberal constitutionalist account of deliberation. First, constitutional structure does not fully determine the kinds of politics that occurs in any system. It is widely observed that the constitution of the United States facilitates pluralist politics, in which interest groups have a wide range of points of access to the political system. Liberal deliberative democrats accept that the reality has often fallen short—for example, in the long exclusion of African-Americans from effective participation. But they believe that such shortcomings can themselves be remedied by constitutional amendment, or by legislation (such as the Voting Rights Act) or by court decisions (such as the famous 1954 Brown vs. Board of Education decision that overturned the 'separate but equal' doctrine). Yet some such inequalities and exclusions cannot be remedied by constitutional means: in particular, inequality between the voice of business and the voices of everybody else (not just labour). Business inevitably holds what Lindblom (1977) calls a 'privileged' position in policy deliberation because government relies on corporations to carry out essential tasks in organizing the economy, without which government itself could not function.

Constitutional structures are not, then, the only forces that order deliberation in the liberal polity. Also important are material forces and discourses (often intertwined). The material forces mostly emanate from the capitalist political economy in which the liberal state is embedded. Discourses matter too. A discourse is a shared means of making sense of the world embedded in language. Any discourse will always be grounded in assumptions, judgements, contentions, dispositions, and capabilities. These shared terms of reference enable those who subscribe to a particular discourse to perceive and compile bits of sensory information into coherent stories or accounts that can be communicated in intersubjectively meaningful ways. Thus a discourse will generally revolve around a central storyline, containing opinions about both facts and values.

Whereas formal rules of the kind that constitutionalists stress constitute institutional hardware, discourses constitute institutional software. The software is important: this is why, for example, when Westminster-style constitutions were parachuted into former British colonies in Africa, the politics they hosted proved vastly different from what happened in Westminster itself.

Discourses can be bound up with material forces. For example, material economic constraints on politics now make themselves felt through the discourse of market liberalism. A competing discourse of ecological modernization enables (moderate) environmentalists to take a more equal place in the policy-making forum from which they are generally excluded by market liberalism. The reason is that ecological modernization ties environmental conservation to business profitability. Other things being equal, a polity where ecological modernization is strong will have more authentic deliberation within governmental structures than one where market liberalism dominates—even if the constitutional rules are identical. In subsequent chapters I will argue that the contestation of discourses is a vital part of deliberative democracy, but that this contestation cannot be confined to liberal constitutional structure. Discourses can be both constraining and enabling, but one cannot wish them away. Critics of particular discourses (for example, Michel Foucault in his classic works on criminality, mental health, and sexuality) often emphasize the constraints.

There are other agents of constraint and distortion generally unappreciated by liberal constitutionalists. Social choice theorists, to be dealt with in Chapter 2, have called into question the possibility of the voting mechanisms that are central to aggregative democracy ever producing stable and non-arbitrary results. Difference democrats, who will appear in Chapter 3, have criticized supposedly neutral liberal premises about access to argument on the grounds that in reality these premises exclude the voices of particular individuals and groups. Those so excluded are generally on the margins of society to begin with, and they do not fit the liberal paradigm of personhood, or fit liberal assumptions about what kind of communication is reasonable.

Sometimes extra-constitutional forces can constitute a *de facto* polity sharply at variance with constitutional appearances. For example, corporatism, defined as co-operative policy-making among government officials (normally from the executive branch) along with leaders of business and labour federations, has nowhere been legislated into existence. Yet it captures the reality of policy-making in a number of countries, such as Austria, the Netherlands, and Sweden, where parliamentary democracy has often proved to be a sideshow. Corporatism is secretive and exclusive, and as such likely to horrify liberal constitutionalists. However, as I will argue in Chapter 4, there are times when this very exclusiveness can actually benefit the deliberative democratic well-being of the polity as a whole, if not the state itself (which is only part of the polity). Thus what seems like an altogether worthy bias to inclusion on the part of liberal constitutionalism turns out to be suspect in practice.

Finally, liberal constitutionalism is largely silent on what should be done when control over important policy issues eludes nation-states. A liberal approach to transnational democratization is conceivable, but, I will argue in Chapter 5, insensitive to the relative weight of the forces that order international politics. Government of the kind favoured by liberals is extraordinarily weak in the global polity, which means that alternative discursive sources of order are especially important therein. The possibility of democratizing these discursive sources of order resonates with the importance to deliberative democracy I accord to the contestation of discourses in civil society.

For all these reasons a complete assimilation of deliberative democracy to liberal constitutionalism is undesirable. These criticisms of liberal constitutionalist deliberative democracy set the agenda for contemplation of what discursive democracy can and should entail. What other resources can be brought to bear in this quest? Let me now take a look at the other major theoretical source of deliberative democracy, critical theory, in this light. As we will see, critical theory has lost its way to the extent it has embraced liberalism, thus highlighting the need to retrieve a truly critical deliberative democracy.

Critical Theory

So far my account has emphasized the liberal roots of deliberative democracy, and thus its accommodation with the constitutional order of the liberal political system. The other major source lies outside liberalism, and so begins (though it turns out not to end) with an attitude of deep scepticism concerning the possibilities for effective deliberation within the vicinity of the liberal state. This root comes from critical theory. My introduction of the 'state' terminology here is deliberate: liberals, especially US liberals, are more comfortable with terms such as 'government' or 'the political system' rather than 'the state'. The state may be defined in the first instance as the set of individuals and organizations legally authorized to make binding decisions on behalf of a society. But those who use the concept, including critical theorists, are often attuned to the manifold constraints upon or opportunities for the state *as an entity*, as opposed to its component parts. (In Chapter 4 I develop a more nuanced definition of the state in terms of the imperatives to which public officials are often but not always subject. In this light, the state is a particular zone of government subjected to these imperatives, not government in its entirety.)

In its broadest sense, critical theory is concerned with charting the progressive emancipation of individuals and society from oppressive forces. It follows that such forces are ideological contingencies rather than structural necessities (from which there is no escape). Emancipation follows understanding of these forces on the part of those at the receiving end, who come to understand both the contingent character of the forces in question and what might be done to counteract them.

This brief characterization of critical theory might suggest that the key difference between liberal and critical theories of democracy is that the latter cannot accept the status quo to which the former is reconciled. But to put matters in these terms would be erroneous. For liberalism itself was once revolutionary—beginning, in a way, as a critical theory of feudalism and absolute monarchy. Bruce Ackerman (1992), for one, thinks liberalism can and should be revolutionary once again. Some critical theorists, for their part, came to accept oppressive forces as so pervasive and immutable that in the end little or nothing worthwhile could be done to oppose them, save perhaps individual artistic expression (see, notably, Adorno, 1973).

When it comes to contemporary political theory, and democratic theory in particular, the real difference is that liberalism operates only on the surface of the political economy. Liberal constitutionalists and critical theorists alike can believe in distortion-free political dialogue as the essence of deliberative democracy (setting aside those liberals like Rawls for whom deliberation does not have to involve actual dialogue). Liberals are keen to devise constitutional and legal arrangements that will counteract distortion: bills of rights, freely-elected legislatures, and so forth. Even Rawls (1997, p. 772) speaks of the need for deliberation to be 'set free from the curse of money' through the remedy of public financing of election campaigns. What liberals fail to recognize is that getting constitutions and laws right is only half the battle. They fail to recognize extra-constitutional agents of distortion that cannot easily be counteracted through such means. These agents include dominant discourses and ideologies, often intertwined with structural economic forces. In today's world, the most compelling of such forces emanate from the transnational political economy, imposing severe constraints on what is possible in terms of both the content of public policy *and* the degree of democracy that can be tolerated in the state's production of policy (see Dryzek, 1996 for a catalogue of these forces).

The critical theory of democracy is not just about the identification of such forces and contemplation of what might be done to counteract them. It is also concerned with the competence of citizens themselves to recognize and oppose such forces, which can be promoted through participation in authentically democratic politics. Liberals believe individuals are left unchanged as a result of political participation; individuals possess preferences that are given, such that before, during, and after participation they are the best judges of their own interests. Critical theorists, in contrast, are among those who take the view that democratic participation can transform individuals, who ideally become 'more public-spirited, more tolerant, more knowledgeable, more attentive to the interests of others, and more probing of their own interests' (Warren, 1992, p. 8).

The major contemporary exponent of critical theory is Jürgen Habermas, who has recently turned to the explication of a theory of deliberative democracy—though, as will become apparent, that theory does not quite fit the requirements of a critical theory of democracy as I have just outlined them. Habermas has long contemplated the sorts of reason that can operate in society since the Enlightenment, distinguishing between instrumental rationality (the capacity to devise, select and effect good means to clarified and consistent ends) and communicative rationality (Habermas, 1984). Communicative action is oriented to understanding between individuals rather than success in achieving predefined individual goals. Communicative rationality is found to the degree that communicative action is free from coercion, deception, self-deception, strategizing, and manipulation. Both forms of reason have their proper place in human affairs. The central problem of modern society to Habermas is that instrumental rationality has invaded and conquered realms where it does not belong, leading to the thorough scientization, bureaucratization, and commercialization of social life and politics. Thus the full potential of communicative rationality has not been realized.

The similarities between communicative rationality and the conditions of effective deliberation should be obvious, and so communicative rationality can be deployed to underwrite a deliberative conception of democracy. It is a straightforward matter to apply the components of communicative rationality as a set of criteria for deliberative democratic authenticity (Dryzek, 1990a, esp. pp. 14–19), though Habermas himself did not at first move in this direction. He did develop the political implications of his theory of communicative action, but only so far as to distinguish between the 'system' and the 'lifeworld' (see especially Habermas, 1987). The system is composed of society's basic steering systems, notably the state and the economy. The lifeworld, in contrast, is where meanings are negotiated and identities constructed by individuals; it is the home of communicative action.

Habermas was careful to relate the lifeworld and the potential for the realization of communicative rationality not to the liberal (or any other) state. Indeed, he treated the state as pretty much inevitably under the sway of instrumental rationality and system imperatives. Habermas looked instead to public spheres that consisted of political association and interaction separate from, and often confronting, the state. Whereas the deliberative paradigm for many liberal constitutionalists is the American Founding, for Habermas the historical exemplar is the early bourgeois European public sphere that flourished in the seventeenth and eighteenth centuries in opposition to the feudal state from which the bourgeoisie was excluded (Habermas, 1989). The early bourgeois public sphere consisted of conversations in meeting places (including informal ones such as coffee houses), debates in newspapers, and political association. It declined along with the commercialization of the press in the nineteenth century and the entry of the bourgeoisie into the state that had once excluded them. In addition, expansion of the franchise meant that propaganda became an efficient political use of newspapers.

Contemporary parallels to the early bourgeois public sphere could be found in new social movements oriented to peace, ecology, feminism, and social justice, and which have often sought or been forced into confrontation rather than accommodation with the capitalist state. Thus theorists of deliberative democracy influenced by Habermas (for example, Bohman, 1996, Dryzek, 1990*a*, and Fraser, 1992) emphasized deliberation in public spheres. Some of them also shared Habermas's tendency to notice only progressive movements, and ignore public spheres inhabited by (say) fundamentalist religious movements, nationalists, or anti-abortion groups. The public sphere as an empirical category encompasses the whole range of such movements, though both far-right militias and leftist groups that have resorted to violence (such as the Red Army Fraction in Germany, or Red Brigades in Italy) can be excluded on analytical grounds because of their lack of any orientation to the state (other than to seek its destruction). Those who use the public sphere as a normative concept should be careful to apply critical standards to the public sphere no less than elsewhere, rather than assume that anything happening therein is by definition praiseworthy, defining out anything that is ugly.

Public spheres can also be linked (in both theory and practice) to the increasingly popular concept of civil society. Civil society remains a contested and sometimes murky concept (for a discussion of the concept's importance in political theory, see Jean Cohen and Andrew Arato, 1992). In the first instance, it is made up of all social interaction not subsumed by the state or the economy. Private life is also normally excluded, though feminist critiques of the public/private distinction make this boundary less hard and fast. From the point of view of democracy it is the political aspects of civil society that are most interesting. Martin Jänicke (1996) defines civil society in functional terms as public action in response to failure in either the state or the economy. Such activity can entail protest against and pressure upon state actors; or it might involve 'paragovernmental' action directed at economic actors, bypassing government. An example of the latter would be a consumer boycott organized to force a company to stop using child labour in its Third World factories.

The politicized aspects of civil society that constitute the public sphere consist of voluntary political associations, whose basic orientation is determined at least in part by the state's activities. For example, peace movements normally only take shape when the state is engaging in warlike activities, such as introducing new missile systems. But these associations in civil society are self-limiting in the sense that they are not pursuing any share of state power (Isaac, 1993). Obviously any emphasis on the public sphere and civil society opens major questions about the relationship of deliberation to public decision as made by and in the state, which I will address in subsequent chapters.

The danger involved in taking Habermas's earlier approach to communicative action and applying it in literal fashion to deliberative politics is that we end up with a political theory that has little to say about political structure—except to condemn it as an agent of distortion. For under communicative rationality—especially in its counterfactual extreme of the 'ideal speech situation'—the only force that applies is that of the better argument. Decision is ideally secured by consensus; implementation of the decision is secured only by the commitment of the individuals involved to the content of that consensus; and subsequent compliance relies on free consent. Such a sequence is not easily related to real-world political institutions and processes, especially those in complex and plural societies.

By the time Habermas finally got around to writing his own theory of democracy in *Between Facts and Norms* (Habermas 1996*a*; the German edition appeared in 1992) he was sensitive to these problems. Indeed, he criticized Joshua Cohen's 1989 formulation for its inattention to the pluralistic complexity of contemporary society and to the question of how deliberation might proceed within differentiated political structures (Habermas, 1996*a*, pp. 304–5). The theory of democracy that appears in *Between Facts and Norms* departs substantially from earlier Habermasian abstractions about communication. While Habermas remains a critical theorist in principle, his reconciliation to a range of immutable facts about the modern world—the pluralistic complexity of society, the intransigence of political–economic structure—means that his distance from liberal theorists of deliberative democracy is now harder to discern. At first glance, Habermas's acceptance of an unyielding world suggests that he has followed the footsteps of one of his foremost predecessors in the Frankfurt School of critical theory, Adorno. But while Adorno turned his back on the world, Habermas decided to try to make the best of it.

In *Between Facts and Norms*, Habermas retains an emphasis on public spheres and civil society, as they form the locus for the formation of truly public opinion via communicative action. The kind of admissible discourse is now extended to include not just issues of truth and morality, but also pragmatic discourse about what should be done in terms of translating consensus into binding decisions capable of implementation, and negotiations concerning what to do when values and interests irreducibly conflict. Habermas is also more attuned to the complexity of contemporary societies, such that opinion formation occurs in a variety of interacting publics. He speaks of diffuse 'subjectless communication' to highlight his contrast with participatory models of democracy that proceed on a face-to-face basis in small communities.

Despite many continuities with his earlier work, Habermas is now much more concerned with how the communicative processes of civil society influence the legislative and policy processes of the state. To begin, the state should be structured so as to guarantee constitutional support and protection to civil society—now treated in more pluralistic terms than before (so there is no unitary republican conception of 'the people' deciding on one common set of ends). Such protection is ensured first and foremost by a set of human rights inscribed in law. Thus law is treated as the main prop for moral and political discourse, not just the force for social control which an earlier Habermas would have stressed. Here Habermas sounds much like the American constitutional theorists I discussed earlier. He highlights 'judicial discourse' concerning how to put collective decisions into legal practice in a way that does not conflict with established rights and other policy programmes.

Habermas addresses the issue of how public opinion can influence the policy practice of the state, no longer treated in obtuse terms. He frames the issue as the translation of the 'communicative power' generated in the public sphere into the 'administrative power' of the state. 'Communicative power is exercised in the manner of a siege.' But the siege is self-limiting: 'it influences the premises of judgment and decision making in the political system without intending to conquer the system itself' (Habermas, 1996a, pp. 486–7). Habermas accepts key aspects of that system, notably elections, law-making by legislatures, and lawful administrative implementation of policy. Indeed, he makes these aspects central to his democratic theory. As he puts it, 'Informal public opinion-formation generates "influence"; influence is transformed into "communicative power" through the channels of political elections; and communicative power is again transformed into "administrative power" through legislation' (Habermas, 1996b, p. 28).

These views would be regarded as old-fashioned by many political scientists (if not constitutional lawyers): that law-making constitutes the *only* rightful mechanism for transforming public opinion into administrative decision. Setting aside the public sphere, Habermas's normative theory of the state is virtually identical to that proposed long ago by Theodore Lowi (1969) under the rubric of 'juridical democracy.' Lowi was widely criticized at the time for proposing a naïve, civics-textbook version of democracy as an antidote to the ills of interest-group domination of US politics and administration.

Habermas's emphasis on elections as the main channel of influence from the public sphere to the state would also strike many political scientists as old-fashioned. What are we to make of the multiple channels of influence that for better or worse do not involve elections—such as protests, demonstrations, boycotts, information campaigns, media events, lobbying, financial inducements, economic threats, and so forth?

Just because a normative theory is old-fashioned does not mean that it is wrong. However, when the theory appears old-fashioned precisely because it does not square with the empirical realities that are its alleged justification, perhaps something deeper is amiss. Here I think Habermas falls prey to a familiar, indeed near-universal, tendency among political theorists: to treat empirical reality in terms of a few stylized facts, rather than attending seriously to the findings of empirical political science (see Gunnell, 1986 on the more general alienation of political theory).

Habermas's democratic theory differs from republican theories in its denial of any undifferentiated popular sovereignty. It differs from communitarian theories in its rejection of the need for any pre-existing community and associated tradition that must impose boundaries on the content of deliberation. And unlike many liberal theorists, he does not accord primacy to rights for the sake only of their bearers—but rather for the sake of securing a space for deliberation. Also unlike most liberals, he does not see ordinary (as opposed to constitutional) politics in terms of the reconciliation and aggregation of interests defined privately, for Habermas recognizes too the need for solidarity to be generated through politics. And he regards debate in the legislature as less important than the more diffuse formation of public opinion.

These differences notwithstanding, it is not hard to discern in Habermas's model of law and democracy an accommodation with key tenets of liberal constitutionalism, especially as interpreted by the liberal American deliberative democrats. There is no sense that the administrative state, or economy, should be democratized any further. All that matters is that they be steered by law, itself democratically influenced. Habermas has turned his back on extra-constitutional agents of both democratic influence and democratic distortion. Earlier

I distinguished the critical theory of democracy precisely in terms of its attention to such extra-constitutional aspects. If this distinction holds, then Habermas's democratic theory is no longer a true critical theory of democracy. The administrative state and its legal system acquire easy legitimacy that was denied in earlier formulations of critical theory, including Habermas's own. Perhaps this shows, once again, that liberalism is the most effective vacuum cleaner in the history of political thought, capable of sucking up all the doctrines that appear to challenge it, be they critical theory, environmentalism, feminism, or socialism. Some liberals, and some of those vacuumed up, might regard this capacity as a strength. I would argue in contrast that it depletes political imagination of the critical distance necessary to think about how dominant political institutions and practices might be changed for the better.

Retrieving the Critical Voice

The assimilation of deliberative democracy to liberal constitutionalism has been strengthened by the seeming defection of Habermas and Habermasians such as Bohman (1998b). Yet there have always been a number of advocates of the theory for whom liberal institutions—and especially the contemporary liberal capitalist state—deserved more in the way of critique than celebration. Theorists such as Benjamin Barber (1984), Seyla Benhabib (1996b), David Miller (1992), Nancy Fraser (1992), Habermas in his earlier work and myself (Dryzek, 1990a) have contrasted the deliberative model to more entrenched models and real-world practices. In particular, they have criticized the limited aggregative account of democracy that appears in much liberal theory and practice (what Barber would call 'thin democracy'). Such theorists have sought either radical reform of the liberal state, to make it more authentically deliberative, or the specification of alternative venues where deliberation might be sought. These alternatives might include civil society in confrontation with the state, or public spheres, or workplace democracy. Again, not all developments in public spheres and civil society need to be endorsed (just as liberal democrats should not endorse everything that happens within liberal governments). The point is simply that from the point of view of democracy there are constraints on the state as a venue that do not apply to civil society.

Bohman (1998b) in a review essay celebrates the 'coming of age' of deliberative democracy in terms of the maturity of the field. On this account, what began as a critical alternative to established liberal democratic practices has matured, to the point where it now sees the liberal institutions which it once rejected in favour of more participatory alternatives as themselves the proper home for deliberation. Bohman himself had until recently favoured an alternative home for deliberation. As he had put it (1996, p. 241), 'public reason is exercised not by the state but primarily in the public sphere of free and equal citizens'.

Bohman's characterization of this coming of age is actually a bit over-simplified. As I have already demonstrated, liberal constitutionalism had a very large presence in the theory of deliberative democracy from the very beginning, and so is not a recent arrival. In this light, 'maturity' means really that the more radical aspect of discursive democracy has been gradually squeezed out. I will set aside the fact that a field of inquiry barely ten years old (at least in its contemporary incarnation) seems a bit young to qualify for 'maturity'.

There remains a rather large question about what this alleged maturation has accomplished. Burkean conservatives would have no problem here: mature judgement involves reconciliation with the status quo that youthful zeal finds it all too easy to reject. Bohman is no conservative, but in the end comes up with no better defense of these developments than a rhetorical invocation of 'maturity' and 'coming of age'. It is hard to see how he could do better, given that the critical edge that was once more pronounced in the deliberative democracy field was never blunted by argument. The fact that no argument has been carried (or so far as I know even attempted) against it means that any celebration of the demise of the critical aspect is untrue to core principles of deliberation, in which of course such matters should be decided by argument rather than assumption, proclamation, or drift.

If I am correct in the contention with which I began, that the agenda for democratic theory is now set by the deliberative turn, and if deliberation has been largely assimilated to liberal constitutionalism, then this loss of critical edge is very serious indeed, for two reasons.

The first concerns the character of democracy itself. Democracy is not a static concept, whose essence could ever be decided once and for all. Rather, it is a dynamic and open-ended project. To seek a model of democracy that is supposed to apply across all times and places, or even to a limited range of particular times and places (such as the set of contemporary developed liberal democracies) is, I believe, pointless. The history of political theory is of course littered with such general prescriptive models. What is striking about recent political theory, especially as it pertains to democracy, is the abandonment by some leading figures of such generalized models in favour of theories that speak to or accept the 'facts' of the contemporary world. Be it Rawls's 'fact of reasonable pluralism' or Habermas's complexity and differentiation, these facts enter political theory in stylized form, off-limits to critical empirical analysis. I would suggest that rather than accept such 'facts' at face value, those faithful to the democratic project should look at the range of constraints and possibilities for furthering that project in particular times and places.

In this light, models of democracy are less interesting than processes of democratization. Democratization in this sense is not the spread of liberal democracy to ever more corners of the world, but rather extensions along any one of three dimensions (Dryzek, 1996, pp. 5–6). The first is franchise, expansion of the number of people capable of participating effectively in collective decision. The second is scope, bringing more issues and areas of life potentially under democratic control (though a polity may deliberatively decide not to regulate particular issues). The third is the authenticity of the control (as defined at the beginning of this chapter): to be real rather than symbolic, involving the effective participation of autonomous and competent actors.

It is on the third of these dimensions that deliberation can make its special contribution. Liberal democrats might argue that there is plenty of scope for increased democratic authenticity within the confines of the liberal state; I would argue that there is not. For this state is increasingly subject to the constraints imposed by the transnational capitalist political economy. The first task of all states in this system is to maintain the confidence of actual and potential investors, to avoid capital flight. This imperative conditions policy-making, for democratic influence on policy-making introduces a dangerous element of indeterminacy, and so becomes increasingly curtailed. Public officials under the sway of such imperatives are highly constrained when it comes to the terms of the arguments they can accept; it is very hard for deliberation to reach them. I have argued this point about the limits of state democratization elsewhere at length (see Dryzek 1996), and will revisit the issue in subsequent chapters (especially Chapter 4).

If we give up on the pursuit of more authentic democracy, then democracy itself is impoverished. The deliberative turn promised to bring new energy to democratic development, and especially to the pursuit of democratic authenticity. If indeed it is accommodating itself too comfortably to the existing liberal state, then this promise is not being fulfilled.

The second reason to lament any loss of a critical edge is that it leaves deliberative democrats bereft of resources necessary to confront both their critics and major challenges presented by the character of today's world. In Chapters 2 and 3 I will show that effective replies to criticisms made by social choice theorists, difference democrats, and post-structuralist sceptics require the stronger and critical version of deliberative democracy which I develop and defend. I will argue in these and subsequent chapters that a domesticated liberal constitutionalist and statist version of deliberative democracy is not well equipped to respond to challenges presented by deep plurality and difference in the political composition of society; by ecological crisis; by economic transnationalization and globalization. In short, for the sake of both democratic theory and democratic development, it is vital that the critical voice in deliberative democracy be retrieved. This is the project of discursive democracy.

CHAPTER 2

Minimal Democracy?
The Social Choice Critique

One defining feature of deliberative democracy is that individuals participating in democratic processes are amenable to changing their minds and their preferences as a result of the reflection induced by deliberation. A competing account of politics emphasizes instead the strategic pursuit of goals and interests on the part of individuals and other actors. Situations are strategic when the outcome of an actor's choice depends on the choice(s) made by another actor or actors also pursuing goals and interests. This competing account is widely held by those who treat politics as a contest in which actors compete for advantage. Many political scientists cast case-specific accounts of the way particular political systems work in terms of the pursuit of power and influence by politicians, interest groups, bureaucrats, parties, or sometimes even the state itself. Some political scientists even aspire to a general theory of politics in these terms.

The most pointed account of politics as strategic interaction has been developed and formalized by rational choice theory, which as I write is the most powerful paradigm in the political science discipline, especially in the United States. Rational choice theorists occupy the lion's share of the pages of the discipline's flagship journal, *The American Political Science Review*, lending that journal scholarly rigour, though too often at the expense of readable prose. The subfield's luminaries and sub-luminaries command the highest salaries in the discipline as top-ranked departments compete for their services.

Rational choice theory examines what happens when *homo economicus* takes leave of the market place to pursue his advantage through politics. *Homo economicus* is an instrumentally rational egoist, concerned only with maximizing a set of predefined elements in a utility function (which might include income, wealth, pleasant leisure time, etc.). As the opposite of public spirit, egoism might be thought to cause problems for politics. Still, rational choice modelling can proceed without the egoism assumption, taking an 'anything goes' approach to the specification of an actor's utility. This utility can therefore include public-spirited as well as narrowly self-interested concerns. What is indispensable to the whole rational choice enterprise, however, is that an actor's preferences, utility function, or goals are not changed in the course of social and political interaction, which otherwise could not be modelled in purely strategic terms. This invariance puts rational choice theory on a collision course with deliberative democracy, whose defining feature is preference change through deliberation. The clash resembles that between liberal and deliberative versions of democracy, which, as seen in Chapter 1, was resolved by a softening of the invariance tenet by some liberals, allowing them to become deliberative democrats. Any such softening is much harder for rational choice theorists to contemplate.

As we will see, some theorists have deployed analysis based on this invariance assumption to develop an account of collective choice that is sceptical of the possibility for meaningful democratic collective decision of any sort, and hostile to deliberation in particular. The prescriptive model associated with this account is a minimal democracy that can at best provide a few safeguards against tyranny. The proponents of this model are therefore anti-democratic liberal extremists. Some of these theorists have made tentative moves beyond this minimal normative model, and I will discuss their suggestions, though exactly where these moves point remains unclear.

Until recently the two traditions proceeded in isolation from—and seeming ignorance of—one another. But for better or worse the inevitable contact has now occurred, and neither tradition is likely to emerge unscathed from it. From the point of view of deliberative democracy, the encounter should be salutary, because rational choice theory is really just a formalization of a much more widely held account of politics as strategic action. This account extends to many observers of politics who would be lost in the pages of the *American Political Science Review*.

I have argued elsewhere that the encounter benefits rational choice theory too, because a recognition of the communicative rationality that underwrites deliberative democracy could help rational choice theorists make sense of phenomena that otherwise elude explanation (Dryzek, 1992; 1996, pp. 92–115). Rational choice theorists have otherwise portrayed in great detail a world in which political order does not and cannot exist. This world hosts bureaucracies that maximize their own revenue with little concern for the public interest, rationally ignorant voters who should always choose to abstain rather than vote, majorities who exploit and oppress minorities, politicians who devise programmes that yield tangible benefits for their constituents at taxpayers' expense, together with 'iron triangles' of self-interested politicians, bureaucrats, and lobbyists conspiring against taxpayers. In short, the main result of the field is 'rational man, irrational society' as Brian Barry and Russell Hardin (1982) put it long ago. What rational choice theory has shown is that a political world of strategically rational actors is a nightmare that illuminates only the worst aspects of the developed liberal democracies that the theory is supposed to model. In this light, it is unsurprising that some practitioners have recognized the desirability of something like the communicative rationality that underwrites deliberative democracy, if not by this name (see e.g. Brennan, 1989; Buchanan, 1986; Vanberg and Buchanan, 1989).

I will not revisit this argument about what communicative rationality can do to solve problems generated by rational choice theory in general. Rather, my intent here is to respond to the attack that has now been launched upon deliberative democracy from a particular branch of theory that treats preferences as invariant. I shall conclude that effective response to this attack requires in the end a strong conception of discursive democracy grounded in communicative action. In this light, many deliberative democrats turn out to have conceded too much to more conventional models of democracy for which voting is central, leaving themselves too vulnerable to a particular choice-based critique of democracy as voting.

The Social Choice Critique of Democracy

The attack upon deliberative democracy has been pressed by a number of social choice theorists. It should be stressed that social choice theory is not exactly the same as rational choice theory, nor is it a subset of the latter. Central to rational choice theory is the assumption that individuals behave strategically in seeking their goals. Social choice theory, in contrast, need make no behavioural assumption of this sort. It is concerned solely with the logical properties and normative desirability of alternative mechanisms, such as voting systems, for aggregating individual preferences into collective decisions. Yet how individuals actually *behave* is not totally beside the point. For one of social choice theory's main results is that all aggregation mechanisms are vulnerable to strategic manipulation. If individuals are not inclined to behave strategically, then there is far less cause for concern.

Two renegade rational choice theorists, Brennan and Lomasky (1993), argue that individuals will not behave strategically in elections featuring large numbers of voters. When numbers are large, the likelihood of any one individual's vote determining the outcome of the election is vanishingly small. Thus there is no point in any individual voting for what is in his or her personal interest. Instead, the individual will vote based on his or her 'expressive' preferences, the social values he or she would like to stand for. Yet the social choice problem of aggregating such expressive preferences remains, as does the vulnerability of any aggregation mechanism to strategic manipulation as soon as we move from the behaviour of ordinary voters to that of activists, politicians, and lobbyists. In short, the Brennan and Lomasky offshoot of rational choice theory does not in the end dispense with the need to worry about social choice problems.

In reality, many of the more prominent social choice theorists are also known for their work in rational choice theory; even though these two enterprises are not formally identical. What rational choice theory and social choice theory share, vitally in the context of the prospects for deliberative democracy, is the assumption that individual preferences do not change in the process of social or political interaction. In what follows I will stress only the social-choice-theoretic critique of deliberation, being careful to identify any rational-choice-theoretic sidebars to the main argument. The social choice critique is powerful precisely because it does not have to rest on any particular behavioural assumption, beyond the invariance of preferences. Thus deliberative democracy has more to fear from social choice theory than it does from rational choice theory.

The seminal work in social choice theory is that of Kenneth Arrow (1963), who was eventually awarded the Nobel Prize in Economics (though not just for his social choice work). Arrow showed that it is impossible for any mechanism for the aggregation of individual preferences into collective choices to satisfy simultaneously five seemingly innocuous and undemanding criteria. The first criterion is unanimity: any unopposed individual choice should be incorporated in the collective choice. The second is non-dictatorship. The third is transitivity: if the collectivity prefers A to B and B to C then A should be preferred to C. The fourth is unrestricted domain: there is no restriction on the preferences individuals can have across the available alternatives. The fifth is independence of irrelevant alternatives: the collectivity's preference between A and B should not be affected by the introduction of option C.

The implication of Arrow's theorem is that it is impossible to devise any voting system (such as majority rule), or collective choice mechanism more generally, which is not highly vulnerable to a lapse into dictatorship, or into the manipulation of agendas and rules by astute actors out to secure the collective outcomes they favour. A straightforward example of the possibilities for manipulation is when majorities can be mustered for option A over option B, option B over option C, and option C over option A. This is the problem of cycling. If an actor wants option A to be chosen, he or she will try to ensure that the first vote taken is between B and C, such that C is knocked out and then A can be introduced to beat B. It is not just majority rule which can be so manipulated, or made the target of strategic behaviour, but any kind of voting system. And when several actors are aware of the possibilities for manipulation and so try to out-manoeuvre one another, the politics can get very complex indeed. The problems are obviously most severe when actors behave according to the strategic precepts of rational choice theory.

Arrow's proof proceeded at a fairly abstract level. The extent to which these sorts of problems are found in practice became, and remains, a matter of contention among social choice theorists. Still, the social choice field remains in the shadow of Arrow and the question mark he placed upon democracy.

The most influential social choice theorist after Arrow is William Riker, who is also the founder of the Rochester School of rational choice theory, which now dominates the pages of the American political science discipline's leading journals. Riker radicalized social choice theory to attack any notion of authentic democracy, particularly what he termed 'populism'. To Riker, a doctrine is populist if it believes that there is such a thing as the will of the people that should be reflected in a collective choice. Any such doctrine is, Riker (1982, p. 241) claims, revealed by social choice theory to be 'inconsistent and absurd'. For there is no popular will that exists independently of the particular mechanism (such as majority rule) used to measure it. Different mechanisms will always yield different collective choices from identical distributions of individual preferences. Moreover, Riker believes that there is no reason to prefer any particular mechanism over any other. If we add McKelvey's (1976) proof that very slight changes in the distribution of preferences across individuals can cause major shifts in the content of any collective decision, then social choice theory has shown voting as a means of collective choice to be not only meaningless because arbitrary, but also unstable (see Van Mill, 1996, pp. 735, 741).

Having dismissed elections and every other conceivable collective choice mechanism in these terms, Riker moves to a prescriptive conclusion: elections are useful only because they periodically provide voters with the possibility to turf tyrants out of office. This is the minimal democracy to which social choice analysis points. But even this weak protection against tyrants is undermined by Riker's own argument, because it implies that dismissal of a bad elected official is in fact the will of the voters. Yet as Riker himself has shown, there is no will of the voters that exists independent of the mechanism used to measure it (Coleman and Ferejohn, 1986, p. 22).

Not all social choice theory has this radically anti-democratic political cast, but within the discipline of political science the most influential strand is indeed that associated with Riker and his followers. Let me move now to how radicalized social choice theory's critique of democracy can be turned against deliberative democracy in particular.

Is Talk Cheap?

At first sight, social choice theory in the shadow of Arrow and Riker would seem to have plenty of bad news for those who interpret democracy in aggregative terms. Seeing this discomfort, some proponents of deliberative democracy and associated communicative notions of rationality have suggested that social choice theory has exposed the limits of instrumental or strategic action as the basis for democratic behaviour. In this light, a turn to deliberation that seeks reasoned agreement rather the mere aggregation of preferences is necessary (Miller, 1992; Sunstein, 1993*b*, p. 244).

The visceral reaction of most *rational* choice theorists here would be to reject any such suggestion on the grounds that talk is cheap—as likely to contain lies as truth, perceived as such by rational actors, therefore of no consequence in explaining or affecting social interaction. A more sophisticated rational choice analysis of talk with direct implications for the prospects for deliberation has been developed in a series of articles by David Austen-Smith (1990, 1992; Austen-Smith and Riker, 1987), who treats talk as a form of signalling. As a rational choice theorist, Austen-Smith believes that speech by one actor can never change the preferences of another, but it can convey information. 'Speech making in politics is presumed to be strategic' (Austen-Smith, 1992, p. 47), designed to transmit information selectively to make it more likely that listener B will behave so as to further the outcome that speaker A desires. As Austen-Smith puts it, 'speech making is potentially influential only insofar as it alters individuals' beliefs about how actions map onto consequences' (p. 57). Listeners, as rational strategic actors themselves, recognize this and so will make strategic calculations as to whether or not to believe speakers. Knowing this, speakers have every incentive to conceal information, manipulate, and deceive, while maintaining the appearance of credibility. To Austen-Smith, talk is not cheap in the sense of being meaningless, but it is in the end costless to the speaker. He assumes there are no punishments for being exposed as a liar (1992, p. 46), except on the very rare occasions when something like a perjury law comes into play. Thus political talk is inherently unreliable.

The implication for collective choice is that deliberation will do nothing to advance the probability that individuals' interests will find effective reflection in collective choice, because deceptive talk can induce people to support courses of action that with better information they would oppose. As Przeworski (1998) points out, deliberation may induce individuals to accept false beliefs about the courses of action that are in their interests. At an extreme, they may accept a complete ideology about what is good for them: such as 'what is good for General Motors is good for America'. Marxists would have no problem in recognizing the problem of false consciousness here.

Gerry Mackie (1998) demonstrates in a thoroughgoing critique of Austen-Smith that this model is over-simplified in crucial ways. The model assumes that political interaction is always a one-shot affair. But if interaction is recurrent, a speaker whose lies are exposed will never be believed again; indeed, will find himself or herself shunned (Mackie, 1998, p. 79). Mackie uses the example of a lobbyist whose deception was exposed on a single issue of only modest importance, and whose career was terminated as a consequence (p. 83). Austen-Smith assumes that information communicated by talk cannot be corroborated or proved, and that there is always but a single speaker and single listener. But in any real democracy there are many speakers and many listeners, thus plenty of opportunities for corroboration of the veracity of speakers and the exposure of flatterers and liars (Mackie, 1998, pp. 85–8). With Mackie's rebuttal, criticisms of deliberation deploying the Austen-Smith kind of rational-choice-theoretic analysis merit no further attention, and we can focus our attention instead on the more trenchant social-choice-theoretic critique of deliberation.

Before moving to that social choice based critique, we need to take note of a troubling charge made by Adam Przeworski (1998). When (to use his example) Mobil Oil takes advertising space in the *New York Times* to argue that the well-being of the United States economy requires an increase in corporate profitability, Mobil Oil's executives and the writers they employ may actually believe this to be true, so there are no flatterers and liars to be exposed. But there are arguments to be countered: a commitment to deliberative democracy does not mean blanket approval of all communication, or blindness to the attempts of corporations and others to use political communication in the interests of ideological domination.[1] Indeed, the *critical* theory of communication that is one source of the theory of deliberative democracy is preoccupied with such agents of distortion and how to counter them (see Chapter 1). That is why close attention needs to be paid to the conditions under which authentic deliberation can proceed. One difference between discursive democracy and liberal constitutionalist deliberative democracy lies precisely in discursive democracy's recognition of, and challenge to, ideological domination. (Later I will address more explicitly the possibility of discursive contestation of the kind of ideological domination feared by Przeworski.)

The Social Choice Critique of Voting in a Deliberative Context

We can safely conclude that political talk is not cheap, and that substantial penalties can apply to those who engage in deceptive talk. But deliberative democracy cannot rest easy here. For collective decisions are not made just by talking. Some deliberative democrats have been rather silent on how collective decisions are in fact made. As such they leave themselves open to critics who point out that deliberation is a radically incomplete democratic theory. Citizens deliberate—and then what? As one critic states, 'No matter how much deliberation takes place, heads have to be counted—aggregated—at some point if a democratic decision to be reached. No adequate model of democracy can fail to be "aggregative". There is no such thing as a "deliberative model of democracy" ' (Saward, 1998, p. 64). Or as Przeworski (1998, p. 141) puts it, 'deliberation theorists . . . wish away the vulgar fact that under democracy deliberation ends in voting' such that 'it is the result

---

[1] Przeworski's argument is actually a bit more subtle than simple manipulation. He argues that false beliefs are not of the 'technical' form—that increasing Mobil's profits really will be good for the economy. Rather, they are of the 'equilibrium' form: individuals believe that most other individuals believe increasing Mobil's profits will benefit the economy, and so feel they must go along with the more widely-held belief. However, this is not then a matter of false belief, but rather a rational judgement about the futility of a particular kind of political action—in this case, opposing Mobil.

of voting, not of discussion, that authorizes governments to govern, to compel' (p. 142).

If and when citizens or their representatives vote, then social choice theory can come charging in with its critique of democracy-as-voting. As Grofman (1993, p. 1578) points out, 'Arrowian aggregation problems ... can manifest themselves in the context of a deliberative search for the public interest unless we posit that all voters share a common notion of the common interest'—which is of course highly improbable. Further, as we will see shortly, social choice theorists can point to some features of deliberative democracy which, if introduced in a context where voting is the main collective choice mechanism, will actually exacerbate instability and arbitrariness in collective choice.

With their increasing stress on voting and elections, deliberative democrats have played into the hands of their social choice critics. To liberal constitutionalist deliberative democrats, the United States constitutional order to which most of them have connected their efforts of interpretation and advocacy does of course feature voting at its heart. Voting can take place in popular elections for Congress and the Presidency, among judges on the bench of the Supreme Court, within Congressional committees, or on the floor of the House and Senate. To Joshua Cohen (1989), voting is second best to consensus, but necessary as a fallback if consensus cannot be achieved. As we saw in Chapter 1, Habermas (1996a; 1996b, p. 28) now sees elections as the main means by which the influence of public opinion is converted into communicative power, which is then converted into administrative power through law-making. Thus David van Mill (1996, p. 743) can claim with some justification that 'the practice of voting is now an integral part of Habermas's theory of discourse' (he should have said 'of democracy' rather than 'of discourse'). This fact in turn enables van Mill to turn his social choice knife against deliberative democracy. Actually Habermas (1996b, p. 29) qualifies his endorsement of elections with the statement that 'The public opinion that is worked up via democratic procedures into communicative power cannot "rule" of itself, but can only point the use of administrative power in specific directions.' So voting in elections does not produce binding social choices. But from the vantage point of social choice theory, 'pointing administrative power in specific directions' can mean little else but producing collective decisions.

Van Mill argues, correctly, that the requirements specified by deliberative democrats for effective deliberation are exactly the 'institution-free' conditions which social choice theorists have demonstrated are most likely to produce meaningless, arbitrary, unstable, and chaotic outcomes in collective choice. These conditions include 'equal access to debate, the absence of a powerful agenda setter, unrestrained access to raise and object to amendments . . .' (van Mill, 1996, p. 735). According to social choice theory, abitrariness and instability stem from exactly such procedural fairness. In Riker's formalization fair procedure means 'monotonicity [that is, if one individual prefers an alternative already chosen more strongly, that alternative will remain the collective choice], neutrality among options, simple majority decision, no agenda setter, equal access to the agenda, equal access to debate, equal opportunity to introduce proposals, and each vote counting equally' (van Mill, 1996, p. 740).

Echoing van Mill, Knight and Johnson (1994) conclude that the real problem with deliberative democracy is that it requires free and equal access, including access for individuals, interests, and groups that were historically excluded from decision-making. Expanding access along these lines will 'unsettle, if not altogether subvert, any extant shared understanding about the dimensions of political conflict' (Knight and Johnson, 1994, p. 289). To Knight and Johnson, it is not just deliberation that is objectionable, but also any associated expansion of the democratic franchise.[2] The fact that deliberation precedes voting is, on the kind of account developed by Van Mill and Knight and Johnson, of little consequence. Social choice theorists can even grant that deliberation can induce replacement of self-interested preferences by ones cast in terms that all individuals can accept via the exercise of free public reason. All that is required for the grim forecast of social choice theory to come into play is that the ordering of these preferences still differs across individuals.

Deliberative democrats can respond here that deliberation will at least make individuals aware of the dimensions of the issue that are at stake. The main reason that cycles and their associated instability and arbitrariness exist is that several evaluative dimensions are combined in a single vote or choice. To contrive an example, consider a hypothetical vote over three proposals about what to construct on a landmark city-centre site: a prison, a shopping centre, and a park. A third of the voters are environmentalists, and favour a park over a prison over a shopping centre (which will increase congestion and pollution). A third fear crime, and so favour a prison over a shopping centre over

---

[2] It is puzzling that in a later essay Knight and Johnson (1997, p. 310) conclude that 'society must take the steps necessary to guarantee that each citizen has the capacity to effectively participate in the democratic arena'. This later essay too is sprinkled with insights gleaned from social choice theory about the difficulties that such equality of access would cause.

a park (where they think drug dealers will congregate and murderers lurk). A third care mainly about the material quality of their own lives, and so favour a shopping centre over a park over a prison. Mere voting could end up by determining that any one of these three options be chosen; it all depends on how the vote or votes are taken. The root of the problem here is that three dimensions of choice—environmental, safety, and material convenience—are being forced into one vote. Deliberation could promote awareness of the three dimensions of collective choice at issue. Alternatives can then be sought on each of the dimensions, and the collectively preferred positions on each dimension aggregated into an overall choice (Miller, 1992, p. 65). Through such a process cycles and associated sources of instability and arbitrariness are made less likely.

An example from the real world of something like this kind of deliberation-induced awareness of the dimensions of choice at issue can perhaps be found in the tortuous multi-actor negotiations leading toward political settlement of the Northern Ireland conflict in the 1990s. If the issue is framed as 'Protestant versus Catholic' or 'Unionist versus Republican', then we have an intractable conflict with no conceivable solution that can conceivably satisfy the two communities in Northern Ireland as well as the governments of the United Kingdom and Irish Republic. Unlike the previous example, the decision rule is not majority voting, but something closer to unanimity across the key players. As time goes on, further dimensions are introduced that relate to respect for identity, guarantees of civil rights, and forgiveness of past politically-motivated crimes (which turns out to unite the gunmen on both sides). Aspirations short of full sovereignty gain purchase; mixed forms of multi-level and cross-national political control and power-sharing surface as options; ways of recognizing and affirming community identity without inter-communal conflict are explored. The process is not exactly a paragon of deliberation, as threats of violence linger in the background, and there is plenty of strategic action on the part of all the key participants. But the deliberative component is also undeniable, and one product of that is that traditionally hostile actors began to learn how to live together despite continuing deep divisions.

Deliberation can multiply dimensions and options, and so it would seem add to the complexity of choice. But complexity should not be equated with intractability, for this proliferation increases the possibilities for stable and non-arbitrary agreement. Deliberation can perform this function even when, as in the Northern Ireland case, it is bargaining that proves decisive in determining the content of the collective choice. Does deliberation uncover latent dimensions that already existed, or are dimensions created in the process of deliberation? Empirically, it is hard if not impossible to tell the difference; and quite possibly some mixture of discovery and creation occurs.

Social choice sceptics such as Jack Knight and James Johnson (1994, p. 287) can criticize any reliance on deliberation-induced awareness on the grounds that a full and shared understanding of the dimensions of conflict at issue is only that. Individuals' preferences across these dimensions remain and so does their potential to cause havoc in collective choices. Indeed, one can imagine a deliberation-induced increase in awareness enabling individuals to behave in still more cunning ways as they attempt to manipulate the process to their own advantage. Yet to accept this dismal conclusion implies excessive reliance on the behavioural assumption of *rational* choice theory, which cannot see in deliberation any potential to curb the proclivity to engage in unremittingly strategic behaviour. The real beauty of deliberation is that it can curb strategic action; if the social and political worlds can be composed *only* of strategic action then in the end Knight and Johnson, are probably justified in their scepticism.

The sceptic might respond here that even if preferences do change as a result of reflection induced by deliberation without deception, there is no guarantee that they will change in a direction which makes the dire predictions of social choice theory less likely to come true. Any acceptance of the possibility of preference change is of course a violation of the assumptions of both rational choice theory and social choice theory, so it involves a major concession to the power of deliberation. Still, it does not necessarily cure scepticism. So Przeworski (1991, pp. 17–18) argues that the information exchanged in deliberation might even make cycles more likely, if individuals are induced to change their preference orderings among the available alternatives in awkward directions. So let me now try to show why deliberation will normally induce movements in the opposite direction to that feared by Przeworski. The key here is restriction of the domain of preferences that can be sustained during deliberation.

Tractable Collective Choice via Domain Restriction

This emphasis on domain restriction is actually pursued by some social choice theorists themselves, or at least those who are unwilling to accept Riker's radical scepticism about democracy and his associated minimalist model. Obviously if the 'unrestricted domain' condition of Arrow's theorem is relaxed then the impossibility result dissipates. That is, individuals are not allowed to have any preferences they like across the available alternatives. Notably, their preference orderings cannot be allowed to violate what is technically called 'single-peakedness'. Single-peakedness means that when the available options are arrayed on a continuum, the individual's preference must fall continuously on either side of the most preferred position. So, for example, an individual confronted with a foreign policy crisis could not be allowed to have capitulation as a first preference, war as a second preference, and coercive diplomacy (threatening war) as a third preference. This ordering has two peaks, one at each end of a continuum. Or particular kinds of extremist views might be ruled out. Social choice theorists such as Johnson (1998, pp. 163–4) can argue here that they are making a similar move to deliberative theorists, who specify that the domain is restricted as part of the deliberative process. But this attempt to 'level the playing field' is more than a little dubious, because deliberation has an endogenous mechanism to restrict domain whereas aggregation does not. Indeed, the whole point of deliberation is to 'restrict domain' as the language of social choice theory would have it, because deliberation in inducing reflection on preferences and requiring that they be defended publicly eliminates preference orderings which cannot be so defended.

Aside from restricting domain on one dimension, deliberation can also facilitate the disaggregation of a non-single-peaked dimension into two or more dimensions which *may* prove to be single-peaked. For example, in a foreign policy crisis a preference for all-out war over no action over moderate intervention is non-single-peaked. But if asked to justify this preference ordering, the individuals in question might reveal two dimensions: one could be termed bellicosity, the other expected net value of military action. Bellicose individuals might also prefer no action to moderate intervention because they think the latter would not succeed in meeting national goals on the 'net value' dimension. Of course, the single-peakedness may be irreducible. The relative incidence of reducible non-single-peakedness and irreducible non-single-peakedness is an empirical question, on which no information exists. But to the extent non-single-peakedness is reducible, deliberation facilitates the explication of the dimensions that reduce it.

An alternative way of resolving Arrow problems to relaxing the unrestricted domain criterion is developed by van Mill (1996, p. 749), who points to the branch of social choice theory that trades in 'structure-induced equilibrium' (the concept was invented by Kenneth Shepsle). Structure-induced equilibrium is one proposed explanation of why the arbitrariness and instability predicted by social choice theorists so rarely appears in the practice of (say) legislatures. The reason is that the circumstances of choice are highly constrained by procedural rules and norms. For example, in the United States Congress committees have gatekeeping powers when it comes to the content of bills that reach the floor of Congress. Normally, amendments cannot be introduced on the floor, so the House as a whole can only vote an entire package up or down. The division of labour within the relevant committee further constrains what can be voted on within the committee itself. These structures induce efficiency, predictability, and stability in the collective choices made in Congress, though at the expense of responsiveness to the distribution of opinion within Congress.

Structure-induced equilibrium is generally deployed as an explanation of stability in real-world voting systems such as legislatures. Van Mill believes it can and should be turned to normative use in institutional design. The problem here is that one must postulate either a benign *deus ex machina* to design the institution in question, or have the process of choice about structure subject to all the instability and arbitrariness that social choice theory has identified. That process could be benign if the participants could control their strategic proclivities in the process of institutional design, although this would not be allowed by a hard-line rational choice theorist. A further problem arises in that it is not clear what normative criteria institutional design should be trying to achieve; recall that one of Riker's arguments is that there is no reason to prefer any particular collective choice mechanism over any other. Moreover, a major design problem enters because introducing additional stability-promoting institutional rules is not cumulative; the interaction of different rules that induce stability in isolation may together induce greater instability (Mackie, 1996, p. 26, following Strom, 1990, p. 105). Thus trying to predict the effects of any combination of institutional innovations would impose an impossible burden of calculation on institutional designers.

But the difficulties associated with any normative application of structure-induced equilibrium analysis should not delay us here. The main reason to concern ourselves with it is that it highlights once again the problems caused by the structurelessness that is associated with the ideal of deliberative democracy. Thus despite the inability of social choice critics to specify any convincing alternative, there remains an important kernel in their critique that still troubles deliberative democracy. For so long as deliberation concludes with voting under structurally unconstrained conditions, the problem of arbitrariness and instability in collective choice remains.

Where, then, does the theory of deliberative democracy now stand in light of the social choice critique? If we stay with the language of social choice theory for the moment, deliberation does have mechanisms to restrict the domain of preferences, thus reducing the probability of the dire outcomes predicted by social choice theorists. There are two ways in which domain can be restricted: by stipulation in advance, and through the process of deliberation itself. In passing, it should be noted that an inability to recognize this distinction vitiates Johnson's (1998) criticism that deliberative democrats engage in arbitrary domain restriction, which I mentioned earlier.

The domain of eligible preferences can be stipulated in advance by specifying the kinds of arguments that are and are not eligible in the deliberative arena: this is deliberation's parallel to the use of structure-induced equilibrium promoted by van Mill (1996). Along these lines, Gutmann and Thompson (1996) rule out in advance arguments that deny political equality (such as racist arguments), and those that do not respect principles of human integrity (such as arguments for unrestricted police powers). In addition, Gutmann and Thompson believe that participants must be committed to core deliberative principles of reciprocity, publicity, and accountability. Reciprocity rules out sectarian arguments—for example, that divorce should be outlawed because it conflicts with the doctrine of a religion. Publicity can screen out narrowly self-interested arguments. Accountability means that arguments must be capable of withstanding the scrutiny of those on whose behalf they are allegedly made. Rawls (1989) specifies a set of deliberative conditions similar in spirit to, but much more restrictive than, Gutmann and Thompson in order to secure discussion that is 'reasonable'. Ruled out are arguments based on self-interest, prejudice, and ideology, or those that attack the core identity of other deliberators.

Johnson (1998, pp. 168–70) argues against deliberative preconditions of this sort by deploying the example of slavery. Clearly, arguments for slavery would be ruled out in advance by the sorts of preconditions for entry into the deliberative process specified by Gutmann and Thompson and Rawls. Johnson notes that in the days when slavery was accepted and slaves themselves were 'socially dead' and 'outside the game of honor' (Johnson takes these phrases from Orlando Patterson) then deliberative resolution of the slavery issue would also be ruled out if we stuck to these preconditions. For any attempt to subject the slavery issue to deliberation by appealing to the otherwise reasonable and civil side of slave-owners and defenders of slavery (Southern gentlemen?) would involve existential challenge to their worldview of a decidedly uncivil sort, and so would be ruled out by any 'civility' preconditions.

This example can actually be used to illustrate a very different point: that the range of issues amenable to deliberation can change across time and space. Today slavery is not amenable to this treatment, and arguments for slavery cannot be admitted if we adhere to anything like the preconditions specified by Gutmann and Thompson and Rawls. In the time of Aristotle, and even Jefferson, slave-owners and defenders of slavery could be men (remembering that only men were citizens) of (deliberative) honour. Thus slave-owners could have been engaged in productive debate by those who opposed the practice. Thus the way these preconditions operates will also change across time and space. How then should deliberative democrats respond to this variability? The answer is surely that the preconditions themselves, and in particular the way they apply, must be redeemable in deliberative scrutiny. In the case of slavery, this might involve asking whether the 'human integrity' principle proposed by Gutmann and Thompson should apply to all humans, and if not why not.

In allowing any preconditions to be themselves redeemed in debate, deliberative democracy scores over social choice theory's competing domain-restricting mechanism of structure-induced equilibrium. Under the latter, the relevant rules and norms can only be introduced in arbitrary fashion, such that there are no criteria and no procedures to distinguish good rules and norms from bad ones. But deliberation's real advantage over social choice theory in the domain restriction stakes is that deliberation has endogenous mechanisms for restricting the range of preferences and options, whereas social choice theory rules out such endogenous mechanisms because it is the prisoner of an assumption that sees preferences as unaffected by political process. Indeed, that is one main point of deliberation—that there are certain kinds of positions that cannot withstand deliberative scrutiny, even if no explicit preconditions are applied on the kinds of arguments that are admissible.

One deliberative mechanism for domain restriction here is what Elster (1998, p. 12) calls 'the civilizing force of hypocrisy', as individuals find that they must stick to the arguments they announce in public, despite any private misgivings they may retain. Individuals find that it is much more persuasive to couch arguments in terms of the public interest rather than the self-interest that may truly motivate them, and they are eventually obliged to follow the public-spirited course of action as a result (or lose face). This is not a matter of just dressing up arguments for private interest, because proposals for a vote will likely only be formulated that respond to the discussion couched in terms of public interest (Fearon, 1998, p. 54). Their need to reduce cognitive dissonance may mean that individuals eventually come to convince themselves of the public interest argument for their position. It is quite likely that talking in public interest terms will lead individuals to think in public interest terms (Goodin, 1992*a*: ch. 7). In this light, Gutmann and Thompson's specification of 'publicity' as a precondition for entry into deliberation is unnecessary, for there are mechanisms internal to deliberation itself that promote publicity in their sense.

In short, deliberation itself possesses substantial endogenous domain restriction mechanisms, such that there is in general no need to introduce the kinds of pre-specified restrictions on the kinds of arguments that can be introduced favoured by authors such as Gutmann and Thompson. Political equality, human integrity, reciprocity, publicity, and accountability are undeniably important values, but the best way for people to learn these values is through the practice of deliberation, rather than through being told (even if it is by Ivy League professors) that they must abide by these principles before they can enter the forum.

From Voting to Communication

My account of deliberation's superior capacity when it comes to domain reduction remains oriented by social choice theory's emphasis on voting, which, as I have noted, many deliberative democrats have come to share, however reluctantly. Downgrading the centrality of voting would involve a substantial ontological shift in our basic conceptualization of democracy. I will now argue that such a shift enables a more compelling response to the social choice critique. The shift has two aspects. The first, which I will deal with in this section, seeks collective choice through reasoned agreement rather than voting. The second, which I will discuss in the next section, looks to make public policy responsive to public opinion through non-electoral means, meaning that public opinion must be conceptualized as something other than the registration of preferences by voting.

Reasoned agreement via deliberation is often characterized as consensus, which in turn is defined as agreement not just on a collective choice, but also on the exact normative grounds for the choice. Not surprisingly, this prospect has been dismissed by social choice theorists as a vain hope that is not worth pursuing in contemporary complex societies (Knight and Johnson, 1994, p. 282). In the language of social choice, consensus means not just convergence on a single dimension of conflict, but also convergence on a single point on that dimension. Even the first of these two steps looks implausible, and there is no reason why deliberation should produce it (Knight and Johnson, 1994, p. 282–3; van Mill, 1996, p. 747).

Among deliberative democrats, a stress on consensus is associated mainly with Habermas, also with Cohen (1989)—though, as we have seen, both eventually concede a central place to voting and elections. In Habermas's communicative theory, under ideal, distortion-free conditions, given long enough to debate, consensus would be achieved on matters of both morality and truth. What distinguishes consensus from mere agreement is that individuals support the outcome for essentially the same reasons. Of course, real-world exigencies and time constraints would in practice get in the way, as Habermas himself recognizes (Habermas, 1979, p. 90; 1982, pp. 257–8). But consensus remains the regulative ideal, an orientation to which real-world arrangements could aspire, though never actually reach. Corresponding to this orientation is disparagement of bargaining. (Though as I have already pointed out, deliberation can have a positive effect even when bargaining is decisive, by multiplying the dimensions on which bargains can be struck.)

Habermas himself has retained this emphasis on consensus in his more recent democratic theory, at least when it comes to the workings of the public sphere (Habermas, 1996). But the stress on consensus has long troubled many of those who are otherwise sympathetic to Habermas's project (see e.g. Benhabib, 1990; Bohman, 1995; Dryzek, 1990*a*, pp. 16–17; Gould, 1988, pp. 18, 126–7; Mackie, 1995). Here it is normal to invoke the implausibility of a strong notion of consensus in plural societies, a plurality which Habermas himself has recognized (though mainly in terms of obstacles on the road to consensus). Now, consensus is not essential or even necessarily central to the theory of democratic deliberation. Allowance for workable agreements (Sunstein, 1997, calls them 'incompletely theorized agreements') in which different participants accept a course of action for different reasons—so long as these reasons have sustained deliberative scrutiny—could quite easily be inserted into the theory of deliberative democracy, and even into the Habermasian edifice in particular (see Dryzek, 1990*a*, pp. 16–17; Eriksen, 1994). One can even retain a focus on public reason through an allowance that public reason can itself be plural (Bohman, 1995, p. 263).

Here, we can usefully take a look at the real world of deliberation. Reasoned agreement as an operating principle finds its place in discursive designs that have flourished in a variety of problem areas. Sometimes it is called the principle of consensus, but it is not consensus in the formal sense specified by social choice theory. Collective choices are indeed produced by near-universal assent; but people can support this decision for different reasons. For example, in the suburb of Melbourne (Northcote) where I live, a community group was organized to object to the level of noxious emissions from a large paper mill in the early 1980s. What began as an acrimonious confrontation in which the company (Australian Paper Mills) successfully resisted further governmental regulation of pollution ended in co-operative resolution in which additional pollution control equipment was installed, and emissions were staggered so as to avoid unfavourable weather conditions, such as still air and temperature inversions. Within the company this course of action had the enthusiastic support of the engineers, for whom emissions reduction was an interesting technical challenge, and the public relations staff, who could now claim with some justification that the company was a good corporate citizen. Obviously the need for such demonstration was increased by the presence of a community protest group. In other cases (but not this one) shareholders and managers have been convinced of the need for pollution reduction on the grounds that 'pollution prevention pays'— pollution is indicative of inefficient use of materials. The reasons that convinced the engineers and public relations staff were very different from the health and aesthetic concerns which motivated the community group, but they only surfaced as a result of the group's efforts.

There is now an extensive literature on experiences of discursive designs (for early discussions, see Dryzek, 1987*a*; Torgerson, 1990). Much of the literature discusses mediation of disputes, ranging from interpersonal conflicts to policy conflicts over natural resource development, and a variety of other third-party facilitated conflict resolution procedures. Other examples range from the community boards of San Francisco, where neighbourhood disputes are negotiated (Schlosberg, 1995) to the Resource Advisory Councils set up in the mid-1990s to manage grazing on the public lands in the Western United States (Welsh, 2000). Discursive designs in practice bear little resemblance to the strategic machinations predicted by social choice theory. Of course, one needs to be on guard against more subtle manipulations of their processes, along with the possibility of ideological hegemony. But those who observe and engage these processes are often aware of possibilities such as co-optation and ideological hegemony, and are indeed on guard against them. The legitimacy of discursive designs depends on their deliberative democratic qualities:

that reasoned discussion should be decisive, that there should be no deference to authority or alleged expertise.

Violations of these principles are readily exposed, and if purportedly open inquiries are in reality a sham they can be criticized as such. For example, public inquiries into nuclear installations and the construction of motorways in Britain have normally been palliative exercises with the terms of reference and rules of evidence and inference stacked against objectors (see e.g. Kemp, 1985). However, the objectors have generally recognized this fact, and sought to expose this character of the proceedings, even as they attempted to make their cases within them.

Reasoned agreement as an operating principle may be easiest to achieve in locality-specific disputes and problems with a relatively small number of identifiable participants who can meet in face-to-face interaction. There are ways of initiating such processes on a larger scale, for example through mechanisms that select participants by lot, such as citizens' juries (Burnheim, 1985; Dahl, 1985; Smith and Wales, 1999). Mechanisms of this sort are an effective response to those who believe that deliberative democracy would in practice entail a self-appointed deliberative aristocracy (e.g. Femia, 1996, p. 391). Still, the larger the scale at which an issue arises, the harder it is to introduce discursive designs to resolve the issue (Femia, 1996, pp. 392–3). For large-scale complex issues a different procedure can come into play, to which I now turn.

From the State to the Public Sphere

For social choice theory, public opinion is some aggregate of individual preferences—though the theory has of course shown just how troublesome such aggregation can be, especially if we try to register it through elections. But there are other ways to think about public opinion and its communication to government. Here I will reintroduce the concept of the public sphere as discussed in Chapter 1. I will argue for a reconceptualization of public opinion in terms of the outcome of contestation within the public sphere as transmitted to the state through a variety of means, notably rhetoric. This reconceptualization constitutes a logically complete deliberative alternative to the aggregative idea that public opinion is transmitted to government through voting that registers preferences. Such an account provides deliberative democracy with a strong response to the social choice critique with which I began this chapter.

Large-scale, complex issues are what Habermas has in mind in his theory of deliberative democracy that involves creation of public opinion in the public sphere, its conversion into communicative power via elections, then translation into the administrative power of the state via law-making. Elections are a crucial link in this chain from public opinion to administrative decision. This stress on elections plays into the hands of social choice critics such as van Mill. But elections are not the only available transmission mechanisms, and if their importance can be downgraded then the critics have a much smaller target. In fact a number of alternative transmission mechanisms are available, and I will explore these further in subsequent chapters, along with some examples of how they work. For the moment it will suffice to emphasize the capacity of the public sphere and its actors to change the terms of political discourse, whose effects can extend to state actors. This transmission mechanism is discursive rather than electoral.

Here it is necessary to think of 'discourse' in (loosely) Foucauldian rather than Habermasian terms: a discourse is a shared set of assumptions that enable its adherents to assemble bits of sensory information into coherent wholes (see Chapter 1 for a more extensive discussion of the meaning of 'discourse' in this sense). The public sphere can be home to a constellation of discourses, some of which are direct competitors, some of which have a looser association with one another. Within the environmental area, the competitors might include the discourses of sustainable development and green radicalism. Within criminal justice policy, they might include emphases on the social psychology of crime versus a more economistic discourse that treats criminals' decisions in terms of rational calculation. Within family policy they might include feminism and a more traditional patriarchal discourse.

The balance of competing discourses matters a great deal; but there is never a vote on which discourse should prevail. Votes may sometimes occur as part of the larger contest; but they are largely epiphenomenal, functioning mainly as markers of the prevailing balance. Sometimes particular individuals can make a great difference in this contest through the power of rhetoric; the achievements of Martin Luther King, Jr., are the exemplary case here (Dryzek, 1996, pp. 152–4). In King's case the effect on United States public policy was eventually profound. But more diffuse and decentralized—and so more democratic—forces are at work in the public sphere too in affecting the balance of competing discourses. The rise of discourses such as feminism and environmentalism in the past three decades was not the work of a few leaders, but the outcome of the combined efforts of thousands if not millions of individuals engaged in many kinds of communication. The public policy changes have of course included major changes in the content of family law induced by feminism, and a spectrum of legislation on the environment (which prior to the late 1960s was barely conceptualized as an issue area). Thinking of the operation of the public sphere in terms of the competition of discourses does, I believe, give more purchase than Habermas's own formulation of fluid 'subjectless communication' that operates in large-scale, complex societies. I will develop this account further in later chapters.

Any mention of rhetoric finds objection in a tradition in political theory extending from Plato to Habermas which equates rhetoric with emotive manipulation of the way points are made, propaganda and demagoguery at an extreme, thus meriting only banishment from the realm of rational communication. Thus some deliberative democrats (e.g. Chambers, 1996, p. 151) see in rhetoric a dangerous potential for emotional manipulation and so coercion. However, one distinguishing feature of rhetoric (in particular, good or effective rhetoric) lies in its ability to reach a particular audience by framing points in a language that will move the audience in question. So Martin Luther King, Jr., could make rhetorical appeals that moved a white audience initially unsympathetic to the civil rights movement through frequent invocation of the language of the Declaration of Independence and the United States Constitution. As liberal documents, these contain grist for rational, dispassionate argument about the content and distribution of rights. But it was the place of the Declaration of Independence and the Constitution in the *hearts* of white Americans that King could reach. The attachment to these documents and the processes that created them is largely, though not exclusively, emotional, rather than a matter of prudent calculation. King's achievement was thus to lead adherents of the established discourse of liberalism to question and ultimately redefine some key terms of that discourse. Certainly there was rational argumentation here too, but the transmission was aided, perhaps even made possible, by the accompanying rhetoric. Without the emotional appeal the argument would have fallen on deaf ears. Such transmission is fully consistent with the orientation of communicative action to reciprocal understanding, so there is no need to banish it to the realm of strategic action, as Habermas would.

Any mention of emotional response might raise fears of demagoguery; but emotions themselves can be subjected to rational justification, because emotions often rest on beliefs. For example, anger might rest on a belief that an individual has been unfairly rewarded, or for that matter unfairly wronged (Rehg, 1997, p. 372; O'Neill, 1998, pp. 19–21). Emotions can be a pointer to ethical judgement (Nussbaum, 1996). In this light, any formal or informal rules of debate that exclude emotional responses may be suppressing particular ways of making a point, and so making it less likely that the force of the point can be established. Still, emotion can be coercive; which is why in the end it must answer to reason.

Several deliberative democrats now recognize that rhetoric has an important part to play in effective deliberation, notably Amy Gutmann and Dennis Thompson (1996, pp. 135–6), William Rehg (1997), and Iris Young (1996, 1998). Young calls herself a communicative democrat, rather than a deliberative one, precisely because deliberation excludes forms of communication such as rhetoric. Gary Remer (1998) points out that many of the cases which deliberative democrats consider exemplary, notably the constitutional debates attending the United States founding, do in reality feature large elements of rhetoric. His defence of rhetoric is perhaps in the end a weak one; if the real world of politics features rhetoric, deliberative democrats are putting themselves at a disadvantage if they renounce it (Remer, 1998, p. 43).

The case for rhetoric is now advanced most forcefully by an emerging Aristotelian school of deliberative democrats, including John O'Neill (1998), Remer (1998), and Stephen Salkever (1998). O'Neill contrasts Aristolelians with Kantians such as Rawls and Habermas. As well as distrusting the emotional component of rhetoric (pathos), Kantians also oppose the degree to which rhetoric relies on exhibition of the virtuous character of the speaker (ethos). Kant himself regarded the defining feature of Enlightenment as escape from the immaturity entailed in taking an argument on trust, based on the character of the speaker. O'Neill points out that when it comes to complex policy issues, lay deliberators operating under time constraints have no alternative but to make character judgements about the experts who are making points, especially when different experts reach contradictory conclusions. However, competent deliberators can make rational judgements: for example, if they know that a researcher receives funds from the tobacco industry, they should not believe his or her claims about the minimal dangers associated with passive smoking, without substantial independent corroboration. In the Melbourne paper mill case I discussed earlier, the company managed in court to discredit an expert witness for the community group by showing that he had once applied unsuccessfully for a job with the company. The community group was unprepared for this; a rejoinder could have mustered cor-roborating experts, or demonstrated that a large proportion of chem-ical engineers in Melbourne must at one point have applied for a job with the company. But the general point here is that in the course of deliberation character judgements must in the end be answerable to reason, just as emotions must. Deliberative democracy can still remain grounded in a critical theory of communication. Habermas's version of that theory would rule out rhetoric; but Habermasian antipathy to deception, self-deception, manipulation, strategizing, and coercion can still be brought to bear.

When it comes to thinking of transmission from the public sphere to the state in particular, then almost by definition there is a need to reach actors whose frames of reference are initially very different from, and potentially unsympathetic to, discourse generated within the public sphere. Thus whatever its role within the public sphere, rhetoric plays an especially important function as a transmission mechanism from the public sphere to the state.

This emphasis on discursive, and specifically rhetorical, transmis-sion from the public sphere to the administrative state takes us a long way from the world as portrayed by social choice theory. Participation in the communicative action of the public sphere is very different from voting as a form of interest aggregation. This does not mean that vot-ing should be banished, because election campaigns do provide one opportunity (among many others) for discursive transmission, and elections themselves constitute a reason for state actors to listen to the public sphere. There is a major ontological shift entailed in terms of thinking of democracy in terms of intersubjective communication within the public sphere, as opposed to voting within the state. Is this still democracy? Yes it is, even if we think of democracy relatively nar-rowly in terms of the generation of public opinion and its translation into state action. I have endeavoured throughout this chapter to main-tain a degree of commensurability and comparability between the social choice and deliberative democracy traditions. And so I hope I have demonstrated that a deliberative democracy can be specified that has communicative parallels to *all* of the mechanisms that theorists of aggregative democracy—including social choice theorists—regard as necessary components for a full democracy. In particular, communica-tive mechanisms can be specified encompassing the public sphere and the state that can resolve contests across alternative positions, once these positions are themselves specified in discursive terms. Thus deliberative democracy is not the radically incomplete theory that its critics caricature and dismiss as impossible or incoherent in principle.

Now, discursive and electoral mechanisms do not exhaust the universe of transmission mechanisms from the public sphere to the state. One noteworthy idea has been developed by James Fishkin (1991, 1995) in connection with his idea of deliberative opinion polls. From the point of view of deliberative democracy, ordinary opinion polls are pointless because they register only unreflective preferences. The idea of a deliberative poll is to assemble a random sample of members of the public, have them deliberate about the key issues of the election, poll them on their positions on the issue, and publicize the results. The intent here is to model the distribution of opinions that the general public would hold if they were able to engage in genuine deliberation, a far cry indeed from the unreflective preferences which ordinary opinion polls register. Fishkin and his associates have conducted such polls on a variety of topics, though the influence on government has been hard to discern—with the exception of a deliberative poll sought by the Texas Public Utility Commission, which (remarkably) resulted in a shift to investment in renewable energy sources and 'green pricing' of energy. The opinion poll administered at the conclusion of deliberation requires the analyst to summarize and aggregate opinions, so it is not clear how this particular transmission mechanism solves the problems of aggregation as defined by social choice theory—except by handing them back to the institutions of government.

Conclusion

In light of the analysis of this chapter, where does the project of establishing discursive democracy as a viable alternative to liberal constitutionalist deliberative democracy now stand? A strong response to the social choice critique requires recognition of the public sphere as a site for the generation of public opinion. But this recognition is not in itself decisive in demarcating the two strands, because some constitutionalists recognize that one function of the constitution is to nurture and protect a realm of public debate. Such constitutionalists (notably Sunstein, 1993*a* and Walzer, 1991) tend not to be liberals themselves, but there is no reason why liberals could not adopt their positions. However, there are three ways in which the analysis of the latter part of this chapter helps to demarcate discursive democracy from liberal constitutionalism.

The first is in drawing a relatively sharp distinction between the public sphere and the state, meaning that the two can be in opposition. Liberals almost always avoid talking of 'the state' as an entity, recognizing instead a political system in which there are no differences in kind between different venues for deliberation, and so no differences in the degree of deliberative authenticity possible. If anything, liberals believe that authentic deliberation should be sought first and foremost within the formal institutions of government—such as legislatures, or supreme courts.

The second difference lies in the emphasis on the contestation of discourses within the public sphere. Liberal democracy treats democracy in terms of the aggregation of individual opinions, and thus does not recognize discourses as real entities with causal force when it comes to both the content and transmission of opinions. Its aggregative character makes liberal democracy especially vulnerable to the social choice theory critique. Discursive democracy emphasizes intersubjective communication across discourses within the public sphere, and treats public opinion as the outcome of their contestation. It can draw on its roots in critical theory to point to the need to counteract the ideological distortions that can often attend particular discourses (though the Habermasian appeal to a world without discourses in this sense should be resisted).

The third difference lies in a stress on discursive transmission of public opinion from the public sphere to the state, and a concomitant downplaying of the electoral mechanisms emphasized in liberal democracy. Here the distinction is a matter of degree, however large; for liberals do not have to rely exclusively on elections, nor do discursive democrats have to completely disregard the opportunities that elections provide.

In the next chapter I show how these three features of discursive democracy enable an effective response to a set of critics who arrive from the opposite direction to the social choice theorists. This encounter will enable further refinement of what democracy based on the contestation of discourses in the public sphere can entail.

CHAPTER 3

Difference Democracy:
The Consciousness-Raising Group
against the Gentlemen's Club

Large sections of the intellectual left of the English-speaking developed countries turned in the 1990s to the politics of identity and difference, which could find support from postmodern thinking in social theory and literary criticism. This turn coincided with an increasingly bleak assessment of the prospects for socialism, or even substantial material redistribution, in any foreseeable future. Progressive politics could, however, be redefined in terms of the emancipation of a growing list of excluded minorities, defined on the basis of gender, race, ethnicity, sexuality, age, disability, as well as social class. The agents of oppression were often treated in cultural terms, but political (and occasionally economic) structures could also be condemned. Much to the surprise of its proponents, deliberative democracy too came to be accused of complicity in the oppression of difference.

Difference democrats are those who stress the need for democratic politics to concern itself first and foremost with the recognition of the legitimacy and validity of the particular perspectives of historically-oppressed segments of the population. Quite what form this politics should take is a matter of continuing debate, as we shall see shortly. Thus the difference democrats are not a self-consciously unified school of thought (a uniformity which would in any case subvert their emphasis on variety). Some stress isolated acts of resistance, others want to replace class struggle with an oppositional politics of unity in diversity. Some propose reform of governmental structures of representation, others scorn the state. Some are self-consciously postmodernist or poststructuralist, others eschew high theory. What they all share is a stress on the variety of oppressions and so subject-positions, leading them to oppose ostensibly neutral rationalistic practices that in fact exclude or silence particular kinds of oppressed subjects.

The case against deliberative democracy here is that its focus on a particular kind of supposedly reasonable political interaction is not in fact neutral, but systematically excludes a variety of voices from effective participation in democratic politics. This charge is the opposite of that made by social choice theorists, who fear that deliberative democracy opens the door to an unmanageable proliferation of participants and positions. Where social choice theorists see dangerous variety, difference democrats see dangerous uniformity. Before I address their critique in a bit more detail, let me lay out in a bit more detail what difference democracy means, and how it relates to the politics of identity.

Models of Difference Democracy

The question of difference as it arises is politics is normally paired with the concept of identity: individuals and groups find their identity only in establishing their differences with others who represent what the individual or group in question is not (see e.g. Benhabib, 1996a, pp. 3–4).[1] In this light, questions of identity and difference can extend to religious fundamentalism and even ethnic warfare, but difference democrats have in mind much more civil and constrained processes. The identities at issue generally relate to social class, culture, nationality, ethnicity, sexuality, and gender, though the list is open-ended.

A case that processes oriented to the exploration of identity and difference should encompass pretty much all we mean by democracy is made by William Connolly (1991a, 1995). Connolly operates within a postmodern idiom, and so opposes any tendency to assertion or recognition of any fixed and timeless identities (of the sort that fundamentalists and essentialists from many points on the political spectrum, not just the religious or nationalist right, trade in). Instead, identities and their associated differences should be treated as a matter for continuous exploration, receiving at best only conditional and contingent statement. Democratic politics in this light should involve the creative questioning of identities through encounter with disparate others. This is not a deadly struggle, more a matter of play; what matters is that the game never ends. Thus a ludic attitude on the part of participants is crucial: they must be prepared to question the com-

---

[1] Iris Young (1997, p. 385) resists the pairing of difference and identity, but her objection is only to sectarian assertions of identity in fixed and unassailable terms.

plexities and ambiguities of their own identities as well as those of others.

Connolly is realistic enough to recognize that such an attitude is not widely shared in a world where the assertion of identity and questioning of the identity of others is frequently treated in deadly serious terms, even within developed liberal democracies. 'Only when both of the hands holding our necks in the grip of resentment are loosened can the politics of agonal democracy be enhanced. Today existential resentments and resentments against injustice in the social distribution of opportunities, resources, sacrifices, and burdens combine to tighten the grip of dogmatism upon the life of identity' (Connolly, 1991*a*, p. 211). To former US Secretary of the Interior James Watt, one could not be an environmentalist and an American; ultimately Watt averred that environmentalists should be defeated using the cartridge box rather than the ballot box or jury box (Dowie, 1995, p. 97). To conservative Christians, denial of feminist and gay identities is integral to their own identity, an article of dogma.

In addition to such obstacles in the world as it stands, Connolly allows that there are material inequalities that have to be remedied before the desired democratic attitudes can be activated. Thus Connolly in the end regards his prescriptive democratic theory as a hope for a better world, but of little contemporary practical applicability. Perhaps the experience of American University life in the 1990s bears Connolly out. The politics of identity and difference pervades campus life, but it is generally accompanied by dogmatism and resentment, on the part of those asserting identities as well as those denying them.

Other difference democrats share Connolly's interpretation of the democratic life, but not his resignation in the face of a recalcitrant world. Instead, they link the negotiation of identity and difference to resistance to a dominant political order that represses difference. Such theorists often write in the shadow of socialism, while recognizing that struggles must be plural, as opposed to socialism's one big struggle. Yet if there is no longer one big struggle, there remains for these theorists one big opponent: the liberal capitalist political order. Thus the politics of identity and difference are played out not just in the unconstrained open-ended interaction of a variety of selves, their identities, and their others, but rather in a conflict with this one opponent.

Marxists would have conceptualized this struggle in material terms; post-Marxists such as Chantal Mouffe (1996) conceptualize it in discursive terms. Mouffe identifies herself as a poststructuralist (as well as a postmodernist) and so a supporter of Michel Foucault. To Foucault, the established order is at any particular time represented by discourses which condition the way people communicate and think. Foucault himself elucidated in great detail the history (or genealogy) of discourses surrounding sexuality, criminality, health, disease, and mental illness, with the intent of exposing the way these discourses simultaneously both constitute and oppress subjects. But oppressive discourses make themselves felt in different ways in different situations. Thus for Foucault there is no hope for any grand project of resistance (of the Marxist sort), only for local resistances; for example, for a group of individuals to refuse their categorization as mentally ill.

Mouffe has greater hopes for the summation of local resistances into some larger radical politics that opposes the discursive order of liberal capitalism. This politics would constitute what she and Ernesto Laclau call a 'radical and plural democracy' composed of the variety of self-defined struggles and movements that respond to the multiple oppressions generated by the dominant order (Laclau and Mouffe, 1985). Such a democracy would pervade social and cultural life, rather than orient itself exclusively to the state (McClure, 1992). At the heart of this democracy would be a politics of identity and difference that contests any attempts to impose universal identities, including supposedly 'rational' and 'neutral' ones advanced by liberal political theorists such as Rawls (Mouffe, 1996, pp. 248–50). Less neutral but still rational and universal identities such as those once sought by Marxists are also ruled out. There is an irony here, because the realization of 'radical and plural democracy' would seem to require the persistence of the unified dominant liberal capitalist order and its multiple oppressions. No liberal capitalism means no oppressions means no radical and plural democracy.

Not all difference democrats connect their efforts to radical resistance to the liberal capitalist order; some believe this order can be reformed from within to better accommodate difference. Thus Anne Phillips (1995) calls for a 'politics of presence' as opposed to a 'politics of ideas', in which efforts are made to ensure the presence of members of disadvantaged groups in the institutions of liberal democracy, such as parliament. Such presence is needed because only members of these groups have the capacity to give authentic voice to the exclusions and oppressions they have experienced. Attuned to the danger of essentializing particular identities, in the end Phillips is confident enough only to recommend quotas in parliament for women, on the grounds that 'women' is an inclusive category that itself contains a number of different identities (see also Phillips, 1993, pp. 96–9). Women who thus enter parliament are not constrained to be *only* women in terms of what they represent; they can also be working-class women, or middle-class women, or black women, or white women, and so forth. Phillips also endorses Lani Guinier's (1991, 1994) suggestions for an electoral system with multi-member constituencies and a system of cumulative voting, with a quota much less than 50 per cent of the total votes needed to elect a candidate. Each citizen would have a number of votes that he or she could divide among candidates, or cast them all for a single candidate. By concentrating their votes on a single candidate, members of a minority group could get a representative elected.

Guinier's proposals constitute a better response to the charge of essentializing identity than do Phillips's quotas. While Guinier is interested mainly in promoting the organization and representation of racial and ethnic minorities, the system of cumulative voting itself is actually neutral when it comes to the kinds of groups that will be induced to mobilize for representation (indeed, it could promote the mobilization of racists and rednecks). This system would encourage the formation of groups in general, also of coalitions that transcend traditional group boundaries (for example, when two ethnic minorities are too small to mobilize enough votes for a representative each, but together could mobilize the threshold number of votes). Thus as identities change, the character of the representatives can change too (see Bickford, 1999). If particular differences, for example class differences, are ever erased, then groups representing those differences will simply fade from view.

More substantial adjustments to representation within the liberal state are advocated by Iris Young (1989, 1990), who argues that disadvantaged groups should have not only representatives, but also guarantees of consultation, and veto power over policies that affect them. Any suggestion of veto power should be greeted with alarm by anyone who has contemplated the workings of voting systems, and not just the social choice theorists discussed in Chapter 2. If group A is allowed to veto policy X while group B is allowed to veto policy 'not X' then the result is deadlock that privileges the status quo, which is presumably not what Young has in mind. Thus some means of softening the idea of veto needs to be found if group representation is to have any practical purchase.

For Young, the politics of difference involves recognition of the group by the state, as well as respect and affirmation across groups in civil society. Like Mouffe, Young begins with a critique of liberalism's universalizing tendencies that in practice repress group difference and mask exclusions. The list of repressed groups to be granted privileged representation will vary for different societies and times. For her own

United States circa 1990, it encompasses 'women, blacks, Native Americans, old people, poor people, disabled people, gay men and lesbians, Spanish-speaking Americans, young people, and nonprofessional workers' (Young, 1989, p. 265). Aware of postmodern warnings against essentializing group identity, Young emphasizes the fact that (oppressive) circumstances beyond its own choosing create the category from which the group then springs (Young, 1997, pp. 385–93). Thus people need not adopt any essential and fixed identity, but only respond to the shared histories and circumstances in which they find themselves. Indeed, Young resists the use of the term 'identity' because it connotes an assertion of essential and unshakeable characteristics, as opposed to the multiple possibilities with which individuals may be faced by virtue of the circumstances into which they are thrown. 'I have only my own identity, fashioned in relation to my multiple group positionings' (Young, 1997, p. 393). Like most difference democrats, Young believes that particular identities should be validated. But it is important to recognize that some differences are disabling, so that they merit elimination rather than validation. Class differences would be the obvious example here (Plumwood, 1998, p. 578).[2]

Does Deliberation Repress Difference?

Support for difference does not have to entail hostility to deliberation. For example, Anne Phillips (1995, pp. 145–65) embraces deliberative democracy, while recognizing the tension between the group interests she believes should always be present and the idea that deliberators should be compelled only by what they hear in the forum (pp. 160–3). However, the difference democrats' suspicion of universal rationality claims has led some of them to attack deliberative democracy. It is

[2] Postmodernism's stress on multiple and contingent differences is reconciled to liberalism still more thoroughly in the hands of Richard Rorty, a self-proclaimed 'post-modernist bourgeois liberal' (Rorty, 1983). Rorty believes that the variety and fluidity in subject positions and their associated differences that postmodernism has highlighted can be negotiated quite adequately through the existing institutions of liberal democracy (Rorty, 1989). In his (postmodern) hostility to the idea that philosophical foundations can be specified for these institutions, Rorty differs profoundly from most liberal political philosophers—but ends up justifying the same institutions nonetheless. He thinks that the world, or at least the American left, needs less philosophy (including postmodern philosophy) and more action to pursue the pluralistic dreams long associated with American thinkers such as Whitman and Dewey (Rorty, 1998). Still, Rorty is an outlier among difference democrats, most of whom believe that the contemporary liberal state requires either thorough reform or radical opposition.

these critics I will focus on here. I shall begin with a poststructural critique of democracy in general, for it is this which acts as the outer boundary for the difference democracy critique of deliberation in particular, and so puts the latter in particularly sharp focus.

Postructuralists follow Michel Foucault in their suspicion of any dominant discourse, because they believe that discourses are the taken-for-granted assumptions that constitute subjects and so subjugate them to power. Fewer discourses today seem more dominant than that of democracy, not just among political thinkers, but also within nearly all the world's regimes, including some very dubious ones. Concerning the way Western political systems have come to be ordered, Foucault himself stressed the idea of a 'governmentality' which constitutes subjects in ways that make them amenable to government control (Burchell, Gordon, and Miller, 1991). Such control comes not through overt coercion or compulsion of any sort, simply through the basic assumptions about politics that people come to share which make them compliant subjects of political regimes. In this light, the contemporary hegemony of the discourse of democracy is just the latest phase of governmentality.

Taking a look at the rise of democracy in the modern era, Barry Hindess (2000) believes that modern political thought and practice could only let go of absolute monarchy once the people were suitably subdued. The threat of force or legal sanction is not crucial here, because the practice of democracy itself contains a variety of mechanisms for taming people. One prominent strand in democratic thinking associated with John Stuart Mill stresses the developmental or educative benefits of participation. But on Hindess's interpretation, these developmental effects have a disciplinary function. For example, individuals called upon to chair meetings must set aside personal convictions, and a quorum will discipline attendance. When it comes to deliberation in particular, 'actual participation in . . . deliberations often requires a considerable degree of self-restraint, an ability and a willingness to conceal one's own views and a capacity to deal peacefully with periods of boredom and intense frustration' (Hindess, 2000). Thus deliberation promotes oppressive self-control.

In this light, democracy acts as a disciplining force by constructing individual identities in ways that make individuals willing participants in and supporters of political systems which can in the end only foreclose their opportunities. Connors (2000) applies this kind of analysis to democratic reform in Thailand. Such reform, he argues, is designed to create new kinds of 'democratic' subjects, more conducive to a liberal constitutionalist political order. This order in turn finds its real justification in being functional for the liberal capitalist political economy developing in Thailand, replacing older traditions of clientelism and deference. Individuals have the impression of choice and participation in control, but they are being constituted to behave in a particular fashion.

Hindess for his part intimates no escape from the disciplinary discourse of democracy, and in this he is arguably more Foucauldian than Foucault. In his later years, Foucault became increasingly attuned to the possibility of reflective choice across discourses, and that some discourses were more consensual and less oppressive than others (Foucault, 1984, p. 343). But for Hindess, all that seems to remain is a resigned acceptance of the status quo, which can be condemned but not changed.

While Hindess emphasizes the universally oppressive character of participation in deliberation and democratic processes more generally, he allows that some people are disciplined more than others, such that deliberation can reinforce existing political hierarchies. Critiques of deliberative democracy that build upon this claim are developed by the difference democrats Lynn Sanders (1997) and Iris Young (1996, 1998). Their basic charge is that deliberation represents a particular kind of communication: dispassionate, reasoned, and logical. The problem is that 'some citizens are better than others at articulating their arguments in rational, reasonable terms' (Sanders, 1997, p. 348). Young for her part allows that deliberative democrats have stressed the importance of incorporating as wide as possible a variety of individuals in deliberative processes (Sanders is not so generous), but none the less argues that deliberative democrats have ignored what she calls the 'internal exclusion' entailed by an emphasis on deliberation.

How do exclusion and oppression work within the deliberative setting? To Sanders, it is partly that some people are good at making arguments and so likely to be heard, while others are less likely to be listened to (see also Bickford, 1996). She points to work on American juries which suggests that when their composition is mixed they tend to be dominated by white, well-educated men (Sanders, 1997, pp. 362–9). Sanders (p. 353) argues that 'Prejudice and privilege do not emerge in deliberative settings as bad reasons, and they are not countered by good arguments. They are sneaky, invisible and pernicious for that reasonable process.' But her essential argument need not rest on such questionable empirical assertions. Rather, the key is that deliberative virtues of civility have a sedative effect that curbs unruly behaviour on the part of the disadvantaged (p. 356). 'Deliberation is a request for a certain kind of talk: rational, constrained, and oriented to a shared problem' (p. 370). Moreover, she argues, public reason's emphasis on interests that can be shared or at least understood by all in practice universalizes the interests of the wealthy and powerful, while simultaneously erasing the particular experiences and interests of poor and powerless minorities (pp. 359–62). In short, 'learning to deliberate in America might be inseparable from indoctrination in familiar routines of hierarchy and deference' (p. 362).

In reading Sanders it is sometimes hard to disentangle the critique of deliberation as such from the critique of how deliberation plays out in the context of a particular unjust political system, that of liberal democracy in the United States. Iris Young's critique is more sharply focused on deliberation as such. Invoking Lyotard's postmodern concept of 'différence', she argues that deliberative frameworks for conflict resolution are systematically skewed when they operate in the idiom of one of the parties to the conflict, while the suffering of the other cannot even be expressed in that idiom (1998, pp. 6–7). The problem here, then, is one of deliberation requiring common premises; but in a world of difference, neutral shared premises are hard to find. Those liberals from Kant to Rawls who have articulated such supposedly neutral premises have in fact only reproduced the standards of a particular political order (see, similarly, Mouffe, 1996, pp. 249–52). Deliberative democracy is charged by Young with privileging certain kinds of speech and so certain kinds of power: speech that is 'assertive and confrontational', 'formal and general', 'dispassionate and disembodied' (1996, pp. 123–4). The first of these in particular advantages stereotypically male as opposed to female speaking styles. Deliberation is not in this light open problem solving, but a confrontation in which there are winners and losers. For all three kinds, 'these differences of speech privilege correlate with other differences of social privilege', while disadvantaging 'the speech culture of women and minorities' (1996, p. 124).

The other main problem with deliberative democracy for Young is its impetus toward unity. For communitarians, that unity is specified in advance by a common tradition. For liberals and critical theorists, the unity is more likely to be reasoned toward rather than specified in advance. Young (1996, pp. 125–6) believes that the former is vitiated by the fact of difference, the latter likely to reach a definition of the common good that favours the privileged.

The force of all these criticisms of deliberation remains something of an open question pending sustained empirical investigation of the degree to which the claims about what actually happens in deliberation actually do describe reality. Are particular kinds of people in reality better than others at arguing in rational terms? Is it really the case that prejudice and privilege are never uncovered and opposed by good argument? Is learning to participate in deliberation really the same as indoctrination in hierarchy? Is an individual's capacity to deliberate really directly proportional to social standing? Is Young's 'speech culture of women and minorities' really disadvantaged in deliberation? The answer to all these questions is that we do not know. So however plausible these claims might seem, their assertion on the part of theorists is no substitute for their empirical investigation in the context of actual cases of deliberation. A body of work does exist that investigates talk in groups, looking at issues such as who talks most, who interrupts most and gets interrupted most (see e.g. Barbour and Kitzinger, 1999). But to the best of my knowledge none of this work addresses directly the propositions advanced by difference democrats about deliberation in particular.

Sanders and Young both argue for kinds of communication other than deliberation. For Sanders, the ideal is testimony, or telling one's own story in one's own language, rather than in the constrained language of deliberation. Rap music is one such kind of testimony. She claims that testimony is 'radically egalitarian' (Sanders, 1997, p. 372), though presumably some people are capable of giving better testimonials than others. Testimony is similar to one of Young's three alternative forms of communication, storytelling. Storytelling 'reveals the particular experiences of those in social locations, experiences that cannot be shared by those situated differently but that they must understand in order to do justice to the others' and 'exhibits subjective experience to other subjects' (Young, 1996, p. 131). Examples here would include womens' stories about the sexual harassment they have experienced.

Young's other two forms of alternative communication are greeting and rhetoric. Greeting involves more or less elaborate recognition of the presence of others, not just at the outset of an encounter, but in expressions of politeness and concern for the well-being of others as the encounter proceeds. In this way, others can be welcomed into the communicative circle, and trust established (Young, 1996, pp. 129–30). Greeting means that the individuals in question can henceforth be treated as subjects in debate, rather than objects of discussion. Greeting resonates with the difference democrats' concern with recognition of identity of the other; it also plays a large part in international diplomacy (Young, 1998, p. 15).

Rhetoric (which I discussed in the previous chapter) involves context-specific attention to the way points are made, with the intention of reaching the perspective of particular listeners and persuading them. Speech without rhetoric can be flat, unpersuasive, boring. Speech with rhetoric can involve jokes, anger, laughter, ridicule, flattery, and hyperbole (Young, 1996, pp. 130–1). Some contemporary deliberative democrats, notably Chambers (1996), Spragens (1990), and Habermas, do indeed want to purge rhetoric from deliberation, on the grounds that rhetoric can open the door to demagogues, manipulators, deceivers, and flatterers. Young argues in contrast that rhetoric can be used to draw attention to previously marginalized concerns, to reach categories of people traditionally excluded from discussion by couching points in terms familiar to them, and to force action on a problem or issue (1998, pp. 23–7).

If greeting, rhetoric, and storytelling are to meet Young's great expectations of them, then it needs to be demonstrated that they do not simply generate other kinds of hierarchy. Young argues that some people are better at argument than others; in the societies with which she is familiar, she believes that the best arguers are well-educated white males. Yet similar differentials can conceivably apply to these other three types of communication. Demagogues might on average be the best rhetoricians. Public relations experts and extrovert Americans who have read books on the habits of highly effective people might be the best greeters. Graduates of creative writing programs and those with lots of accumulated experience might be the best storytellers. The empirical validity of Young's claims about the degree to which these three forms of communication equalize across difference depends on the hierarchies within argument, greeting, rhetoric, and storytelling compensating for, rather than reinforcing, one another.

Any such hierarchies associated with alternative forms of communication notwithstanding, difference democrats have placed some serious question marks next to deliberative democracy. Thus we need to determine the degree to which deliberative democracy must stress rational argument, and the extent to which it can and should admit alternative forms of communication. This will help determine how deliberation might best accommodate the fact of radically different identities and subject positions. I will now try to show that effective responses to the difference democrats' critique can be crafted.

Deliberating across Difference

If the recognition of difference means simply the recognition of the different kinds of communication enumerated by Young, then the solution might at first sight appear to be simple: let them in! For greeting, rhetoric, and storytelling on the one hand and familiar forms of argument on the other are not mutually exclusive, and can coexist in any real discursive setting.[3]

This accommodating reaction is in fact too easy. A more defensible response is that all forms of communication should only ever be admitted conditionally. There are two tests that can be applied. First, any communication that involves coercion or the threat of coercion should be excluded. Second, any communication that cannot connect the particular to the general should be excluded (Miller, 1999, p. 15 applies this second test, but only to testimony). These two tests can be applied to any form of communication, be it storytelling, testimony, rhetoric, greeting—and even argument. My introduction of these tests for the various kinds of communication is not designed to rule any of them out in blanket terms. To use the language of Foucault (1984, p. 343), 'My point is not that everything is bad, but that everything is dangerous.' Advocates of the alternative forms are generally blind to the dangers. So let me give some examples of how each form of communication can fail on the two tests, and consider what might be done about such failure.

Storytelling and Testimony

Storytelling is a coercive form of communication when group norms constrain the range of acceptable stories. For Young (1998, p. 32), the paradigm of a forum hospitable to storytelling is the consciousness-raising group, in which members 'identify one another, and identify the basis of their affinity' through telling stories about their own experience. But there is a danger that such groups will require correct storylines, and punish incorrect ones which cannot easily withstand the normalizing gaze of the group. The storyline must begin with oppression whose character is not recognized by the victim, and proceed through recognition of the oppression to the search for a need to contextualize that realization in a more general framework. Such disciplining of story lines is not of course unique to consciousness-raising groups (see Patai and Koertge, 1994, for some cautionary cases). It can be found equally in fundamentalist religions, where the newcomer to the group must offer a story based on past sin leading to realization of

---

[3] This is recognized, for example, in Patsy Healy's deliberative approach to public planning, which, though based on a Habermasian framework of the sort Young finds objectionable, is open to 'the power of ideas, metaphors, images, and stories' (Healy, 1993, p. 244).

god's mercy and the hope for redemption; and the bigger the sin, the better the story. Disciplined stories may also be required in particular kinds of therapy, in order to fit the theoretical framework of the therapist.

Turning to the second test, if an individual's story is purely about that individual then there is no political point in hearing it. The reason the consciousness-raising group or the religious sect wants to hear stories is because they illustrate the general situation of those in the group. When it comes to deliberation beyond the particular group the tests are a bit more demanding: the story must be capable of resonating with individuals who do not share that situation—but do share other characteristics (if only a common humanity). Thus a truly effective story about a particular repression will also involve implicit appeal to more universal standards. The story of a refugee from a war zone may be full of harrowing episodes particular to the conflict in question, perhaps the repression of a particular ethnic group. But such stories are moving precisely because they involve gross violation of more general standards of human dignity, not because listeners have to identify with the oppressed ethnicity in question. The latter is likely only to perpetuate cycles of revenge.

Greeting

Greeting at first sight might seem an innocuous form of communication, perhaps even a necessary beginning for the recognition of other parties to communication. Yet greeting too can be coercive. Think, for example, of the bone-crushing handshake. The New Zealand national rugby team, the All Blacks, always precedes its matches with the *haka*, a Maori greeting ceremony designed to intimidate opponents. Greeting can also fail to connect the particular to the general. For example, the secret handshakes of Freemasons are presumably designed to mark them off immediately from other people, and establish an exclusive communicative relationship (in some cases, such as the British police and judiciary, or the P2 Lodge that was long part of Italy's 'invisible government', one with real political force).

Rhetoric

Rhetoric can be coercive when it is deployed by demagogues and emotional manipulators, which is precisely why some deliberative democrats (such as Habermas, Chambers, and Spragens) wish to purge it. Think, for example, of the power of Nazi rhetoric, and the fate awaiting those who were not swayed by it. Rhetoric can raise the emotional stakes by casting issues in terms of threats to the core identity of the group, especially when it is defined on ethnic or national lines. Less dramatically, when an expert recites his or her credentials in order to silence lay criticism, that is also rhetorical coercion.

According to Miller (1999, p. 17–18), rhetoric requires a context of a community of like-minded people, taking force only 'when people are united in their aims', igniting their passions and making it less likely that their differences with those outside the group can be resolved. If so, then by definition rhetoric must always fail in its capacity to connect the particular with general. However, rhetoric can also be effective in making appeals across different frames of reference, perhaps with a view to their reconciliation, or the expansion of a particular frame. Good rhetoric on behalf of the disadvantaged can induce a sense of the need for redress on the part of the powerful. The rhetoricians of the Civil Rights movement in the United States in the 1960s, notably Martin Luther King, Jr., deployed exactly this kind of rhetorical capacity to good effect. Rhetoric oriented to reciprocal understanding is often essential in reaching others when simple argument cannot. One of the most important 'others' to be reached will often be those with access to the levers of governmental power. In Chapter 2 I argued that rhetoric can enable transmission to the state of public opinion formed in the public sphere, without that transmission requiring subordination to strategic action, such as that entailed in voting and elections.

Argument

At first, it is perhaps less easy to see how argument can be coercive. If an argument is backed by a threat, then it is not really argument at all. For if only one side can make credible threats, then the kind of communication at issue is more like command, while if both sides can make threats, then the situation is one of bargaining rather than arguing. Habermas speaks of 'the forceless force of the better argument', which is why he values argument above other forms of communication. Yet argument is only forceless if all the individuals involved share an equal communicative competence: the capacity to raise and challenge validity claims. When such equality does not hold, then in practice some individuals will be able to make their arguments prevail as a result of denial of access to the premises of argument to other individuals. Indeed, this is the basic worry of the difference democrats who first challenged deliberation's stress on argument: that *in practice* it involves communication in the terms set by the powerful, who almost by definition are those best able to articulate their arguments in terms of the dominant speech culture of a society. It is this speech culture that will often be embedded in the informal and formal rules of dominant institutions.

Coercion in argument occurs as a result of failure to connect the particular to the general—or, rather, the suppression of any challenge to the particular. For example, if a supreme court rules that a law must be struck down because it contravenes the constitution, that is an argument in terms of the particular. The constitution may be unfair to a particular group in society—for example, if it specifies the sanctity of private property, thus disadvantaging those who have little or no property. If deliberation ends with 'because this is what the constitution says', rather than allowing the challenge 'but should the constitution mean this?' then it has failed the second test. Legalistic forums are especially problematic in the restrictions they impose upon admissible argument and so free dialogue. But similar logic can be applied to argument that ends with appeal to the authority of tradition, precedent, or supposed laws of nature. Of course, this does not mean that to pass the test of connecting the particular to the general argument must always be taken to philosophical first principles. All it means is that challenges should not be foreclosed.

Argument, then, can also be coercive, and fail to connect the particular to the general. Yet argument is also capable of exposing these failings—in itself, but also in testimony, greeting, and rhetoric. If a group censors storylines, the way to overcome that censorship could be to tell an unacceptable story—but if impasse then results, argument can break the logjam through discussion of the grounds for admitting stories. If a greeting is aggressive, it can be challenged with a hug; or by an argument about aggression. If rhetoric whips up passion directed against an out-group, that can be challenged by more inclusive rhetoric—but also by an argument pointing to the consequences of exclusion.

When it comes to the key question 'what is to be done?' about communicative failures of the kind I have discussed here, argument always plays a central role. When it comes to 'what is to be done?' in terms of collective action in response to a social problem, argument also must enter. Thus argument always has to be central to deliberative democracy. The other forms can be present, and there are good reasons to welcome them, but their status is a bit different because they do not *have* to be present.

At this juncture I conclude that deliberative democracy can cope with the issue of difference by conditionally admitting a variety of forms of communication, as well as being attuned to plurality in subject positions and associated ways of life. Thus critics who charge that deliberative democracy 'posits a simplistic opposition between private interest and general interest' (Femia, 1996, p. 381) are mistaken; partial interests intermediate between the private and the general can be recognized. Deliberative democrats themselves have long recognized and grappled with the issue of plurality (e.g. Bohman, 1995; Dryzek, 1990*a*, pp. 16–19; Hanson, 1985; White, 1988, p. 70). Thus Iris Young's observation that for *all* such theorists 'the goal of deliberation is to arrive at consensus' (1996, p. 122) is simply wrong. Even Habermas, who has clung to the ideal of consensus longest and hardest, long ago recognized the practical difficulties that precluded the realization of consensus in practice (Habermas, 1979, p. 90; 1982, pp. 257–8). (Young's observation also fits oddly with her claim on the very next page (p. 123)—equally mistaken in my view—that 'Deliberation is competition. Parties to dispute aim to win the argument, not to achieve mutual understanding.' This claim grounds deliberation in strategic rationality, as opposed to the communicative rationality that underwrites discursive democracy.) Some notion of reasoned agreement that allows for different individuals to retain different reasons for subscribing to an agreement is widely held among deliberative democrats (see also my discussion in Chapter 2). However, this notion of reasoned agreement as opposed to consensus does call into question Rawls's (1993) reliance on a unitary public reason. In this Rawlsian language, Bohman (1996, pp. 83–5) points out that the solution is to think of public reason as itself 'plural', such that 'agents can come to an agreement with one another for *different* publicly accessible reasons' (emphasis in original).

Deliberative democracy need not fear difference, let alone repress difference. Indeed, were it not for difference, deliberation would be a very dull affair, a conversation among those who had already settled upon basics. As Phillips (1995, p. 151) puts it, 'Deliberation matters only because there is difference.' Many of the most fundamental questions confronting a polity entail confrontations with difference of some kind, be it in terms of nationality, social class, gender, ethnicity, or ecological situation. Schlosberg (1998, p. 605) can argue with justification that 'Deliberative democracy is the procedure of a revived pluralism. As such, I read much of the literature of deliberative democracy as designs for the intersubjective banquet that both James and Connolly imagine.' The kind of pluralism to which Schlosberg is referring here is the critical strand, that begins with William James's century-old account of how the variety of ways in which human beings can experience the world must be accommodated in an open and evolving political order. This strand covers William Connolly's more recent pluralism of agonistic respect across difference. (Such critical pluralism is very different from the mid-century celebration of the range of competing interest groups in the United States by pluralists such as David Truman, Edward Banfield, Nelson Polsby, and Robert Dahl—who later changed his mind.) While endorsing Schlosberg's observation here, I would note in passing that deliberative democracy is more interested in the production of collective outcomes in problem-solving contexts than is Connolly, such that the fit may not be quite as comfortable as Schlosberg believes.

Conceiving of deliberative democracy in terms of an intersubjective banquet should also help allay the fears of Foucauldians such as Barry Hindess, which I introduced earlier, even though it could never banish those fears entirely (nor could any political theory). Hindess, recall, portrays deliberation in the image of a committee meeting in which individuals restrain themselves, conceal their views, and subject themselves to boredom and frustration. Deliberation may have moments like this; but then all forms of political life fall short of a perpetual carnival. An expansive notion of deliberation across difference is probably better than most kinds of politics at constituting subjects in non-oppressive ways.

But what about the very different fears of the social choice theorists as discussed in the previous chapter? The recognition of multiple modes of communication entailed by this more expansive notion of deliberation might at first sight seem to contradict the point I made there about the need for domain restriction to promote tractability in collective choice. I argued that deliberative democrats can respond to the social choice critique by pointing to the capacity of deliberation to restrict the range of admissible preferences, and so limit the possibilities for cycling across alternatives. Allowing a variety of modes of communication across difference into a deliberation would seem to work in the opposite direction: to expand domain by increasing the range of subject-positions allowed in the forum.

How is this apparent contradiction to be resolved? Here we need to take a close look at what different modes of communication actually accomplish. Certainly, they act in the first instance to reveal additional dimensions of collective choice—if they did not, there would be no point in introducing them. But, as I argued in Chapter 2, introducing additional dimensions can make social choices *more* tractable. These modes of communication can help to uncover dimensions that were previously compressed into a single choice, thus making it more likely that responses can be crafted responsive to the various dimensions at issue. Deliberation is about good and authentic communication, and all the mechanisms that deliberation possesses to restrict domain operate in argument, in rhetoric, and storytelling alike. Expanding the kind of communication admissible also expands the grounds on which particular positions may not survive deliberative scrutiny, so there is no reason to suppose that such expansion will make social choice more rather than less difficult.

Difference as the Contest of Discourses

Deliberative democrats should not simply rest here and congratulate themselves on their ability to accommodate difference. James's (1979 [1896]) intersubjective banquet serves only diners who will not throw food at each other or seek to banish beggars from the table. Similarly, Connolly's hopes for agonistic respect extend to people differently situated—but who are enlightened enough to reject dogmatism and sectarianism, and to open themselves to engagement with others. That is why Connolly sees little possibility for the adoption of his prescriptive model of democracy in contemporary circumstances, where identities linked to the denial of respect loom large.

Here, it is noteworthy that Schlosberg's (1998) paradigm for deliberation across difference is the United States environmental justice movement and its network form of organization. Yet whatever the differences the movement accommodates when it comes to race, urban/rural location, ethnicity, or even social class, the recognition and respect that the movement achieves is, at least in the first instance, among those with a common interest in fighting the environmental risks imposed upon them. Unlike many difference democrats, Schlosberg also highlights the character of the interactions that the movement seeks to establish with governmental and corporate actors with no commitment to or interest in communication across difference. Here the record is more mixed. Participants in the movement have often insisted on interactions with such actors that involve mutual respect rather than condescension, substantive rather than symbolic participation in decisions. Such insistence often meets with resistance from state and corporate actors. This situation illustrates the fact that there is another half to the problem of identity and difference: what to do in deliberative terms about oppressive identities and discourses, and those that appear in locations other than the 'progressive' end of the political spectrum. Difference democrats invoke the image of the gentlemen's club in criticizing the excessively civil image of deliberation. If they have replaced the gentlemen's club only with the consciousness-raising group, that is not good enough.

A serious response to the challenge of difference requires an account of democracy that can address difference across repressive and emancipatory identities and discourses, both of which will populate political life for the foreseeable future. Here I believe it is useful to reintroduce the account of the public sphere developed in the previous chapter, which highlights contestation across discourses rather than engagement across identities, and so establish a link to discursive democracy as opposed to liberal constitutionalist deliberative democracy. There is of course a tight connection between discourses and identities, which are constituted in whole or part by discourses. Discourses, recall, are shared sets of assumptions and capabilities that enable their adherents to assemble bits of sensory input into coherent wholes, or organize them around coherent storylines (see the more extensive conceptual discussion in Chapter 1). One way of interpreting the whole idea of difference is therefore in terms of discourses rather than identities.

A hard-line Foucauldian usage of the discourse concept (as deployed, for example, by Hindess) treats discourses in hegemonic terms. In this light, a discourse is not just a partial view of the world, but something that constitutes even seemingly competing views (such as, for example, market liberal and social democratic viewpoints on capitalist political economy). Yet however hegemonic discourses may have been historically, *our* age—enlightened in part by Foucauldian exposés of the power of particular discourses!—is home to a variety of discourses about which people can be aware. This awareness does not mean that Foucauldian hegemony must be discarded in favour of an Enlightenment universalism that can scrutinize all assumptions and storylines. Rather, it recognizes that discourses are powerful because they can and do constitute identities; yet reflective comparisons across discourse boundaries can, if only occasionally and with some effort, be made.[4] In the concluding chapter I will show how this openness to comparison resonates with the idea of reflexive modernization.

This interpretation of the public sphere in terms of the contestation of discourses has the advantage of being able to address the question of what to do about repressive or recalcitrant discourses. Think, for example, of the discourse of market liberalism, which constructs individuals as consumers, profit-maximizers, and rent-seekers. Or

[4] As I noted earlier, this position is consistent with remarks Foucault himself made toward the end of his life.

racist discourses with elaborate constructions of reasons for the denial of interracial equality. Or Leninist discourses which subordinate absolutely everything to the strategic struggle for revolution, with a grim fate for deviants from the party line. Or a 'realist' discourse of anarchy in international relations, which constructs actors only as states always at the edge of violent conflict with one another. The presence of these discourses drives home the point that it is a mistake to conceptualize the public sphere or civil society only in terms of a set of progressive discourses or groupings (such as new social movements).

There are, then, many discourses that provide little grist for agonistic respect of the sort that difference democrats favour. But they do have a place in the public sphere thought of in terms of contestation across discourses. This latter model is not in the first instance a prescriptive one: it is an interpretation of the way the world is. Market liberalism does contest more social democratic and interventionist discourses. Racist discourses do contest alternatives that stress tolerance or affirmation of other races, and also discourses that deny the relevance of race as a category. Leninism (inasmuch as it exists still) contests more libertarian approaches to radical politics. Hobbesian anarchy as an interpretation of international relations is contested by a liberal discourse which stress the possibility of co-operative institutional construction. So the issue is not whether to welcome or bemoan such contestation of discourses, but what to about it.

A prescriptive model of the public sphere in terms of contestation, of publics rather than discourses, is advanced by Nancy Fraser (1992). Fraser believes that contestation is different from deliberation: 'the discursive relations among differently empowered publics are as likely to take the form of contestation as that of deliberation' (1992, p. 125).[5] But this contrast holds only to the extent deliberation is characterized in the narrow terms criticized by difference democrats. As I argued in the Introduction and Chapter 1, deliberative authenticity exists to the extent that communication induces reflection on preferences in non-coercive fashion. Provided that this standard is met, the kinds of communication admissible can be quite wide-ranging, and contestation in particular should be welcomed for its ability to induce reflection. Contestation also helps respond to those who believe that

[5] For Fraser, contestation is engaged by 'subaltern counterpublics' which constitute 'parallel discursive arenas' (p. 123) within which similarly-situated individuals can find their voices. They are publics rather than enclaves because their members 'aspire to disseminate [their] discourse to ever-widening arenas' (p. 124). Her paradigm is the feminist movement in the United States.

deliberation will produce only a conformist 'groupthink' (Femia, 1996, p. 386–7).

Discursive contestation can proceed in more or less democratic terms; the mere fact of contestation does not signal the presence of democracy. Contestation is undemocratic to the extent it is controlled by public relations experts, spin doctors, and demagogues. Contestation is democratic to the extent that it is engaged by a broad variety of competent actors under unconstrained conditions of the kind that deliberative democrats, or at least those discursive democrats influenced by critical theory, have always championed.

In this light, the real democratic contribution of the network form of organization celebrated by Schlosberg (1998, 1999) lies less in its internal relations of agonistic respect across difference, more in its capacity to promote dispersed control over the terms of discourse. (In Chapter 5 I will explain why there are intrinsic features of the network form that are conducive to the achievement of equality in deliberative competence.)

The United States environmental justice movement analysed by Schlosberg is indeed an exemplary network. It arose in the 1980s and flourished in the 1990s as a result of the mainstream environmental organizations' perceived indifference to the distribution of environmental risks on the basis of race and social class. The movement grew out of a series of local actions against waste dumps, incinerators, pesticides, uranium mining, and other hazardous activities. These local actions eventually grew into the sharing of information and resources through networks co-ordinated by bodies such as the Citizens' Clearinghouse on Hazardous Wastes and the Southwest Network for Environmental and Economic Justice. But the organization has always been bottom-up rather than top-down; there is no hierarchy and central leadership of the sort characterizing the mainstream groups.

This movement and its networks have been successful in reframing environmental issues related to risk and social justice, and so extending deliberative democratic control on these issues. Its discursive contests have been with more entrenched environmentalist discourses that conceptualize risks in terms of their collective and common character, as well as with industrialist discourses that deny the severity of risk, or subordinate risk to the pursuit of material prosperity. The environmental justice discourse is not organized and promoted centrally. Instead, it emerges from a wide variety of local struggles that together help to define what environmental injustice and justice can mean. Those schooled in social choice theory might look at the emergence of this movement and see only potential trouble for tractable social choice, inasmuch as the movement increases the number of subject positions that have to be addressed in collective choices. A series of localized 'not in my back yard' actions would seem to have this effect. Yet the emergence of the network form and its associated discourse actually presents a coherent perspective on issues of environmental risk; in the terminology of Maarten Hajer (1995), the movement has constituted a discourse coalition organized around a common story-line about the generation and distribution of environmental hazards. The picture here is one of struggle between the environmental justice discourse coalition and an industrialist discourse coalition, with a more established mainstream environmentalist discourse coalition also involved. What we see is a relatively small number of competing discourses, rather than a wild proliferation of subject positions of the sort that would alarm social choice theorists.

The environmental justice movement has also succeeded in affecting the content of public policy—for example, through an executive order on environmental justice signed by President Clinton in 1993, and the establishment of an Office of Environmental Justice in the United States Environmental Protection Agency in 1992. This success high-lights a further advantage of thinking in terms of the contestation of discourses rather than the engagement of identities: the recognition of difference can coexist with an orientation to collective decision. One of the standard criticisms of deliberative democracy is that it is rad-ically incomplete as a model, because it specifies no mechanism for collective choice; we deliberate, and then what? Difference democracy is still more subject to the same criticism. In the hands of Connolly, for example, democracy is redefined as the creative interplay of subject positions. There is no suggestion that there are collective decisions to be made, social problems to be solved. Sanders's emphasis on testi-mony suffers from the same difficulty: individuals testify—and then what?[6]

In Chapter 2 I responded to such charges of incompleteness by pointing to the degree to which the relative weight of competing dis-courses in the public sphere can be transmitted to the administrative state, in part through the deployment of rhetoric, thus affecting the content of public policy. Democratic life is not just the endless inter-

---

[6] Iris Young is careful to specify that she does not want to banish argument about what is to be done from deliberation—simply to supplement rational argument with other kinds of communication that better represent difference. Thus she can present her own model of communicative democracy as a development of the deliberative model, rather than a nega-tion of it, and so she is no more subject to the charge of incompleteness than is deliberative democracy.

play of discourses. There have to be moments of decisive collective action, and in contemporary societies it is mainly (but not only) the state that has this capacity. Discourses and their contests do not stop at the edge of the public sphere; they can also permeate the understandings and assumptions of state actors. Yet it is important to maintain a public sphere autonomous from the state, for discursive interplay within the public sphere is always likely to be less constrained than within the state. It is within the public sphere that insurgent discourses and identities can first establish themselves. In this light, liberal statist difference democrats such as Phillips (1993, 1995) can be over-optimistic about the capacity of the state to promote difference, at least in terms of anything more than limited corrections to mechanisms of representation.

In Chapters 2 and 3 I have tried to show that a conceptualization of democracy that emphasizes the contestation of discourses in the public sphere enables discursive democrats to reply effectively to the criticisms of both social choice theorists and difference democrats. Yet is such a conceptualization vulnerable to the charge frequently leveled at postmodernists and poststructuralists who deploy the discourse idea that an over-emphasis on language means that the influence of governmental structure, political power, and material interest are ignored? Moreover, can there not be moments of decisive collective action that do more than simply confirm the power of the dominant discourse?

To Foucault and Foucauldians discourses are the prime causal factors in human affairs, including politics. My account of the contestation of discourses is quite different, because it allows that there is much more to life and politics than discourses. The claim is only that the contestation of discourses in the public sphere is the most defensible way to think about discursive democracy on a society-wide basis. The outcome of this contestation is in reality not always decisive; in authoritarian states, for example, it might even be irrelevant in affecting public policy outcomes. Even in liberal democracies, the outcome may well be overridden by the exercise of political power by dominant interests tied to government, or by government's need to maintain investor confidence and keep the markets happy. However, the same might be said for deliberation of *any* kind.

Still, there are times when discursive shifts do make a difference, and are decisive in changing the content of public policy (see, for example, the case studies of Hajer, 1995, and Litfin, 1994). Civil rights legislation in the United States in the 1960s marked a demise of a discourse that saw little wrong in denying individuals full humanity on the basis of skin colour. The flurry of environmental legislation, administrative action, and institution-building around 1970 was evidence of the sudden arrival of the discourse of environmentalism. At this time environmental groups were not a significant presence in terms of exerting pressure on policy-making, nor were environmental issues especially contentious in election campaigns.

A sceptic might still argue that such influence of discourse shifts is sporadic and indirect. Yet the same might be said of elections—especially in light of their distortion by money, and the arbitrariness revealed by social choice theory. And interest group influence can be just as tenuous. Pluralists who once pinned their hopes on interest groups as more effective channels of influence than elections eventually conceded the systematic dominance of particular kinds of groups, especially corporations (Lindblom, 1977). Democracy as discursive contestation should be compared with these real and so defective alternatives, not with some unattainable ideal of how the will of the people can take effect directly in policy-making.

The relationship between this kind of contestation in the public sphere and more conventional kinds of democratic politics in closer association with the state is a tough question for discursive democrats and difference democrats alike.[7] When should efforts to advance democracy emphasize action through the state, and when should the public sphere be highlighted? How should the two kinds of action be connected? I believe these questions can only be answered in terms that are both historical and comparative. Different times and places, and different states, will yield different answers, as I will demonstrate in the next chapter.

---

[7] See Fraser (1992, p. 136) for a difference democrat's admission of the difficulty she has in specifying an appropriate relationship.

CHAPTER 4

Insurgent Democracy: Civil Society and State

In previous chapters I highlighted possibilities associated with the public sphere and civil society as political venues for the pursuit of discursive democracy that are in important ways distinct from the state. Earlier I recognized that many deliberative democrats now regard the institutions of the liberal state—constitutional assemblies, legislatures, courts, and public hearings—as the most significant venues for deliberation. An emphasis on the public sphere and civil society does not preclude recognition of these state-based possibilities—for example, in connection with the discursive designs mentioned in Chapter 2. Further, the state remains the main (though not, as I will point out later in this chapter, the sole) entity for making enforceable collective decisions in response to social problems. Moreover, the public sphere only takes shape in the presence of the state—however oppositional the stance taken by its key actors and movements. The discursive democratic well-being of civil society depends crucially on how the state organizes or obstructs interest representation. For all these reasons, a focus on civil society cannot mean turning one's back on the state.

The key question then becomes that of *when* should democratic advances be sought in the state, and *when* should they be sought in the public sphere and civil society? What should be the balance between these two options? Contrary to almost all analysts who have contemplated these questions, I do not believe they admit of any universally valid answers. We should not generalize from the situation in particular liberal democracies at particular times (for example, the present-day United States). Rather, such questions should be investigated in terms that are both comparative and historical. This chapter begins such an investigation. The answers turn out to be quite different for different times, places, and kinds of states.

In previous chapters I paid close attention to the precise definition of 'the state' and 'civil society', two concepts central to contemporary thinking about democracy but contested in their meaning by social scientists and political theorists. Most simply, the state may be defined formally as the set of individuals and organizations legally authorized to make binding decisions for a society. This chapter's exploration of the relationship between civil society and the state will enable more nuanced explication of the relationship between these two concepts, and so clarification of their meaning in the context of the prospects for democracy. I will show that 'the state' can be characterized in terms more useful than the simple definition just given, through reference to a set of imperatives for collective action. The state should not be equated with the broader set of society's institutions of government. The implication for normative democratic theory is that the fact that particular kinds of political interaction can be observed somewhere within these institutions does not imply that the form of these inter-actions can be prescribed straightforwardly for the state.

In practice, key political actors will sometimes face a choice between action in the public sphere and action within the state. Sometimes there will be no choice, if for example the state adopts exclusive patterns of interest representation, refusing to recognize the legitimacy of a particular social movement. When such a choice does arise, as it has done in the history of many social movements, it may often seem that there are instrumental benefits to be gained by entry into the state, in terms of achieving the group's substantive goals. Such entry can take many forms, from lobbying through conventional channels to taking part in co-operative policy-making mechanisms organized by government. Yet voices may also be raised warning of being bought off cheaply, and being co-opted into the existing power structure.

In contemplating any choice between action in civil society and the state, two kinds of concerns come into play. The first concerns the substantive goals of the group: are they more likely to be furthered by action in the public sphere, or more directly through the state? The second concerns the implications for democracy: does the democratic gain in terms of a more democratic (because more inclusive) state outweigh the democratic loss caused by a less vital and authentically democratic public sphere?

As I have already indicated, I do not believe that such questions admit of any universal answers. Rather, from the points of view of both particular movements and the well-being of democracy as a whole, the answers will depend upon the particular configuration of circumstances. Different times and places, and different kinds of states, will yield different answers. I will argue in this chapter that, from the point of view of democracy, benign inclusion in the state is possible only when two conditions hold. First, a group's defining concern must be capable of assimilation to an established or emerging state imperative. Second, civil society's discursive capacities must not be unduly depleted by the group's entry into the state. These criteria help determine whether any particular group's inclusion in the state constitutes a democratic gain or loss, for the group in question and, more importantly, for the polity as a whole. Absent such conditions, oppositional civil society may be a better focus for democratization efforts than the state.

A state imperative is any function that governmental structures must perform if those structures are to secure longevity and stability. Imperatives are always in the *interests* of public officials. The idea of an 'autonomous state' in Skocpol's (1985) terms is that public officials have collective interests of their own that are not reducible to the interests of a dominant class in society (such as the bourgeoisie in Marxist theory). But imperatives exist irrespective of the *desires* or *preferences* of particular public officials, and override these preferences and desires in case of conflict. For example, an incoming government may be elected on a platform of income redistribution and freedom of information about governmental activities, and its leaders may be sincerely committed to these values. But if they find that redistributive policies frighten the markets, and that freedom of information threatens to undermine national security in the face of a hostile international context, these officials' own interests in avoiding economic crisis (and so maintaining government revenues) and securing the state against adversaries override their preferences.

Examples of state imperatives include the need to keep domestic peace, respond to external threats, prevent capital flight, and raise revenues. The content and relative weight of these imperatives vary with time and place (as I will show later). The existence of such imperatives does not mean that all public officials have to give them priority all of the time. If that were the case, the state would appear as an entity with sharp boundaries, those on the inside pursuing a common purpose, those on the outside free to pursue a variety of interests. In practice, governments feature both internal differences and permeable boundaries, and their different parts can pursue contradictory policies. For example, agriculture ministries or departments will typically make common cause with farmers' organizations against central budgetary departments wishing to restrict subsidies and tax concessions for farmers. One department of government may administer subsidies to tobacco growers, while another conducts anti-smoking campaigns. Such internal differences and porous boundaries led almost all American political scientists to banish 'the state' from their vocabulary from the 1930s to the 1980s, in favour of the supposedly more realistic and scientific concept of 'the political system' (see especially Easton, 1953). However, the concept of the state made a comeback in the 1980s (for a celebration, see Evans, Rueschemeyer, and Skocpol, 1985; for a lament, see Almond, 1988).

How can a preference for 'the state' over 'the political system' be justified once we accept internal conflict and contradiction in government, along with porous boundaries? The only defensible answer proceeds, I believe, through reference to the idea of imperatives. We can isolate core functions made necessary by these imperatives. When we speak of 'the state' in the active voice, it is *only* these functions that can be at issue. Within this core, the actions of public officials are co-ordinated so as to be consistent with imperatives (irrespective of the precise wishes of these officials). Though not using the terminology of 'the state', Charles Lindblom (1982, p. 335) usefully distinguishes between 'imprisoned' and 'unimprisoned' zones of policy-making. The imprisoned zone covers the policies that must be pursued—in Lindblom's case, to keep actual and potential investors happy, though the idea can be generalized to other imperatives. The unimprisoned zone is the residual set of policy areas, featuring more indeterminate political bargaining, conflict, and compromise.

The core functions of the state constitute the essential areas of state activity—indeed, they define the need for the state—and it is these that I will emphasize in all the analysis of this chapter. All significant matters relating to national security and foreign policy, fiscal, monetary and trade policy, the welfare state, civil and criminal justice, environmental and natural resources policy are located in the core. In practice, governments will also be involved in many activities that have little connection to this core. Yet it would be a mistake to define the core and the periphery of government in terms of two fixed and mutually exclusive sets of policy issue areas. For when the stakes become high in just about any issue area, then core functions enter the picture. For example, if policy towards a small indigenous minority is only a matter of removing discrimination and securing equal political rights, then however important such questions may be to the well-being of this minority and to the larger society, the state's policy core is not at issue. But if the question becomes one of that minority's claims to a large land area rich in natural resources or agricultural production, then core economic imperatives do become relevant. Areas such as arts policy or the promotion of sport might have little conceivable connection to the core (assuming that the era of social control through bread and circuses has gone for good)—but they do as soon as the sums of money at issue become large.

In light of the two criteria for guiding choice between action in civil society and through the state that I proposed earlier, concerning respectively connection of a group's defining interest to a state imperatives and avoidance of depletion of civil society, democratic theorists who advocate a strategy of progressive inclusion of as many groups as possible in the state fail to recognize that the conditions for authentic as opposed to symbolic inclusion here are quite demanding. When these criteria are not met then inclusion in the polity beyond the state is more appropriate. There are times when benign inclusion in the state can occur, but I will conclude that any such inclusive move should also produce exclusions that both facilitate future democratization and guard against any reversal of democratic commitment in state and society. The dynamics of democratization turn out to reveal a subtle interplay between inclusion and exclusion, the state and civil society. The history of the expansion of the effective democratic franchise is largely one of insurgencies beginning in oppositional civil society. Sometimes these insurgencies end up being absorbed by the state, sometimes they do not. Sometimes such absorption is a democratic gain, sometimes a democratic loss. To set the scene for this account of insurgent democracy, let me begin with a closer look at what the basic idea of political inclusion entails.

Democratization as Inclusion

The difference democrats' critique discussed in the previous chapter highlights the degree to which formal political equality (of the sort that universal adult citizenship rights imply) can in practice mask the continued exclusion, and even oppression, of particular categories of people. Difference democrats are certainly not alone in calling for political change that would lead to the more effective inclusion of a fuller variety of individuals, groups, and categories of people in political life. Deliberative democracy itself began (even if it did not end) as a theory for which democratic legitimacy depends upon the ability of *all* those subject to a decision to participate in authentic deliberation. As the social choice critics of deliberation have been quick to note, this implies a commitment to the maximization of free, equal, and authentic access to debate, which should extend to individuals, interests, and groups traditionally excluded from decision-making.

In this light, democracy can be made more substantial and effective through greater efforts to include a variety of disadvantaged categories and groups for which the formal promise of democratic equality has masked continued exclusion or oppression (see Phillips, 1995). This feature of contemporary liberal societies—continued exclusion— provides one basic justification for a focus on democratization to begin with. However, this justification is contingent on a particular set of inequalities. A more general reason for caring about democratization is democracy itself: a democratic society is in important respects one that is continually striving to make democracy better, rather than a settled order of any sort (see Dryzek, 1996, pp. 4–5 for more extensive justification of this point). Democratization can take place along three dimensions: franchise, scope, and authenticity. Franchise refers to the proportion of the population that can participate effectively in politics. Scope is the range of issues under democratic control. And authenticity is the degree to which participation and control are substantive as opposed to symbolic.[1] In this chapter I emphasize franchise, understood as effective inclusion beyond formal citizenship rights. Candidates for such inclusive efforts currently include ethnic and religious minorities, indigenous peoples, women, the old, gays and lesbians, youth, the unemployed, the underclass, recent immigrants, people on the receiving end of environmental risks, and (if only by proxy) future generations.

While recognizing that the effective inclusion of more groups and categories in the polity is central to democratization, in this chapter I want to question any predisposition toward inclusion sponsored by or sought in the state. Entry into the state can come through organization as an interest group and associated lobbying activities, or participation in policy development and implementation through ongoing negotiation between group leaders and public officials, or participation in conventional party and electoral politics either by organizing as a party or in formal affiliation with an established party, or acceptance of governmental appointments by group leaders, or having enhancement of the group's ability to participate in policy-making itself being a target of public policy. This sort of inclusion or entry into the state therefore involves more than the attainment of basic citizenship rights such as the right to vote and associate, which I shall take for granted.

[1] In Dryzek (1996, pp. 5–9) I argue that an advance on any one of these dimensions should never be bought at the expense of a retreat on one of the two others.

Democratic theorists have of course always assumed that the state is the main locus of their concerns; indeed, this assumption is so universal and unremarkable that it is not often even noted. A rare explicit acknowledgment is made by Robert Dahl (1989, p. 37): 'Advocates of the democratic process have always meant it to be applied to the state.' I would suggest in contrast that much of the time we should look instead to the polity beyond the state. In the past, the main non-state focus emphasized by democratic theorists was the workplace. More recently, some emphasis has shifted to civil society, and as previous chapters should already indicate, I support this emphasis. Still, the civil society concept remains both contested and ambiguous, especially in terms of its relationship to the state. Here, I wish to do more both to advance this emphasis on civil society, and to clarify its appropriate relationship to the state.

Wariness of political inclusion is common in the ranks of conservatives and classical liberals. Conservatives want to repel destabilizing threats to the established order, and liberals want to protect their project of universal rights assigned equally to individuals irrespective of their characteristics, rather than to particular categories or groups. My own argument for highly selective inclusion is different in that it proceeds from the point of view of democratization itself. It is important to distinguish between inclusion in politics and inclusion in the state. I will attempt to show that democrats, including deliberative democrats, should generally favour a state that is in important aspects exclusive, for exclusion properly arranged can actually benefit democracy and democratization, even from the point of view of those excluded. (That exclusion can do so from the point of those included has been a staple of republican thinking through the ages, from antiquity to Arendt, 1958.)

An examination of the history of democratization indicates that pressures for greater democracy almost always emanate from insurgency in oppositional civil society, rarely or never from the state itself. In most West European countries, the franchise was gradually extended beyond a narrow group of property-holders as a result of agitation from the working class and its organizations (see Rueschemeyer, Stephens, and Stephens, 1992)—perhaps most famously, the Chartists in early nineteenth-century England. Women's suffrage was in the pioneer cases the culmination of a long struggle by women themselves, organized into suffragette movements.

If a group leaves the oppositional sphere to enter the state then dominant classes and public officials have less to fear in the way of public protest. There may be democratic gain in this entry, but there is also democratic loss in terms of a less discursively vital civil society, the erosion of some existing democratic accomplishments, and a reduced likelihood of further democratization in future. Moreover, the democratic gain is itself uncertain. I will argue that such gain can only be secured when the defining interest of the entering group can be connected quite directly to an existing or emerging state imperative. This connection can be made when an equivalence is discovered between the goods sought by a group and some aspect of what the state must do in terms of public policy. If the group's interest cannot be so assimilated, then the group in question is confined in its operations to peripheral aspects of public policy, or at best receives only symbolic rewards. Such co-option has been a standing concern of observers of the role of groups in democratic systems. Co-option was defined long ago by Selznick (1966, p. 13) as 'the process of absorbing new elements into the leadership or policy-determining structure of an organization as a means of averting threats to its stability or existence', though in co-option's normal pejorative sense such absorption comes without any real power-sharing.[2]

Before analysing in detail the circumstances in which the different venues for more inclusive democratization are appropriate, let me discuss approaches to inclusion that are unequivocally statist.

Inclusive States

Proposals for democratic inclusion have been pursued most assiduously by the difference democrats introduced in the previous chapter, many of whom have turned their attention to how states might be made more inclusive. Difference democrats believe that merely granting members of oppressed groups the same formal rights and the same access to the state as everyone else effectively extinguishes any political manifestation of difference (Young, 1989; 1990). So, for example, indigenous peoples in Canada, the United States, or Australia are enfranchised under 'one person, one vote'. But given their numbers and geographical dispersal, this effectively denies them any representation in national legislatures. New Zealand has long recognized this problem, and (until the recent reform of the electoral system) set aside a number of Maori seats in parliament.[3] It is not just electoral systems

---

[2] For a detailed analysis of the hazards of co-option, especially for resource-poor groups, see Saward (1992).

[3] One parliamentary seat in the German *land* of Schleswig-Holstein is reserved for the tiny Danish minority.

which can exclude disadvantaged groups. Many other aspects of political systems, including cultural aspects, can make it difficult for disadvantaged groups to attain real recognition and access, even when these groups are large.

To some difference democrats, notably Anne Phillips (1993, pp. 96–9), these considerations suggest only measures such as setting aside quotas of seats in parliament for particular categories of people, such as women. Political parties in Scandinavia have adopted quota systems of just this sort, and the British Labour Party has also tried to specify that a certain percentage of its candidates in winnable seats be women. Phillips is otherwise keen to preserve the basic structure of liberal democracy. There is no suggestion that the representatives in question have a special charge to speak for women and only as women; it is enough that they simply *are* women.

As we saw in Chapter 3, more radical implications are drawn from the principle of difference by Iris Young, who believes that oppressed groups need more than just representatives in the legislature. Groups should also have veto power over policies that affect them, and guarantees that public officials will respond to their concerns. In other words, the group is represented *qua* group, rather than merely yielding representatives with the characteristics of the group.

Now, the idea that the representation of groups rather than individuals should be the locus of democratic politics is not unique to contemporary difference democrats. Pluralists have always interpreted state-related politics in terms of the interaction of groups, and public policy as the output of that interaction. Mid-century United States pluralists such as David Truman (1951) and Robert Dahl (1956) may not have had the same set of interests in mind as the difference democrats, but they shared an emphasis on different experiences producing different interests which should then be pursued by interest organization through groups.[4]

These pluralists saw the state in passive terms, as reacting to whatever groups happened to emerge. Given that they recognized few barriers to the emergence of interests and the organization of groups, they saw no need for public authority to intervene to affect the pattern of group representation (though they had no objection to the removal of barriers to group assertiveness, through for example civil rights legislation in the United States). In contrast, difference democrats see a variety of barriers to the emergence, recognition, organization, and

[4] Early 20th-cent. pluralists such as Harold Laski (1919) and Mary Parker Follett (1918) have more in common with contemporary difference democrats than do Truman *et al.* (see Schlosberg, 1998).

assertiveness of groups. These barriers come mostly in the form of hierarchy and oppression, with cultural and economic as well as political causes. Whereas mid-century US pluralism is *passively* inclusive in its pattern of representation in that it is prepared to accept whatever constellation of groups society throws towards politics, difference democrats are more attuned to the need for *actively* inclusive representation, in which efforts are made to promote the ability of groups to recognize an interest and pursue it in politics. In this respect, they reveal a surprising affinity with James Madison's view of groups, or factions as he would have called them; for Madison too did not believe that a desirable pattern of group representation emerged automatically.

Difference democrats are not always clear as to who does the recognizing and promoting here. Joshua Cohen and Joel Rogers (1992) are more forthright in their answer: the state. Sharing with both Madison and difference democrats the recognition that desirable patterns of interest organization and representation do not arise automatically (1992, p. 426), they believe the state should play an active role in sponsoring and certifying groups, removing obstacles to their exercising political influence, and creating channels for that influence to be felt in government. In particular, inequality of representation in their 'associative democracy' should be remedied by state promotion of the organization of disadvantaged groups (Cohen and Rogers, 1992, p. 425). The kinds of associations Cohen and Rogers have in mind are mostly economic ones, especially categories of workers. Their emphasis on the economic basis of interest formation is shared by mid-century pluralists, though the latter were not, Dahl excepted, particularly interested in the working class.

State-sponsored association is proposed by Michael Walzer as an antidote to a rampant individualism which is producing 'dissociated individuals' who are easy prey for anti-democratic demagogues (Walzer, 1994, p. 189).[5] In the United States at least, Walzer (1991, p. 125) believes conditions have deteriorated to the extent that 'it makes sense to call the state to the rescue of civil society'. Walzer recommends governmental sponsorship and subsidy for trade unions, for 'cultural associations' defined in ethnic or religious terms that provide welfare, education, and health services, for 'charter schools' designed and managed by parents and teachers, for tenants' housing co-operatives, for workers' co-operatives, and for a wide range of community projects (1994, p. 189). Group life enhanced along these lines

[5] Here, Walzer echoes the long-standing fear of mass society theorists such as Kornhauser (1959).

will, Walzer hopes, produce efficacious and tolerant citizens, but it requires 'certain background or framing conditions that can only be provided by state action' involving 'a political strategy for mobilizing, organizing, and, if necessary, subsidizing the right sort of groups' (1994, p. 191).

Once mobilized, Walzer's 'right sort of groups' are left free to participate in politics without further state support. In contrast, Cohen and Rogers believe such support should continue through the creation of channels and mechanisms for groups to influence public policy. With this continuation, the state-sponsored pattern of representation advocated in the associative democracy of Cohen and Rogers does, as they recognize, have more in common with corporatism than with liberalism.[6] Corporatism as a form for the organization of national political systems may be defined as a tripartite concertation of government, labour, and business, the last two represented by encompassing associations. All three partners are involved in the making and implementation of policy; institutions such as parliament play a comparatively minor role, as it is the executive that represents government. The essence of the corporatist bargain is that business supports policies geared to redistribution and full employment, and does not disinvest in response to these policies. Labour, for its part, promises not to make life difficult for business through strikes or other forms of militancy. Government fosters the organization and representation of business and labour, guarantees their exclusive participation in policy-making, and in turn expects both business and labour associations to discipline their members (for further details, see Schmitter and Lehmbruch, 1979). Corporatism of this sort has been practised most effectively in Scandinavia, Germany, the Netherlands, and Austria, though elements exist in other European countries (and in Australia).

The democrat's problem with corporatism has always been that it is exclusive: only business and labour are represented, and even the grass roots of labour have little influence. Interests defined on a non-economic basis are shut out completely. Thus recent theoretical works in the corporatist tradition (e.g. Schmitter, 1992) have addressed themselves to how corporatism might be made more inclusive by granting a place at the table to non-economic groups such as environmentalists.

---

[6] A somewhat different model going by the same name is developed by Hirst (1994). But whereas Cohen and Rogers propose an actively inclusive state, the state in Hirst's associative democracy is passively inclusive. In Hirst's model, democracy is built from the ground up by citizen associations which would then take on many of the functions now performed by the state. The state's role is restricted to enabling such a process to occur, rather than actively promoting it.

The latter might agree not to sponsor boycotts, protests, or legal action against polluters and despoilers in return for commitments on the part of government, industry, and labour to anti-pollution measures and wilderness protection. Real-world corporatist systems have shown some signs of extending themselves in this direction. Notably, in Norway moderate environmental groups (such as Friends of the Earth) are partially funded by the state and have a recognized place in corporatist policy-making. Such extension—though for the most part only to interests defined on an economic basis—is exactly what Cohen and Rogers desire.

Iris Young applauds this kind of state-sponsored extension of representation, though she wants it to apply to the whole range of oppressed groups, not just economically-defined ones. Connecting her earlier work on group representation with the idea of associative democracy, she avers in her commentary on Cohen and Rogers that 'the state could decide to promote the self-organization of members of oppressed groups where such organization is weak, or to provide greater resources to existing associations representing oppressed or disadvantaged groups, and to create compensatory political forms to ensure that such groups have an equal voice in agenda setting and policy formation' (Young,1992, p. 532).

Theorists who seek democratization in the shadow of corporatism believe that corporatism's best quality is its ability actively to include particular interests; the problem is only that historically a very limited range of interests has been included. I will suggest in contrast that the real beauty of corporatism is in its passive exclusion of many interests in society—and that it does this with a state that seems quite good at promoting economic justice at least in comparison to all the alternative forms of state organization that have been tried from time to time (see below for evidence on this last point).

Actively inclusive states exist mostly in the proposals of political theorists such as Cohen and Rogers, Walzer, and Young. Yet there is one real-world example, though not one these theorists are likely to endorse. The Mexican state's longevity and stability can be attributed to its brilliantly successful incorporation of successive waves of potential troublemakers. Until recently both the means (patronage and coercion) and the ends were authoritarian. But the 1988–94 Salinas administration's PRONASOL (National Solidarity Campaign) added the trappings of grassroots participatory democracy to centralized state guidance. PRONASOL was directed at the social movement activists involved with the Cardenista opposition, which had probably won the 1988 presidential election (the government claimed otherwise). Oriented to the organization of peasants, workers, and disadvantaged communities, PRONASOL dismantled the opposition and employed many of its activists (see Carruthers, 1995). Thus could the Mexican tradition of a strong state dominating a weak civil society continue, though now with an inclusive democratic aspect, or at least veneer.

Let me now try to add an historical dimension to the analysis which will justify suspicion of the actively inclusive state, and so demonstrate why the Mexican outcome might well follow from the proposals of actively inclusive democratic theorists, however unwelcome this outcome might be to them. I will then outline the consequences of this suspicion for any strategy of democratization, and proceed to consider where and how democrats might do better.

Inclusion in Historical Perspective

A democratizing strategy of progressive inclusion of as many interests as possible in the state implies that the content of public policy is essentially indeterminate. Mid-century pluralists were most explicit on this point in seeing public policy through a physics analogy as the resultant of the direction and strength of whatever pressures were applied by different interest groups. Yet this picture of indeterminacy is manifestly false, as pluralists such as Dahl and Lindblom themselves eventually came to recognize. Irrespective of what interest groups seek, there are certain imperatives that all states simply must meet. Unfortunately for advocates of state-sponsored group representation such as Cohen and Rogers and Young, promoting the organization of disadvantaged groups is not one of them, and I can imagine no scenario under which it becomes one. If so, then to advocate such representation may work as moral philosophy, but not as political theory, for the latter must attend to practical constraints (see even Rawls, 1987, p. 24). But luckily for democrats, the imperatives of states are not constant over time; and it is this very inconstancy which enabled democratization of the state to take place in the past. The implication here is that democratization of the state in future is possible only to the extent state imperatives continue to change. Before exploring this last point in more depth, let me turn to the content and history of the imperatives facing states.

According to Skocpol (1979), all states must survive in a hostile world, keep order internally, and extract the resources to finance survival and order, through some combination of taxation and compulsion of their own population. When states alienate their own upper classes by leaning on them too heavily in order to finance their response to external threats, these classes may withdraw support from the state, allowing revolution to commence. Skocpol applies this analysis to revolution in the agrarian bureaucracies of France, Russia, and China.

Though Skocpol writes as though these three imperatives apply unchangingly to all states, in fact their severe conjunction applies only in a Hobbesian world in which violent international conflict is a normal feature and the economic resource base available to states is more or less fixed. Conditions have changed for states now fortunate enough to belong to the global core, enabling them to meet their imperatives in ways that have had positive consequences for democracy. (Life for states in the global periphery remains more Hobbesian; see Goldgeier and McFaul, 1992 on the difference between the situations of states in the global core and in the periphery.)

The first such modification comes with the rise of capitalist economies, and with them the potential for economic growth on a scale never seen before. States need no longer rely on punitive taxation or confiscation in order to finance themselves against external threats; economic growth can help perform the same function in less painful fashion. Thus the first imperative facing states in capitalist systems is what (post-)Marxists (e.g. Offe, 1984; O'Connor, 1984) call *accumulation*. States simply must provide the conditions that facilitate capitalist investment and economic growth; if they pursue anti-business policies, then they are punished by 'capital strike', recession, falling tax revenues, and unpopularity in the eyes of the public. Block (1977) and Lindblom (1982) have detailed the degree to which this 'exchange-dependency' constricts the policies of states; markets, according to Lindblom, 'imprison' government policy, and 'pluralism at most operates only in an unimprisoned zone of policy making' (Lindblom, 1982: 335). It is markets, especially financial ones, which are the sounding-boards for public policy, not public opinion or parliament. And if policies are constricted, then so is democracy, for policies that contradict the fundamental interests of business must be vetoed, no matter how popular. As Bowles and Gintis (1986, p. 90) put it, 'the presumed sovereignty of the democratic citizenry fails in the presence of capital strike.' The ever-increasing mobility of capital across national boundaries intensifies this constraint (Dryzek, 1996, pp. 77–83).

Though today exchange dependency figures mostly as an impediment to democratization, the opposite was once true. The importance of the accumulation imperative in the development of democracy is that it brought the interests of the state and of the emerging bourgeoisie into harmony, and so participation in policy making could be extended to the bourgeoisie. It is easy to forget that the bourgeoisie was once an oppositional force in Western societies, constituting a democratic civil society hostile to the state. Habermas (1989) details the deliberative democratic life of the early bourgeois public sphere, manifested in newspapers, coffee houses, and public association. He also charts the subsequent migration of the bourgeoisie from civil society to the state.

This migration was followed somewhat later (the timing of course varying by country) by the industrial working class; and again, this development can be related to the shifting content of state imperatives. Capitalism produces an industrial working class; and, as Karl Marx recognized, the conditions of its existence in urban centres and large factories enable it to constitute a political threat to the state in capitalist society. At the time Marx was writing the activists of the organized working class constituted an oppositional sphere that confronted the state. Marx himself thought that opposition would culminate in revolution. What happened instead is that opposition gave way to inclusion. That choice was far from easy for socialist parties to make, and syndicalists, anarchists, and revolutionary Marxists mounted a protracted resistance to it in the early twentieth century (see Przeworski and Sprague, 1986, pp. 13–28). But for better or for worse, workers' parties and trades unions did come to play significant roles in electoral politics and public policy-making in many industrial societies. However, the degree of their inclusion remains quite variable, reaching a high point in social democratic corporatist societies, and this inclusion has for the most part proved less easy and less complete than the earlier inclusion of the bourgeoisie. Strikes and demonstrations have been, at least until the last decade or so, part of the organized working class's political repertoire.

Industrialization meant that the long-established state imperative of keeping internal order was no longer a matter of control of enough coercive force to keep potential malcontents in line. Far more efficient, if it can be secured, is the *voluntary* acquiescence of potentially rebellious subordinate social classes and categories to the dominant political–economic order. Thus the imperative of keeping internal order mutates over time into what neo-Marxists or post-Marxists such as Habermas (1975), Offe (1984), and O'Connor (1973) call legitimation. And the most effective device for legitimation so far devised, these authors aver, is the welfare state. In part, the working class can be induced to accept the capitalist political economy if it delivers the goods in terms of material prosperity, in which case legitimation can be assimilated to accumulation (assuming enough wealth trickles down). But the business cycles and employment insecurity endemic even to growing capitalist systems mean that something more is required, and this is where the Keynesian welfare state comes in. The fact that the Keynesian welfare state is now on the way out, or at least under attack, has some major negative consequences for democratization which I will address shortly.

Legitimation is secured when subordinate classes and categories with the capacity to destabilize the political economy instead support or accept that structure. The best example of such a class or category in industrial societies has often been the working class, though groups defined on an ethnic or religious basis may also possess the capacity to destabilize. The threat to political stability posed by permanent ethnic or religious minorities forms the core of Arend Lijphart's argument for a consociational state which recognizes and incorporates the organizations of such minorities (see e.g. Lijphart, 1977). (Shortly I will discuss the emergence of another threat to legitimation.) It should be stressed that the legitimation imperative does not reduce to a need for governments to court popularity. If it did, then every interest held by every group in society could be assimilated to the legitimation imperative, and the whole concept of a state imperative would dissolve into pluralism, thus losing all force. Only when the class or category in question has the capacity to destabilize government or block policy effectiveness is legitimation at issue.

Emerging State Imperatives and the Prospects for Inclusion

The moral of the preceding historical tale is that, at least when it comes to action in the vicinity of the core functions of the state, oppositional groupings can only be included in the state in benign fashion when the defining interest of the grouping can be related quite directly to a state imperative. Under this condition, groups can help determine the content of public policy, at a minimum in terms of how imperatives are met (for example, legitimation might be promoted by either universalistic or means tested welfare state programs), and how trade-offs between competing imperatives are made (for example, to what extent should economic growth be sacrificed for the sake of redistribution?).

If the interest of an oppositional group cannot be so related to an imperative, then inclusion means being co-opted or bought off cheaply, like the leaders of environmental interest groups who secured not only access but also employment at high levels in the Clinton administration, but found themselves unable to achieve much in the way of policy substance. As Jay Hair, leader of the National Wildlife Federation, the largest of the co-opted groups, eventually put it, 'What started out like a love affair turned out to be date rape' (quoted in Dowie, 1995, p. 177). The group in question receives symbolic rewards only. Goodin (1980, pp. 123–56) argues that such rewards are defensible if the symbols in question (e.g. religious rituals, flags, seeing a member of one's ethnic group in the mayor's chair) have intrinsic value to the group. Symbolic rewards are correspondingly indefensible if they are offered as promissory notes for more tangible goods, but turn out to be substitutes for these goods.

There are, as I pointed out earlier, areas of public policy where state imperatives are at issue only weakly, if at all. In such areas, a group's defining interest may well have little bearing on any imperative. Thus the degree to which the inclusion of the group in the state is benign is a matter untouched by my foregoing analysis. Yet this possibility provides little relief, for it implies that inclusion in the state is unproblematic only in relatively peripheral policy areas. And even if a group is operating freely in this 'unimprisoned' zone of policy-making, this seeming freedom is contingent on the group not transgressing boundaries that threaten the core. For example, gay and lesbian rights groups may lobby successfully for legal recognition of same-sex unions on a par with heterosexual partnerships, with few obvious implications for core imperatives. But if the financial costs to government or private companies (in terms of claims for health benefits, etc.) look like they will be substantial, the economic imperative comes into play.

To the extent public policy remains under the sway of state imperatives, groups whose inclusion coincides with no imperative at all cannot easily find the tangible goods they value advanced. They may be allowed to participate in the policy process, but outcomes will be systematically skewed against them. Anything more would introduce a dangerous degree of indeterminacy into the content of public policy. There is a high price to be paid by any group included on this basis. For if state officials have no compelling reason to include the group anyway, then presumably the group in question must moderate its stance in order to fit with established state imperatives. Moreover, in entering the state the group becomes constrained in the kind of interactions it engages. In particular, the group may have to develop a more hierarchical internal structure in order to produce a stable leadership for government officials to recognize and deal with. Life in the state is, then, bought at the expense of relatively unrestricted democratic interplay and deliberation in the oppositional public sphere. The democratic loss

experienced by entry into the state can, as with the cases of the bourgeoisie and the working class in the past, be justified through reference
to the instrumental benefits so achieved. But if there are few or no
instrumental benefits, the loss is harder to justify.

Of the group claims now endorsed by difference democrats and
other advocates of inclusion, which if any can be related to established
or emerging state imperatives? Their experience in the Clinton White
House notwithstanding, I would consider the best claimants to be
environmentalists, and the relevant emerging state imperative to be
environmental conservation. This imperative itself develops out of the
accumulation and legitimation imperatives. Now, accumulation and
environmental conservation have traditionally been cast in a zero-sum
relationship: economic growth has to be foregone to enjoy environmental values. But recent thinking reconceptualizes this relationship.
Albert Weale (1992), among others, argues that the essence of the new
environmental politics is 'ecological modernization': the idea that economic growth and environmental values now stand in a positive-sum
relationship, as a clean environment is good for business. Why? First,
a pleasant environment can substitute for monetary income for
employees. Second, dirty air and water hurt productivity. Third, consumers increasingly demand environmentally-benign goods and services. Finally, pollution indicates inefficiency in materials usage. Weale
argues that ecological modernization has been incorporated into government policy most effectively in Germany; Hajer (1995) compares
its limited progress in Britain with its more substantial gains in the
Netherlands. In the United States, the kind of green capitalism advocated by Vice-President Albert Gore (1992) is consistent with ecological modernization, though he does not use the term.

Environmental conservation can be linked to the legitimation
imperative via Ulrich Beck's (1992) notion of 'risk society'. To Beck,
politics is increasingly organized around the production and distribution of risks (mostly related to chemical, radioactive, and biotechnological hazards) rather than material goods. Those on the receiving end
of risks are so numerous, and so capable of political mobilization, that
they threaten the stability of the political–economic order, and so
legitimation becomes at issue. In the face of widespread public mistrust of arrogant scientists and technologists and of their corporate
and governmental employers, Beck believes that legitimation in risk
society can only be achieved by public participation in risk selection,
allocation, and amelioration.

Even if the ecological modernizers and risk democrats are correct,
not all environmental concerns can be easily assimilated to state

imperatives. Endangered species protection, wilderness preservation (especially when the wilderness contains valuable extractive resources), animal rights (especially when the profits of companies relying on animal testing or factory farming are threatened), and deep ecological conceptions of how to live in relation to nature are some of the aspects of environmentalism not easily assimilated. The solution here might be a 'velvet divorce' in which part of the environmental movement enters the state, and part chooses to continue to confront the state from the public sphere. This describes the situation in a number of countries. Until their demise in the early 1990s, Green 'Fundis' in Germany maintained a confrontational stance while their 'Realo' counterparts pursued an ever more conventional electoral strategy. In the United States, there remains a clear distinction between mainstream environmental groups on the one hand and radicals such as Earth First!, animal liberationists, and networks organized around toxics and environmental justice issues on the other.

One might perhaps analyse contemporary feminism in similar terms: liberal feminism is destined for the state, whereas cultural feminism is more suited to the public sphere. The feminization of work means that women's concerns about employment can be related to the accumulation imperative, as the removal of discrimination against women can actually be good for business in general. If the patriarchal family is a remnant feudal structure (as Fraad, Resnick, and Wolff, 1994 argue), then capitalism is now destroying feudalisms's last holdout by bringing women into the paid labour force (see also Beck, 1992, p. 105). The feminization of poverty might indicate that aspects of feminism could be assimilated to the legitimation imperative, given the latter's association with the welfare state. But given that poverty-stricken female-headed households do not constitute much of a political threat to the established order (in comparison with the organized working class of old), this assimilation seems unlikely. Cultural feminist demands for a different kind of politics based on ethics of care and nurturing have no obvious connection to any state imperative, and so should not expect advances therein, especially if they aspire to anything more than languishing on the periphery of governmental concerns.

To Civil Society

The main alternative to the state as a site for democratization in general, and deliberative democracy in particular, is civil society. As discussed in Chapter 1, civil society in its politicized sense (that is, the public sphere) consists of self-limiting political association oriented by a relationship to the state, but not seeking any share in state power. Prominent examples of politicized civil society in action would include the early bourgeois public sphere discussed by Habermas (1989), the insurgent 'free spaces' in US political history constituted by women, blacks, workers, farmers, and others (Evans and Boyte, 1986), the democratic opposition in Eastern Europe prior to 1989 (Arato, 1993), and, in the West, feminist, anti-nuclear, peace, environmental, and urban new social movements. Such public spheres often feature relatively egalitarian and authentically discursive politics in their internal workings (for further details, see Dryzek, 1996, pp. 47–53). They do not pursue power as interest groups or through electorally-oriented parties; yet they are of course concerned with public affairs. Often this concern casts them in opposition to the state and prominent economic actors, though sometimes state and corporate power can be ignored.

Civil society is a heterogeneous place, home to the Michigan Militia as well as the movements I have mentioned. Other groups may be less hostile to democratic values, but still quite hierarchical—for example, Greenpeace. Not everything in oppositional civil society represents discursive democratic vitality. So how do we distinguish between civil society formations that contribute to democratization and those that do not? It is possible to exclude terrorists of both the left and right on analytic grounds: if a group has no orientation to the state other than seeking its destruction, then that group may be part of civil society, but it is not part of the public sphere. Offe (1985, p. 853) excludes the religious right in the United States and neofascists in Europe from his purview by applying the criterion of commitment to 'a selective radicalization of 'modern' values'. Thus to Offe social movements are relevant to democratization to the degree they fit an account of progress toward fulfilment of modernity's potential. Offe's viewpoint dovetails quite easily with my analysis of evolving state imperatives and their relation to changing patterns of inclusion and protest. However, while it is rare in practice, oppositional civil society groups can be both conservative in aims and democratic in internal structure. The US anti-abortion group Operation Rescue might fall into this category. Their conservatism alone does not warrant their dismissal. Nor is hierarchy alone sufficient reason for dismissal: despite its internal hierarchy, Greenpeace contributes to the democratic interplay of oppositional civil society.

It is less easy to see how groups that are both conservative and hierarchical make any such contribution. Yet even here, we should be open to surprises. There is some evidence to suggest that white supremacist groups can provide a temporary lifeline to troubled young adults, enabling their future integration into more truly 'civil' society; and even right-wing militias may actually reduce violence by providing a structured outlet for individuals who would otherwise be off on their own, bombing and killing (Rosenblum, 1998, pp. 9, 16). In evaluating such groups, we need to look at what they actually do for their members, and not just rush to make moral judgements based on the groups' stated goals.

Self-limitation does not mean that civil society is a powerless realm. Power can be exercised from and in civil society in several ways. First, political action in civil society can change the terms of political discourse, and so affect the content of public policy. The rhetorical achievements of Martin Luther King are exemplary here. As I noted in Chapter 2, King drew upon and reshaped the discourse of American constitutional liberalism in order to advance an agenda of civil rights for African-Americans. The women's movement has succeeded (not without resistance) in changing the ways in which gender, family, and the dividing line between public and private affairs are conceptualized in policy debates. The communicative power that the public sphere can exert over the state is diffuse and pervasive, felt in the way terms are defined and issues are framed, not in the direct leverage of one actor over another. The relative weight of competing discourses in civil society can have major implications for the content of public policy.

Second, as Tarrow (1994, pp. 184–6) argues in reply to those who believe waves of political protest leave behind only burned-out or co-opted activists, social movements can produce lasting effects in political culture by legitimating particular forms of collective action such as the sit-in, and by establishing a permanent place for issues on the public agenda.

Third, policy-oriented deliberative fora can be constituted within civil society. A good example is the Global Forum which assembled as the civil society counterpart to the 1992 United Nations Conference on Environment and Development in Rio. Composed of non-governmental activists from all over the world, the Global Forum influenced what transpired in the official proceedings of the Conference, in part by shaming and embarrassing some of the official participants. Domestic environmental policy is sometimes influenced by such fora, concerned with issues such as renewable resources (Berger, 1985) and toxic wastes (Fischer, 1993).

Fourth, protest in civil society can create fear of political instability and so draw forth a governmental response. Piven and Cloward (1971) interpret the history of the US welfare state in these terms: welfare provision increases only in response to unruliness on the part of the poverty-stricken. Piven and Cloward themselves do not draw any implication that protest should be confined to civil society, and advise the poor to step up their demands on the state through conventional channels. Yet their historical account can be deployed as evidence of the power of civil society over the state.

These four civil society activities involve the more or less democratic exercise of power *over* the state, but they do not reduce to the inclusion of civil society *in* the state. In addition, civil society can reclaim power *from* the state—and from the economy. Indeed, Jänicke (1996) defines civil society in functional terms, as public action in response to failure in government and the economy. This functional definition highlights the idea that civil society can itself feature problem-solving, not merely cheap talk. Thus enforceable collective decisions can sometimes be made without reference to the state, even if the state remains the most significant entity so engaged. Civil society can, then, be home to 'para-governmental' activity, and not simply act as a source of influence over the more obviously governmental activities of the state. There are numerous examples here. When feminists and others speak of 'empowerment' they do not mean influence over government, but rather control of their own lives, facilitated by support groups and the like. Disputes within communities can be settled through alternative dispute resolution without involving courts, as for example in the community boards of San Francisco (Schlosberg, 1995). Community groups (such as churches) can provide social services. Citizens can exercise power directly over economic actors through means such as boycotts of corporations or products. Thus in 1995 Greenpeace organized protests against the Shell Oil corporation's plan to dispose of the redundant Brent Spar oil platform in the North Atlantic. Shell eventually capitulated, much to the annoyance of the British government, which was prepared to use force to dislodge protesters from the platform. Paragovernmental interventions can be less benign: sectarian militias can evict families of a different ethnicity or religion from a neighbourhood (a practice of long standing in Northern Ireland).

A final and somewhat different way in which power can be exercised through civil society is in terms of cultural change affecting power relations. Think, for example, of the extent to which feminism has changed power relationships both within the family and outside (and not just as a consequence of changes in family law). So even if civil society actions leave public policy untouched, they can have real social

effects. Along these lines, Tesh (1993) sees the success of social movements in terms of the changes they produce in ethics, culture, and so
behaviour in everyday life, for example in relationships between the
sexes, or in the way people conceptualize pollutants and the environmental friendliness of products.

Civil society can constitute a site for democratization because it can
be a place where people choose to live their public lives and solve their
joint problems. This can be as true for postmodernists such as
Connolly (1991*a*), who conceptualize democracy in terms of the
negotiation of identities across difference, as for deliberative democrats. Different again, Hannah Arendt's democratic 'oases in the
desert' of a sterile modernity can only be found in civil society. Critics
of Arendt argue that she was happy to purchase deliberative democratic authenticity at the expense of democratic franchise. But as Isaac
points out, the 'elites' populating these oases are self-selected and can
come from any social class, ruling over themselves, not over anyone
else, which is why a workers' council can be for Arendt an exemplary
'elite' (Isaac, 1994, p. 158).

But why should civil society often be more attractive than the state
as a site for democratization, and deliberative democratization in particular? The answer is that it is relatively unconstrained. If we think of
political action in civil society in terms of the contestation of discourses rather than voting across alternative positions, then strategic
action of the sort whose destructive consequences have been exposed
by social choice theory (see Chapter 2) looms less large. Thus deliberation need not be muffled in the interests of strategic advantage. In
addition, goals and interests need not be compromised or subordinated to the pursuit of office or access, and there is less reason to repress
the contributions to debate of embarrassing troublemakers. Perhaps
most important of all, the indeterminacy of outcome inherent in
democracy need not be subordinated to reasons of state. Given that
deliberative democratic authenticity consists of communication that
induces reflection on preferences in noncoercive fashion, there are
therefore several coercive agents of distortion less pervasive in civil
society than in the state.

The Democratic Benefits of Exclusive States

There is, then, much to be said for deliberative and democratic life in
civil society as opposed to the state. But even if we focus on civil society alone, the state and its structure cannot be ignored, for how states

are organized turns out to have major implications for the democratic vitality of civil society. Research on the history of social movements shows that the way they emerge depends crucially on the character of state structures. Indeed, social movements first emerged only in reaction to the development of the modern nation-state, which, to a much greater extent than its monarchical and feudal predecessors, proved amenable to policy change as a result of social pressure (Tilly, Tilly, and Tilly, 1975). Yet if the impetus for democratization begins with insurgency in oppositional civil society rather than the state—and historically, I would suggest this has almost always been true—then, counterintuitively, a degree of *exclusion* in the pattern of state interest representation is desirable in order for civil society and so democracy itself to flourish. But what kind of exclusionary state is at issue here?

I have already noted that inclusive states can be either passive (in the sense of accepting whatever groups society throws up) or active (in taking steps to mobilize particular groups and shepherding them into the state)—and that both passively and actively inclusive states have their hazards for democracy in civil society. Similarly, states that pursue exclusion can do so in either active or passive fashion. Active exclusion implies a state that attacks and undermines the conditions for public association and deliberation in civil society. Passive exclusion implies a state that simply leaves civil society alone.

Examples of these two kinds of exclusion can be found in the histories of both the West and of the former Soviet bloc. In the Soviet bloc, active exclusion characterizes true Stalinism, under which any sign of political organization separate from the state is sought out and snuffed out. With time and the loss of true believers, the Stalinist state's energies flagged in this respect. The more passive exclusion of half-hearted Stalinism, especially in Poland, Hungary, and Czechoslovakia, proved far more conducive to the establishment and survival of oppositional public spheres (see Bunce, 1992). Movements such as Solidarity in Poland and Charter 77 in Czechoslovakia had no access to the state, but neither were they obliterated (even though their members were harassed and occasionally imprisoned).

In the West, the main available actively exclusionary form of state interest representation is authoritarian liberalism, practised with varying zeal in the Anglo-American world in the 1980s (and in some cases beyond). Authoritarian liberalism involves maximization of the role of the market in organizing society, in combination with an attack on the conditions of public association and so the deliberative capacities of civil society. Along these lines, Britain under Margaret Thatcher experienced attacks on the ability of trade unions to organize workers, on press freedom, on the ability of civil servants to divulge information (even about government activities unrelated to national security), on the legal rights of defendants in court cases, on the autonomy of local authorities from central government control, on the independence of the British Broadcasting Corporation, and on the political neutrality of the police (for details, see Kavanagh and Seldon, 1989). Not only the collectivism of the left came under attack; organic 'one nation' Toryism was also destroyed by the Thatcherites. Authoritarian liberals even tried, with some success, to reverse the historical inclusion of the working class in the state. The Trades Unions Congress was expelled from the quasi-corporatist National Economic Development Council, and unions were subjected to new legal restrictions on their ability to organize workers and take industrial action. The inclusion of the working class had never been very pronounced in the United States, but the expulsion of organized labour was symbolized by the Reagan administration's unopposed destruction of PATCO, the air traffic controllers' union, in 1982. In both cases, the legitimation or welfare state imperative associated with the initial inclusion of the working class also came under attack, and more coercive means of social control came back into fashion. All this could happen in part because of de-industrialization and the associated dissolution of the working class. The organized working class became less of a threat than it once was, and so its link to the legitimation imperative could be weakened, if not severed.

These sorts of governmental attacks on the conditions for association in civil society can be hindered, if not prevented, by constitutional restraints. Walzer (1991) argues that the Bill of Rights in the United States Constitution protects not just a private realm of individual life, but also an associational realm of civil society. On Walzer's account, the authors of the Bill of Rights assumed the existence of this associational realm, whose subsequent atrophy meant that the Bill came to be interpreted as protecting private individuals rather than public associations. Still, the absence of any comparable constitutional defences in Britain may help explain the relative ease with which the Thatcherite agenda for the individualization of civil society was implemented in the 1980s. Earlier I argued that one should not expect a great deal in the way of positive commitment to the associational life of civil society on the part of governmental officials, the hopes of Walzer and others notwithstanding. However, constitutional and legal defences for civil society should be welcomed when they can be obtained from governments. Beyond the Bill of Rights, other US examples can be found in connection with the 1935 National Labor Relations Act's establishment of the rights of unions to engage in collective bargaining, civil rights legislation in the 1960s, and more recent changes in family law. Such measures do not have to be accompanied by the entry of the protected associations into the state in the terms I defined at the outset.

Such constitutional and legal restraints are less necessary under corporatism. Corporatism, as I noted earlier, is characterized by a bargain involving government, business, and labour, the terms of which do not allow other interests to have any say in policy formation and implementation. Corporatist states do not attack or undermine the conditions for public association in civil society; they simply ignore it by offering few channels of access to the state. Thus the passive exclusion associated with corporatism is more benign for democracy in civil society than is the active exclusion of authoritarian liberalism.

Empirical research on social movements, once dominated by social-psychologial work on the attributes and beliefs of movement activists, took a more political turn in the 1980s. The new paradigm focused on how the 'political opportunity structures' presented by states affected the form taken by social movements, protests, and 'contentious politics' (see e.g. Kriesi, 1995; Tarrow, 1994). The relevant aspects of such structures include the degree of consensus or division within governing elites, the stability or instability of partisanship in leadership configuration, and how closed or open state policy-making structures are. Corporatism features consensus and stable partisanship within governing elites and closed decision-making. Corporatism's political opportunity structure was therefore conducive to the development of 'new social movements' such as those representing environmental, feminist, anti-nuclear, and peace values in Europe in the 1970s and 1980s in countries such as West Germany, the Netherlands, and Austria (Kitschelt, 1988). Such movements developed an unconventional action repertoire, 'self-limiting' in that they did not seek a formal share of state power.

The other main line of empirical research on the consequences of corporatism concerns its implications for economic performance and social stability. Most of the extensive literature on this topic concludes that corporatism has been successful in delivering the goods when it comes to growth, income redistribution, and stability, at least for the period from the 1950s to the 1980s (see e.g. Freeman, 1989; Pekkarin, Pohjola, and Rowthorn, 1992). Stability is usually defined in terms of the regulation of class conflict, as measured by industrial disputes. More recently, cross-national comparative work on work on 'capacity-building' in environmental policy has found that the consensual style associated with corporatism is conducive to effective environmental outcomes (Jänicke *et al.*, 1997), and that a positive statistical relationship exists between degree of corporatism and environmental policy performance (Scruggs, 1999).

An examination of contemporary states conducted in terms of comparative statics would conclude that corporatism is the state model most conducive to a discursive and democratic civil society (see Dryzek, 1996, pp. 64–70). But a historical extension of the analysis reveals that corporatist states are themselves the product of inclusion in the state of groups previously operating in civil society, first the bourgeoisie and then the organized working class. These two inclusions could proceed only under particular conjunctions of group interest and changing state imperatives. As I have indicated in discussions of environmentalism and the women's movement, changing circumstances might lead to a revision of this provisional verdict on corporatism, especially if the latter is defined in strictly tripartite terms. The provisional conclusion in favour of passive exclusion, of which tripartite corporatism is the most visible contemporary example, is less easily shaken. (Other examples of passive exclusion would include consociational democracy, featuring government by co-operation among the leaders of historically warring social blocks, normally defined on the basis of religion or ethnicity.)

For better or for worse, corporatist states may continue to change in response to groups operating in civil society claiming access to the state (or indeed forsaking the state in favour of civil society). Sometimes such claims are futile, if the state has no obvious point of access. But even strong corporatist states (classified by Lehmbruch, 1984, as Austria, The Netherlands, Norway, and Sweden) sometimes open up access points—for example, for environmentalists in Norway in the 1990s, as I noted earlier. And most contemporary states in developed societies are not strongly corporatist, instead falling somewhere on a continuum between corporatism and pluralism (see Lehmbruch, 1984, for a classification of countries in these terms). What, then, should guide the strategic choices of groups when the possibility of access to the state does arise?

Movement Strategy and State Response

Observers of social movement dynamics often argue that eventually there comes a point at which groups have to choose the state over civil society. Given that mass activism is hard to sustain, protest movements often end up incorporated into the state, at least in liberal democratic societies, if indeed the movement can escape fading into oblivion. More authoritarian systems may see the movement end in repression. To the extent such life cycles are inescapable, then entry into the state (through any, some, or all of the means I defined at the outset) may be a matter of pragmatic necessity, not free strategic choice. Along these lines, Claus Offe (1990) argues that movements normally pass through three stages. The 'take-off' phase in civil society is informal, spontaneous, and militant. Such inchoate, unfocused energy fades as the movement moves into what he calls a 'stagnation' phase ('consolidation' would have fewer pejorative connotations), involving definition of group membership, leadership, and organization. The third stage is 'institutionalization', what I have termed inclusion in or entry into the state. Offe believes such institutionalization can be expected as a rational use of limited resources of time, energy, and finance, as a way of sustaining a movement when supporters are not ready to contribute anything more than votes and money. The movement can then 'cash in' the resources it has mobilized in its take-off and consolidation phases to achieve access to real political power (Offe, 1990, p. 243). Thus Offe believes entry into the state can be a good bargain. Other observers believe such entry normally means co-option (for example, Lowi, 1971). I would suggest in contrast that one cannot generalize about and evaluate such entry in any sweeping terms. Whether the third stage of the life cycle should be welcomed or lamented depends crucially on the particular configuration of movement interests and state imperatives.

A close look at the historical record casts doubt on this life cycle interpretation of social movements. Offe himself admits that when the available range of public policy solutions to movement concerns is manifestly inadequate, then there are good reasons for a section of the movement to resist institutionalization—an insight he applies to the German Greens (Offe, 1990, pp. 246–7). Rucht (1990) notes that new social movements, in particular environmentalism in France and Germany, have featured simultaneous and sustained action in the state and civil society. Jean Cohen and Andrew Arato (1992, pp. 555–7) make a similar observation about feminism in the United States. This record suggests that groups are not locked into any simple life cycle; they do have choices. Faced with such a choice, should a group choose civil society, the state, or both simultaneously?

Cohen and Arato (1992) advance a blanket 'both' guideline, which they call a 'dualistic' strategy for social movements. They regard the women's movement as exemplary: 'The dual logic of feminist politics

. . . involves a communicative, discursive politics of identity and influence that targets civil and political society and an organized, strategically rational politics of inclusion and reform that is aimed at political and economic institutions' (Cohen and Arato, 1992, p. 550). In civil society, movements would act 'to redefine identities, to reinterpret norms, and to develop egalitarian, democratic associational forms' (p. 531). In the state, groups would not only pursue group goals, but also seek the development of a supportive constitutional, legal, and policy context for continued movement activity in civil society. Legislation and policy in turn would draw sustenance from a supportive civil society cultural context (p. 552). A large part of the justification for their dualistic strategy therefore turns out to be the degree to which the state can influence the democratic condition of civil society, for better or for worse.

A similar 'both' position is argued by Hilary Wainwright (1994), though for the sake of achievement of substantive group ends rather than the democratic vitality of civil society. She avers that movement goals related to (say) ecological and equity values 'require democratic decision making with binding national and international authority' which can only be supplied by the state (Wainwright, 1994, p. 195). Without movement activism in civil society, such public policy action is unlikely (p. 197); but again, echoing Cohen and Arato, 'non-state forms of political action need a supportive and independent relationship to political power if they are to be effective agents of economic and social change' (p. 190). Though sympathetic to Offe's life-cycle reasons for entry into the state, she believes that parliamentary activity can involve permanent sustenance for the extra-parliamentary movement, rather than constituting a permanent substitute for the latter (Wainwright, 1994, p. 196).

These arguments for a 'both' answer or a 'dualistic' strategy are on the face of it good ones. But they imply a benign view of the actual or potential motivations of government officials even in the vicinity of state imperatives, motivations that can be reflected in the content of public policy without structural impediment. One might hope that public officials would recognize the need for a discursively lively civil society, and formulate policies to promote it, perhaps even along the lines proposed by Walzer that I discussed earlier. The problem remains that there is absolutely no reason for public officials to behave in the way Walzer suggests, and every reason for them collectively to act otherwise if the strengthening of particular civil society groups clashes with an established state imperative. Walzer's own agenda of stronger unions, housing co-operatives, workers' co-operatives, and subsidized community-based welfare provision promises plenty of trouble along these lines.

Beyond laws protecting basic citizenship rights of expression and association, one should not expect much in the way of positive state action to promote the well-being of civil society. Cohen and Arato and Wainwright might object here that, unlike Walzer, they do not seek much in the way of positive commitment by state actors, merely acceptance of the legitimacy of movement goals, and of the continued linkage of group leaders with more uncompromising extra-parliamentary movement wings. But such tolerance may be stretched to the limit if movement goals, especially as articulated in radical terms by the civil society wing, clash with state imperatives. In this light, let me suggest that two criteria are relevant to any group's choice between civil society, the state, and a 'dualistic' strategy. First, the group should consider whether its defining interest can be assimilated to any state imperative. If the answer is 'no', then entry into the state is a poor strategy in instrumental terms, for it is unlikely the group's goals will be embodied in public policy, and bad from the point of view of democracy, because the vigorous and discursive democratic life of the public sphere has been forsaken in favour of co-option and a politics of symbolic rewards.

This first criterion may not always allow a once-and-for-all answer. I noted earlier that state imperatives change with time. Such changes are not easily predicted. But if they do occur, a group should be prepared to change its choice. Around 1980 it would have been hard to predict the assimilation of environmental concerns to the imperatives of accumulation and legitimation. Developing notions of ecological modernization and risk society have made this assimilation possible, as I noted earlier. In Germany, these developments help to justify the 'Realo' Green Party's eventual choice of wholehearted entry into the state, to the point of coalition government with the Social Democratic Party following the 1998 federal election. (One might argue that these developments are themselves due in part to a social learning process initiated by the Greens, but such learning can issue from civil society just as easily as from or in the state, and so provides no argument for pre-emptive entry into the state.)

Changing state imperatives might also lead a group to reconsider a past decision to enter the state. Such entry may have been a good bargain for the organized working class for most of the twentieth century. More recently, deindustrialization and the consequent decline in the numbers of industrial workers and of the scope of the Keynesian welfare state means that working-class interests are no longer so easily aligned with the legitimation imperative as they once were. However, these developments and difficulties have not persuaded the leadership of social democratic parties to contemplate a return to oppositional civil society. To the contrary, their normal response has been strategic moderation in the hope of appealing to non-working-class constituencies, or positioning the party to secure what Kitschelt (1994) calls the 'pivotal' vote in coalition politics, having abandoned any desire to govern on behalf of an electoral majority garnered from the working class. But this strategic moderation has itself led some activists to abandon the party in favour of civil society alternatives.

The second criterion to be considered is whether the group's entry into the state leaves behind a flourishing civil society. If the answer is no, then a depleted civil society means a less democratic polity, even though it might mean a more democratic state. But even the latter is unlikely. For if all disadvantaged and oppositional groups commit themselves to conventional political channels, then there is less reason for the state to include them. In this context, Fisk (1989, pp. 178–9) argues that 'Only if there is a continuation of politics by extraparliamentary means will democracy be able to establish limits to the power of a dominant class,' because extraparliamentary protest is a standing warning to this class of what might happen if it is unresponsive to demands made through conventional channels (see also Wainwright, 1994, p. 197). And of course much is lost with the depletion of civil society. This loss is not always noted, still less lamented, for example in connection with the success of socialist parties in electoral politics. Yet, as Przeworski and Sprague (1986: 184) observe, with this apparent success these parties 'demobilized those potential efforts—cooperatives, councils, and communes—that could not be channelled through elections; they deprived grassroots initiatives of a chance to experiment and grow autonomously; they turned nascent movements into compliance with electoral tactics.'

Consider also, in light of this second criterion, the migration of East European civil society into the state during and following the successful revolutions of 1989. This migration left behind little or nothing in terms of oppositional public spheres. The gain was a liberal democratic state; the loss was in terms of discursive democratic vitality. There was a real sense of loss experienced by former participants in and observers of oppositional civil society (see Ash, 1990). Such losses can also be observed in connection with the entry of the Campaign for Nuclear Disarmament into the British Labour Party around 1960, the entry of the 1960s US civil rights movement into the Democratic Party, the demise of the 'Fundi' Greens in Germany in the 1990s, and the Mexican opposition's participation in the regime's PRONASOL initiative after 1988 (discussed earlier).

Now, not all civil society groups care about democracy, be it in their internal workings or in the polity more generally. Some groups might therefore see no reason to apply these two criteria, if it is only the well-being of democracy that is at issue. However, both criteria have an instrumental as well as a democratic aspect. The first criterion asks a group to consider whether its presence in the state will indeed be accompanied by real influence. The second asks the group to contemplate the potential impairment of its influence resulting from the loss of a standing warning to dominant actors attendant upon the group's wholesale commitment to conventional politics. Thus the two criteria are relevant to group strategy irrespective of the degree of commitment to democracy in general, or deliberative democracy in particular.

Whether a group should choose the state, civil society, or both simultaneously depends on the particular configuration of movement interests and state imperatives. None of these three answers is right for all movements at all times and in all places. I would argue that the popular 'dualistic' strategy is appropriate only when some but not all of a movement's defining interests can be assimilated to state imperatives. As I argued earlier, liberal feminism may be at home in the state, whereas cultural feminism should remain in civil society. Similarly, environmental concerns that can be connected to risk, ecological modernization, or sustainable development can be expressed in state-related action, while the dimensions of environmentalism that pose a more radical challenge to the imperatives of industrial society and its governments belong in civil society. Sometimes the two wings may choose to part company. For example, the emerging network of groups concerned with environmental justice and toxics issues in the United States have distanced themselves from mainstream groups to the point of refusing the label 'environmentalist.' On the other hand, mainstream groups may, overtly or covertly, welcome the activities of their more radical counterparts in civil society; note the variety of reactions mainstream environmentalists have to the radical Earth First! group in the United States. At any rate, in such 'dualistic' circumstances the identity of the movement as a single entity should also be on its agenda (for an account of these tensions in American environmentalism, see Dowie, 1995).

A group's calculus in terms of the two criteria will be influenced by the mode of inclusion available to it. No unrestricted choice of mode is at issue here, for different political systems have different opportunity structures. For example, in the United States there are many barriers and few opportunities made available for new political parties, which is why movement entry to the state normally comes via interest group politics. Germany, in contrast, provides public subsidy and free media access for any party once it has gained a small percentage of the vote, but relatively few opportunities for US-style interest groups, and so inclusion is more likely via a party route. It is hard to generalize about the impact of these variations in opportunity structure, if indeed they do make a difference; a lot depends on the details of particular cases. For example, the national list system of proportional represent-ation in Israeli elections makes inclusion via the party route very easy, but at the same time mandates the specification in very precise detail of a national party hierarchy. Other proportional representation sys-tems work on a constituency basis, and so provide more scope for local party organizations to retain some autonomy. One might hypothesize that the latter would be more conducive to the continu-ing democratic vitality of civil society than the former, and so to a 'dualistic' movement strategy; but this is just a hypothesis. Observers of social movement dynamics and life cycles rarely draw any distinc-tions between or make comparisons across the different ways a move-ment can end up being incorporated in the state, so there is little useful comparative literature to draw on here.

Life-cycle theorists and dualists alike hold that some degree of association with the state is eventually necessary and desirable, if only to maintain a powerful and permanent presence for a movement. But, as I argued earlier, choosing civil society rather than the state does not necessarily imply choosing powerlessness. Nor does this choice imply impermanence. Movement concerns can persist even as movement action is less visible, for civil society can be sustained in social and political networks and reproduced through cultural transformation after more spectacular manifestations of the movement have passed (see Melucci, 1989, p. 206; Tarrow, 1994, pp. 176–7).

Conclusion

Let me now summarize my account of the dynamics of democratiza-tion. First, democratization is largely (though not exclusively) a matter of the progressive recognition and inclusion of different groups in the political life of society. This general inclusion is in turn sometimes manifested in inclusion in the life of the state. However, recognizing that pressures and movements for democratization almost always orig-inate in insurgency in civil society rather than the state, a flourishing oppositional civil society is the key to further democratization. This sort of civil society is actually facilitated by a passively exclusive state. A truly inclusive state would corrode the discursive vitality of civil society (as the Mexican case illustrates), and so undermine the conditions for further democratization. Thus every historical inclusive step taken by the state should produce a pattern of exclusions as well as inclusions. These exclusions are the seeds for, if nothing else, future and further democratization of the state; and they offer protection against the state reversing its democratic commitments. Exemplary here is the creation of the social democratic corporatist state: labour was explicitly included, a whole range of other groups implicitly excluded by the very way in which labour was included. Thus democrats, even difference democrats, should not interpret democratization as a matter of the state recognizing and welcoming an increasingly diverse range of groups and interests. Inclusion of this sort is only benign when a group's defining interest can be associated with an established or emerging state imperative, and when entry into the state does not unduly deplete the civil society left behind. Occasionally these criteria allow a group to operate in both civil society and the state; but often they dictate that one or the other be chosen.

The analysis of this chapter has proceeded on the assumption that the main alternative venues for democracy and democratization are the state and a civil society whose orientation is given by a particular state. This emphasis is justified on the basis of the continued importance of states, for the present and foreseeable future. Yet today's world increasingly features a migration of the locus of political control away from nation-states, a movement which constitutes one aspect of transnationalization, or globalization at an extreme. The next chapter examines the degree to which democracy in general, and discursive democracy in particular, can also be transnationalized. I will show that the comparative and historical analysis of alternative sites for democratization that I have developed in this chapter can also be applied to international politics, though not in quite such clear-cut fashion.

CHAPTER 5

Transnational Democracy: Beyond the Cosmopolitan Model

The theory and practice of democracy have close historical ties to the state, to which the democratic ideal of the self-governing community can be applied more straightforwardly than to any other political unit. In previous chapters I examined the possibility for democratization in civil society as an alternative venue, but as pointed out in Chapter 4, that possibility itself only takes form in a context largely provided by the presence of a state. Yet this is the age of globalization as well as democracy. And globalization means that important issues increasingly elude the control of nation-states. Can democracy follow this migration of issues, problems, strategies, and solutions into transnational society?

Democratic theorists have recently begun to pay attention to the issue of how this internationalization of the political economy might be matched by an internationalization of democracy. To date this quest has emphasized the development of transnational mechanisms for government that resemble those long employed within states. However, the defining feature of the international polity is that it lacks a state or state-analogue at the system level. Thus any attempt to introduce such mechanisms faces an uphill struggle. I believe that it makes more sense to examine the possibilities for democratization in connection with discursive sources of order already present in the international system that do not require any organization of international government. Discursive order of this sort can be connected quite directly to the analysis of discourses and their contestation developed in previous chapters as key aspects of discursive democracy.

Deliberative democracy should be more at home in the international system than liberal aggregative models of democracy, though only so long as it can escape its ties to liberal constitutionalism, because there are no constitutions worth speaking of in the international system. A precondition of aggregation of preferences or interests is specification of the boundaries of the *demos*, the self-governing community. Such boundaries are very hard to specify in international politics. But while aggregation across boundaries is hard to conceptualize, deliberation across boundaries is straightforward. Some rather large questions then arise about how to translate such deliberation into collective decisions. I will try to show that ideas about democratic control of the contestation of discourses in civil society affecting the content of collective decisions can be deployed in transnational settings too. Indeed, such mechanisms may be more important in the international system because of the weakness of alternative sources of order therein. The network form of organization introduced in Chapter 3 turns out to play an important role.

As things stand, collective choice in the contemporary international system is at best only a thinly democratic affair, at most thoroughly undemocratic. It is thinly democratic when nation-states gather and negotiate on international agreements; at best, this is democracy at one remove, piggy-backing on any degree of democracy present in the states involved. Yet even here we know that foreign policy is the main area where 'reasons of state' override democratic decision-making, and that it is likely to be foreign ministries and the executive branch of government that play the major role in negotiations (Smith, 1986). At worst, the world is sometimes the dangerous place that realist theorists of international relations describe, with self-help the only prudent strategy in an anarchy where violence is an ever-present possibility, such that state democracy cannot be allowed to impede the overarching survival imperative (Gilbert, 1992; Johansen, 1992). More insidiously, the international system bears witness to the consolidation of regimes for trade and finance that entrench the authority of the market and of those actors and organizations (such as the International Monetary Fund and World Trade Organization) designated as economic police officers. There is again little evidence of democracy here.

These impediments to democracy notwithstanding, the contemporary international polity is also a highly decentralized system in which substantial amounts of co-operation, conflict resolution, and joint problem-solving can occur. It is in this light that the more positive prospects for democracy—and in particular discursive democracy—can be pursued.

In Search of Transnational Democracy: Government or Governance?

With the growing salience of international issues in mind, democratic theorists have, as I have already noted, at long last begun to think about extending democracy to the international system itself. Thus William Connolly (1991*b*) and Alan Gilbert (1992) both call for an international democratic movement, though in the end they have little more than exhortation to offer. The most straightforward such extension would apply devices already used by or in states to the international context. Along these lines, Thomas Pogge (1992) proposes 'nested territorial units' ranging from the local to the global across which sovereignty might be dispersed. Such dispersion would occur both up and down from existing sovereign states, producing a large and complex federal system. Later, Pogge turns his attention to how international organizations like the European Union might be constructed in more democratic fashion through series of national referenda (Pogge, 1997). In both endeavours Pogge emphasizes institutional hardware of a familiar state-like sort.

The indeterminacy of spatial boundaries in international politics (and elsewhere) is taken more seriously by John Burnheim (1985) in his proposals for what he calls 'demarchy'. Burnheim proposes functional authorities of variable geographic coverage, the area of coverage depending on the issue in question. These authorities would replace states, and be operated by individuals chosen by lot from among all those with a material interest in the issue in question. Burnheim's proposals are a bit utopian. In addition, while they dispose of one boundary problem, they create another: between functional issue areas (such as energy, population, and the environment).

In the most thoughtful and comprehensive exploration of issues relating to democracy in the international system, David Held proposes a long list of procedural and substantive changes that would help constitute what he calls 'cosmopolitan democracy' (Held, 1995; see also Archibugi and Held, 1995, Archibugi, Held, and Köhler, 1998). The approach of Held and his associates is grounded in the evolution of the international states system, such that the character of that system and its associated constraints and opportunities are taken more seriously than by Pogge. In the short term, Held's proposals include a more effective and inclusive United Nations Security Council, increased regionalization, cross-national referenda, stronger international courts, and more effective international economic and military authorities. In the longer term, he envisages 'cosmopolitan democratic law' and a global legal system, a global parliament to which all global bodies would be accountable, and military consolidation leading eventually to global demilitarization (see Held, 1995, pp. 279–80 for a summary of these prescriptions). Held attends too to the place of the economy and civil society in cosmopolitan democracy. Concerning the economy, he foresees substantial political intervention into and control of economic affairs in order to secure basic incomes, and the application of social criteria to investment decisions. When it comes to civil society, he envisages a plurality of active groups in transnational civil society.

Held's vision is in some ways quite compelling, proposing as it does a humane, inclusive, and social-democratic global polity, the foundations of which lie in existing governmental practices and associated democratic theory. Though drawing on themes in republican and participatory traditions, the project is in large measure an extension of liberal democracy, for he believes that

a defensible account of the proper meaning of democracy must acknowledge the importance of a number of fundamental liberal and liberal democratic tenets. Among these are the centrality, in principle, of an 'impersonal' structure of public power, of a constitution to help protect and safeguard rights, and of a diversity of power centres within and outside the state, including institutional fora to promote open discussion and deliberation among alternative political viewpoints and platforms. (Held, 1995, p. 15).

The building blocks are familiar, even if the institutional architecture is novel, as 'democracy can result from, and only from, a nucleus, or cluster, of democratic states and societies' (Held, 1995, p. 22). Thus substantial reservoirs of within-state democratic theory and practice can be drawn upon.

What Held wants, then, is more government of a more deeply liberal and democratic kind. His cosmopolitan democracy 'is based upon the recognition that democracy within a particular community and democratic relations among communities are interlocked, absolutely inseparable, and that new organizational and binding mechanisms must be created if democracy is to develop in the decades ahead' (Held, 1995, p. 235). Yet the defining feature of the international system for the past few hundred years has been precisely its lack of government, if government is understood as authoritative organization at the system level. Since 1945 matters have changed somewhat with the development of the United Nations and its agencies, the Bretton Woods monetary regime, regional groupings such as the European Union, and—perhaps   most   significantly—the   World   Trade

Organization (WTO). None of these system-level institutions is especially democratic.

That the introduction of stronger system-level institutions is not necessarily a democratic advance is driven home by the recent establishment of the WTO, which has no democratic features. The danger in establishing governmental bodies with an economic mandate at the international level is that they will be subject to the economic constraints on states, and so reproduce those limits to democracy at an international level. The first task of all states with capitalist economies is maintenance of the confidence of actual and potential investors, as Held himself recognizes (1995, pp. 246–7). One source of the structural power of capital over the state is the threat of capital flight to another country, and so this threat would not apply to any 'global state', which would preside over a closed economy. Yet even in closed economies, the possibility of simple disinvestment remains as a structural constraint on the state (as an examination of the history of the relatively closed capitalist economy of the United States would demonstrate).

There are dangers too in the introduction of cosmopolitan principles and practices into a world characterized by gross inequalities of power. As Danilo Zolo (1997) argues at length, such principles can serve to legitimate dubious military interventions, such as those led by the United States in Somalia and Iraq in the early 1990s, or that undertaken by France to prop up a genocidal regime in Rwanda. Zolo fears that such interventions actually work against the achievement of the 'peace of reconciliation', which cannot be imposed from outside upon warring parties. In this light, cosmopolis is autocratic, not democratic.

These suspicions notwithstanding, we should not lightly dismiss the introduction of government into the international system, even if it is in practice undemocratic. For if realist theorists of international relations are right, the alternative may be perpetuation of a brutal Hobbesian anarchy where self-help is the only prudent strategy in a world always at the edge of violence, in which the only source of order is the balance of power. Yet to pose the choice as government *or* anarchy is to miss a third possibility, styled 'governance without government' by international relations theorists such as James Rosenau and Oran Young (Rosenau, 1992; Young, 1994). This possibility draws on 'the growing realization that the achievement of governance does not invariably require the creation of material entities or formal organizations of the sort we normally associate with the concept of government' (Young, 1994, p. 14). Governance so defined does, though, require institutions, interpreted as formal or informal rules 'capable of resolving conflict, facilitating cooperation, or, more generally, alleviating collective action problems in a world of interdependent actors' (Young, 1994, p. 15).

The concept of governance without government is used somewhat loosely in the international relations literature. Clearly those who propose a global super-state or world federalism favour government, while those with unlimited faith in spontaneous co-operation in decentralized systems favour governance without any government. Exactly where the dividing line falls between these two extremes is less clear. Let me suggest that any proposal to populate the world with systems-level authoritative organizations buttressed by international law is on the 'government' side of the dividing line. This would include Held (despite the 'governance' in the subtitle of his 1995 book, and his opposition to any kind of global super-state), also Burnheim, whom I mentioned earlier.

In the interests of pinning down these concepts more precisely, government in international politics may be defined as explicit and binding collective decision at the system level. Treaties, international courts, organizations such as the World Trade Organization with the capacity to impose penalties on states for noncompliance, and the Security Council of the United Nations are all examples of government. Governance, in contrast, may be defined as the creation and maintenance of order and the resolution of joint problems in the absence of such binding decision structures.

Despite any parallels in institutional structure, government in the international system should not be equated with the state in domestic society. With the exception of regional super-states like the European Union, international government does not normally involve pursuit of the kinds of imperatives introduced in Chapter 4, which help to define what is meant by 'the state' in the first place.

Here I will focus on the possibilities for democratizing the governance that does exist in the international system rather than the government that might. The prospects for democracy in the context of such governance have recently been addressed by Rosenau (1998) himself. However, Rosenau fails to advance the issue very far, because he believes that if 'Global governance is the sum of myriad—literally millions—of control mechanisms' then 'the world is too disaggregated for grand logics that postulate a measure of global coherence' (1998, p. 32). When it comes to the prospects for democracy within this overwhelmingly complex 'crazy-quilt' (p. 31) system, Rosenau believes that 'clear-cut answers to these questions are not yet available', such that any 'democratic procedures' in 'Globalized space' are currently, and inevitably, 'ad hoc, non-systematic, irregular and fragile' (1998, p. 39). *Contra* Rosenau, I suggest that there is in fact a 'grand logic' that can be deployed in the search for 'clear-cut answers'. This logic emphasizes discursive sources of governance and order.

Such discursive sources are ignored by Held (whose seven sites of power are the body, welfare, culture, civil society, the economy, coercion, and the state—see Held, 1995, pp. 176–85; discourse would be an eighth site). Whether this approach is more or less plausible than the cosmopolitan project of Held and his associates remains to be seen. But at least in principle my road is a shorter one, because it deals in the democratization of sources of order that are already present, rather than those that might be introduced.

The International System and its Discourses

The most striking political feature of the international political system is that, for better or for worse, it lacks any kind of effective central authority analogous to the state. For realist theorists of international relations (for example, Waltz, 1979), this has always been for the worse. The absence of a state or state-analogue means anarchy, and operating successfully within an anarchical system means having first and foremost to maximize state survival in an environment of actually or potentially hostile competitors. Liberal theorists of international relations (for example, Ruggie, 1992) look at the world system and see something very different: a system populated by sources of order such as international regimes, international law, and international organizations. Fans of 'governance without government' such as Rosenau and Young constitute a subset of the liberal camp; many if not most liberals are quite keen on bringing more government into the system, often of a super-statist sort. Liberal theorists of all stripes have not generally been especially interested in the prospects for international democracy.

The discursive sources of international order I stress have received less attention than they deserve, and they prove especially interesting in the light of the prospects for democratization. Recall that a discourse is by definition a shared set of assumptions and capabilities embedded in language that enables its adherents to assemble bits of sensory information that come their way into coherent wholes. Because discourses are social as well as personal, they act as sources of order by co-ordinating the behaviour of the individuals who subscribe to them. In previous chapters I have argued that the contestation of discourses should be central to a model of deliberative democracy, provided that the contest can be engaged by a broad variety of competent actors under unconstrained conditions.

Discourses are intertwined with institutions; if formal rules constitute institutional hardware, then discourses constitute institutional software. In the international system, the hardware is not well developed, which means that the software becomes more important still. Many observers of the international system lament the absence of institutional hardware, but it may turn out that its absence can be turned to good democratic use, especially if institutional software is less resistant to democratization than is the hardware.

To demonstrate the importance of discourses, and their role in co-ordinating action and achieving governance, so preparing the ground for a discussion of the possibilities they allow for reflection and reconstruction under democratic conditions, let me introduce some of the more important discourses present in the international system.

Anarchy. Anarchy is treated by realist theorists of international relations as a given and immutable feature of the international system, but what theorists, state leaders, and other actors *make* of anarchy is in large measure a social construction (Wendt, 1992). As constructed by realist actors and analysts, anarchy is Hobbesian: the only entities in the international system that really matter are states. States maximize power and security, and their natural relationship is rivalry or conflict in which violence is always possible. Non-state actors are treated as unimportant by assumption, and interactions transcending state boundaries involving such actors are ignored.

Market Liberalism. Market liberalism has emerged as a very different discourse to that of anarchy. Market liberals stress relationships not between states, but between economic actors such as corporations, banks, and consumers. States enter in a secondary role, to facilitate the conditions for markets to operate. Natural relationships involve competition rather than conflict, with the potential for positive-sum outcomes in which everyone gains from trade (realists deal only in zero-sum relationships). From market liberalism's microeconomic origins comes a metaphorical structure that is essentially mechanistic.

Sustainable Development. The contemporary contest over the meaning of sustainable development takes place within boundaries. The first boundary is set by an older discourse which sustainable development largely displaced in the 1980s: the discourse of limits and survival. The latter reached its zenith with the efforts of the Club of Rome in the early 1970s (Meadows *et al.*, 1972), echoed a decade later in the *Global 2000 Report to the President* (for details of the global transition from a discourse of limits to one of sustainable development, see Torgerson, 1995). Sustainable development denies the existence of global ecological limits; it cannot demonstrate (or even really argue) that such limits do not exist, but instead it assumes them away. The ground is thus cleared for commitments to continued economic development and environmental conservation proceeding in tandem—with social justice both within and across generations thrown in for good measure. A natural relationship of harmony between these various values is assumed.

Sustainable development differs from market liberalism in having an organic rather than a mechanical metaphorical structure, recognizing the existence of nested social and ecological systems. The actors and agents highlighted in the discourse are not realism's states or market liberalism's economic actors, but rather political bodies above and below the state, international organizations and citizens' groups of various kinds. Thus sustainable development is a discourse of and for international civil society (Lafferty, 1996, p. 203; Dryzek, 1997, p. 131). Sustainable development is further delimited by its rejection of a green radicalism which looks to a future beyond capitalism; for the moment at least, sustainable development is accommodated to the capitalist economic system (though there are those who wish to radicalize the discourse).

Sustainable development's function in the international system is to provide a conceptual meeting place for many actors, and a shared set of assumptions for their communication and joint action. It is these shared assumptions and capabilities which define the discourse. Nowhere is sustainable development an accomplished fact, or even a demonstrable possibility, or even a concept that can be defined with any precision. The concept is essentially contestable. Just as one can nowhere see or even envisage a true democracy, one cannot see or envisage true sustainable development.

Sustainable development exists in a constellation with a number of other discourses: survivalism (the discourse of limits), market liberalism, and green radicalism. The interplay of these discourses is quite crucial in setting the agenda for global environmental affairs. But what does this interplay have to do with the prospects for transnational democracy? Some of these discourses are indeed more conducive to democracy that others: for example, green radicalism is far more hospitable to citizen participation than is the grim authoritarianism of survivalism. Sustainable development seems reasonably conducive to democracy inasmuch as it emphasizes the role of transnational civil society (I will return to this point in due course). More importantly, though, the balance of these discourses is quite crucial, more crucial than in domestic society, because discourses play a much greater role in co-ordinating action in international politics than they do in domestic society, where the institutional hardware is stronger. So it does matter a great deal which of these discourses holds sway, or more likely what balance of them obtains. This balance or interplay can be brought under conscious, collective, and ultimately democratic control—as I will now argue.

Some Discursive Contests

Let me give some examples of contests between discourses, as a prelude to contemplation of democratic control of their content and relative weight. In this section I will show how this content and weight can be affected by the actions of international actors, for better or for worse. I should stress that these examples are not intended to illustrate discursive *democracy* in action. Rather, they are introduced in order to show that shifts in the relative weight of discourses or discourse positions can have real consequences. The degree to which these shifts can be made amenable to democratic control will be addressed later.

The Law of the Sea. The agreements negotiated in the long and painstaking processes of the United Nations Conference on the Law of the Sea in the 1970s represented an attempt at liberal institution-building that eventually secured the near-unanimous approval of the world's states. In 1981 the newly-elected Reagan Administration announced that the United States was withdrawing its support from the agreements, thus vitiating them. Equally important, this action at a stroke established that the deep ocean and its resources would henceforth be subject to a discourse of Hobbesian anarchy, in which no authority has any right to restrict access to the deep ocean. The implications were felt beyond the specific issue of the Law of the Sea. The reinstated discourse of anarchy meant that no significant global environmental agreements were reached in the 1980s (with the important exception of the 1987 Montreal Protocol for the protection of the ozone layer and its subsequent elaborations).

Ozone Discourses. In her study of the ozone issue, Karen Litfin (1994) argues that the breakthrough which moved international negotiations on the ozone issue from impasse to agreement was a shift in the discourse which dominated the proceedings. The breakthrough came with the victory of what she calls a 'discourse of precautionary action,' which framed existing—and far from decisive—scientific knowledge in a new way. But this shift did not just *happen*; it came with the rhetorical force of the idea of an 'ozone hole' over the Antarctic, which was a way of simplifying seasonal and variable depletions of ozone levels in the Southern hemisphere. By the time of the 1987 Montreal Protocol there was still no proof that chlorofluorocarbons actually damaged stratospheric ozone; but a precautionary discourse means that action does not have to await proof. A key part in shifting the terms of discourse was played by a group of 'knowledge brokers' in the US Environmental Protection Agency, and their like-minded contacts in environmental agencies in other countries (Litfin, 1994, p. 81).

Prospectors and Pirates. The world contains many species that have found local use, but whose global commercial potential has not been exploited. Multinational corporations and university-based researchers have in recent years intensified a global search for such biological sources of drugs, crops, natural pesticides, and cosmetics. These corporations and universities have sought and obtained patents on the biological material itself, chemicals extracted from it, or products synthesized from it. Those engaged in this industry describe it as 'bioprospecting' in a search for 'untapped pharmaco-industrial resources'. The allusion here is to mineral prospectors, travelling into virgin territory looking for viable deposits. Their opponents (for example, Shiva, 1997) call the practice 'biopiracy': practitioners are pirates because they are stealing the ecological, medicinal, and agricultural knowledge accumulated over centuries (if not millennia) by the human inhabitants of particular ecosystems, often indigenous peoples. For the corporate search is often guided by traditional knowledge and practices. The locals generally receive no share of the patent, and in some cases may even have to pay to buy back rights to develop their use of the biological material. For example, in 1994 the University of Toledo in the United States took out a patent on the endod plant from Ethiopia, which has long been used to kill the snails that carry schistosomiasis (and which proved able to kill the zebra mussels that plague the North American Great Lakes). In 1995 the University of Toledo offered to allow scientists in Ethiopia to carry out further research on endod—provided they paid $US 25,000. For this action the University of Toledo gained a 'Marie Antoinette Napkin Ring' to accompany the 'Captain Hook Award' which it had already been given by the Coalition Against Biopiracy (see http://www.cscanada.org/~csc/text/CptHook.htm).

Clearly it matters a great deal which of these two discursive constructions prevails. If it is the prospector, then the intellectual property rights confirmed through patents place the search for and utilization of biological material firmly within the global liberal market regime and its associated legal conventions concerning legitimate commerce, competition, and private property. So far, the supremacy of the prospector has been confirmed by GATT and WTO rulings. But if prospectors were reconstructed as pirates, their practices would become dubious and even illegal, bringing punishment for theft rather than reward for discovery. At one level, the piracy construction might prompt a reallocation of private property rights and so a redistribution of income to the traditional 'owners' of the biological knowledge in question. But when such knowledge is diffused through the community, or through multiple and overlapping communities, it may be harder to identify the individuals or collective bodies that might claim the private property right. Here the assumptions of private property that underpin commercial law are undermined, and so the piracy construction can point to different systems of common property and their associated practices which will need to be negotiated in non-market fashion.

Whaling. A moratorium on commercial whaling was imposed by the International Whaling Commission (IWC) beginning in 1986; exceptions were allowed for Iceland, Japan, and Norway to engage in 'scientific' whaling. Scientific whaling is actually a cover for a continued (but sharply reduced) commercial catch; the whale products are still used as before, and precious little science comes from the dead whales. These three countries wish to resume full-scale commercial whaling, arguing that stocks of species such as the minke whale have recovered sufficiently to allow a sustainable harvest. While some might dispute this point, the real issue here is the discursive construction of the whale. What is a whale? On the one hand, it is a natural resource, providing useful products such as meat and baleen. On the other hand, a whale is a magnificent sentient creature whose intelligence perhaps equals or surpasses that of we humans, with an intrinsic right to exist and flourish. The IWC moratorium reflects not a sober consideration of the depletion of whale stocks and what might be done to restore them; evidence of exhaustion verging on extinction of many species had been available to the IWC for decades, with precious little response. Rather, the moratorium is the outcome of a discursive shift, a reconceptualization of what a whale is, and what oceanic ecosystems are. Eventually this newer discourse captured a large majority of the national delegations to the IWC. Iceland, Norway, and Japan have an interest in a shift away from this newer discourse. But rather than just return to the older discourse of resource harvesting, they frequently invoke the idea of science: the whaling they want to engage in is now 'scientific', though it still means killing whales to eat them.

Sustainable Development versus Market Liberalism. I have already noted that sustainable development has over the last decade or so largely (but not totally) displaced the rival global discourse of limits and survival. However, that decade has also witnessed the continued ascent of another global discourse: market liberalism (whose roots of course go back a long way). In terms of impact on the shape of the transnational political economy, market liberalism has been much more successful than sustainable development in this period. So far the clash of the two discourses has taken the form of a few border skirmishes. For example, to a number of business interests (represented, for example, in the World Business Council on Sustainable Development, and Global Climate Coalition), sustainable development is a good thing because 'sustainable' means 'continued' and 'development' means 'growth'. Thus can market liberalism press its claims on sustainable development, and try to push the discourse in a particular pro-business direction. Other border skirmishes have taken place in connection with international trade. For example, under World Trade Organization (WTO) rules it is clear that environmental restraints on trade must give way; the WTO's environmental committee deals almost exclusively with such restraints. Such restraints include government subsidy of pollution control equipment and limits on the kinds of pesticides that can be used on imported food. Prior to the establishment of the WTO, in 1991 a committee of the General Agreement on Tariffs and Trade (GATT) ruled that the United States ban on tuna imports caught in ways that involved the deaths of large numbers of dolphins was a violation of the GATT. The GATT also ruled against Indonesia's ban on raw log exports, thus diminishing the prospects for sustainable forestry. When it comes to national developmental paths, it is clear that market liberalism precludes sustainable development conceptualized as anything other than unrestricted economic growth. For example, countries such as Mexico which commit themselves to export-oriented development along lines approved by the International Monetary Fund and World Bank find that in so doing their locally-grown produce cannot compete with cheap imports. Peasants are forced from the land, giving way to export-oriented agribusiness, which generally farms in ecologically unsound fashion. The displaced peasants either exacerbate congestion and pollution in Mexico City or move across the border to the United States.

Contesting Sustainable Development. At the Rio Earth Summit in 1992 there were two sets of proceedings: the official meeting of heads of government and other state representatives, and the unofficial Global Forum made up mostly of non-governmental organization (NGO) activists. In both fora, the discourse of sustainable development held sway. But there was still a contest between the sustainable development being negotiated in the official United Nations Conference on Environment and Development proceedings and the kinds of sustainable development on display in the Global Forum. The former were more closely linked to conventional industrialist notions of economic growth and its benefits, the latter to more radical redistribution of resources from rich to poor, and redistribution of power from government and business to community and citizens. The contest remains; there is quite a gulf between the vision of the World Business Council on Sustainable Development and the various environmental groups which have also endorsed the concept. It is unlikely that any of the sides will score a clear discursive victory; but clearly the relative weight of these competing conceptions matters enormously for the future of sustainable development and its global impact. Rhetorical interventions by particular actors continually change this balance—both locally and globally. So for example when Kai Lee (1993) declares that sustainable development has been successfully launched in the Columbia River Basin in the Pacific Northwest of the United States, he advances a notion of sustainable development as centrally managed ecosystem restoration. When the World Business Council on Sustainable Development collects success stories from its member corporations, it advances the notion of sustainable development as an environmental gloss on corporate business as usual (Schmidheiny, 1992).

In the examples I have given, it is probably fair to say that the actors involved did not have any strong conception of a theory of collective choice in terms of the contestation of discourses. Most of them may well have had little or no interest in democracy as such, caring more about the pursuit of substantive interests. Any connection of these interests to the pursuit of democratic values would stem from the fact that, in the international system no less than elsewhere, it is the materially disadvantaged who have the most to gain by expansion of the effective democratic franchise (for domestic politics, see Shapiro, 1996, pp. 224–5). But these examples illustrate the power of discourses, not democracy in action. I would argue that the more intelligent among these actors may well have had a good tacit grasp of how their actions affected the prevailing content and balance of discourses—though they may not have framed the question in this sort of language.

Having established the importance of the discourse dimension in international affairs, the next step is to contemplate how the contestation of discourses might be subjected to democratic control.

Democratic Theory and Transnational Practice

I have argued that democratic action in the international system can be rooted in dispersed and competent control of the prevailing balance of discourses. I will now try to be a bit more explicit about how and by whom such control is exercised.

Political theorists used to think about democracy solely in terms of the ideal of a self-governing community within precise territorial boundaries (many of them still do). Extending this idea of democracy to the international system has always been quite hard. But as I noted at the outset of this chapter, this extension is made easier by the degree to which we think of democracy not in terms of voting or the representation of persons or interests, but rather in terms of deliberation and communication. This rethinking does not automatically lead beyond the self-governing territorial entity. Thus Miller (1995: ch. 4) argues that deliberation is facilitated by a common national identity that overrides group identities. Yet deliberation does not *require* such an identity, still less one that stops at national boundaries, especially if we think about deliberation in terms of the contestation of discourses and their component identities. Such a model of democracy is particularly conducive to international society, because unlike older models of democracy, it can downplay the problem of boundaries. These older models always saw the first task in their application as specification of the boundaries of a political community. Deliberation and communication, in contrast, can cope with fluid boundaries, and the production of outcomes across boundaries. For we can now look for democracy in the character of political interaction that generates public opinion, without worrying about whether or not it is confined to particular territorial entities.

The idea that we can have democracy without boundaries means that the intimate link between democracy and the state can be severed. Democracy need no longer be confined to the processes of the state. As I have already emphasized, there is no state-analogue for the international system, and if one were to be created it would reproduce the constraints to which existing states are subject. First and foremost

among these constraints upon democratic control is the need to maintain the confidence of actual and potential investors (Lindblom, 1982).

In earlier chapters I linked discursive democracy to a strong conception of civil society and the related idea of the public sphere. Civil
society and public spheres also exist in the international system.
Martin Jänicke's (1996) functional definition of civil society as public
action in response to failure in either the state or the economy might
seem less easy to apply here because there is no system-level state to
fail. But there are formally constituted political bodies such as the
United Nations and its agencies, the World Bank, and the World Trade
Organization, which can fail frequently and sometimes spectacularly.
So while there is not state failure, there is plenty of political failure to
which civil society action can respond. The role of transnational civil
society has been explored by, among others, Martin Köhler (1998),
Ronnie Lipschutz (1995), Paul Wapner (1996). The most prominent
actors here are non-governmental organizations (NGOs) and what
Wapner, concerned mainly with environmental affairs, calls TEAGS,
'transnational environmental activist groups'. Köhler speaks of 'civil
society organizations'. These groups can work within, with, across,
and often against states and international governmental organizations
(such as the World Bank)—and of course with each other. They may
form coalitions with state actors in particular countries to push other
states in a desired direction—especially when the latter kind of state is
resistant to pressure from its own people (for example, when the
Nigerian government is oblivious to the plight of indigenous peoples
in oil-producing areas). Politics in transnational civil society is also a
matter of promoting the social and ecological sensibilities of citizens
and of exerting pressure on multinational corporations to behave in
more responsible ways. Civic politics of this sort was in particular
evidence in the Global Forum at the 1992 Rio Earth Summit.

The idea of an international public sphere has recently been explored
by James Bohman (1998a), Molly Cochran (1998), and Marc Lynch
(1998) (see also Dryzek, 1996, pp. 89–91). While one can quibble about
definitions here, and the supposed association of civil society with
either narrow, rights-based conceptions of political action or unremit-
ting distance from state power, in practice little is lost by treating
transnational civil society and transnational public spheres as covering
similar territory. As in domestic society, the transnational public sphere
can be treated as the politicized aspect of transnational civil society; that
is, it has an orientation to power, as constituted in states or elsewhere.

Observers and (especially) critics of transnational civil society often
ask about the extent and sources of its own power. To those schooled

in conventional analyses of power, that possessed by civil society actors looks very weak and indirect, something like that of interest groups or pressure groups in domestic politics, only less influential because there are few well-developed channels for pressure to be exerted. But the kind of discursive analysis that I have developed highlights the real power of transnational civil society, which is communicative power of the sort introduced in earlier chapters.

How does this communicative power work in the international system? The politics of transnational civil society is largely about questioning, criticizing, and publicizing. Again, a cynic might see this as capable of generating only a few pinpricks in the hides of established powers such as states, IGOs, and multinational corporations. But—crucially—these actions can also change the terms of discourse, and the balance of different components in the international constellation of discourses that I have described. Compared to the realm of states and their interactions, transnational civil society is a realm of relatively (though of course not perfectly) unconstrained and uncoerced communication. Actors within it are not bound by reasons of state, by the conventions of diplomatic niceties, by the fear of upsetting allied or rival states, or (more important) fear of upsetting actual and potential investors in one's country, or the financial markets. For these reasons, one should expect civil society and its actors to take the lead when it comes to interventions affecting and helping to constitute and reconstitute the discursive aspect of international politics. In the international system no less than elsewhere, the main cumulative effect of the past thirty years of environmental activism may be precisely such reconstruction

This capacity to affect the terms of discourse and change the balance of competing discourses is widely distributed. One does not need an army, control over governmental bureaucracies, massive wealth, or even large numbers of activists to be effective. One does need a certain minimum of conventional political resources: money, personnel, access to the media, and credibility. More importantly, actors need to be astute enough to recognize the importance of the discursive realm, and to figure out how to act effectively within this realm. Effective action here often means reasoning constitutively: instead of asking the instrumental question 'will action X promote goal Y?' one asks the constitutive question 'will action X help bring into being the kind of world I find attractive?'—especially the terms of communication and discourse in that world. This sort of consideration might give pause, for example, to groups such as the Rainforest Alliance that argue for the preservation of tropical rainforests on the grounds that they are storehouses of potential pharmaceutical products. While this argument might enlist the help of drug companies in preservation efforts, it reinforces a discourse that conceptualizes Third World ecosystems only in terms of economic value for the developed world.

This account of communicative power and its effects in transnational democracy notwithstanding, those attuned to more conventional models of democracy might still scratch their heads and ask questions such as: how do we determine exactly whose interests should be represented? Where are the moments of binding collective decision, and how exactly are these decisions to be made? The first question is actually not answered well in conventional theory. When it comes to specifying whose interests should count by specifying the boundaries of the political unit, Robert Dahl (1989, p. 209) admits that in the end answers to the question of how to define the boundaries of the polity 'are far more likely to come from political action and conflict, which will often be accompanied by violence or coercion, than from reasoned inferences from democratic principles and practices'. While pragmatic judgement can be applied in drawing boundaries, this judgement receives little guidance from democratic theory as such.

The second question can be answered through reference to the distinction between government and governance that I made earlier. Explicit, binding collective decisions are the province of government, not governance. They can sometimes be made by intergovernmental organizations or treaties, but more often they are made by states acting individually. Yet the decisions and policies of states acting individually can be influenced by the discursive force of transnational civil society. Indeed, even if states were the only decisive actors—as they are in conventional models of democracy—the account of transnational democracy developed here would stand unchanged. We would have governance across states in terms of the order provided by transnational discourses, and government within states in terms of what states did under the influence of these discourses. For example, the policies of the Mexican government toward the Zapatista rebels in the 1990s were strongly influenced by the Zapatistas' ability to connect their cause to a supportive transnational discourse.

Dennis Thompson (1999) proposes extending deliberative democracy into the international system in somewhat different but complementary fashion. He wants deliberators in state decision-making to take into account the interests of 'moral constituents' beyond the boundaries of the state who are influenced by the state's policies. Though Thompson positions himself against 'civil societarians', I can think of no better way of ensuring that policy makers take such interests into account than via influence exerted by and in transnational civil society. (Thompson himself prefers devices such as a 'Tribune for non-citizens'—p. 122.)

Institutionalization: The Role of Civil Society Networks in Promoting Deliberation

Any account of democracy (transnational or otherwise) can expect to be asked about the institutions that will house it. In a system and a model of democracy where governance but not government is central, these institutions will not be governmental organizations. But what kind of institutions might promote the communicative processes that I have stressed? Can we identify institutional forms conducive to decentral-ized, deliberative control of the relative weight of rival discourses? Let me suggest that for the international system no less than domestic pol-itics, the most promising such institutional form currently available is the network, which in turn finds a home in civil society.

Networks of this sort are beginning to appear in international civil society around issues such as the *maquiladoras* on the South side of the United States–Mexico border (and their tentacles elsewhere). These factories produce goods for the United States market, but their working conditions, rates of pay, and environmental abuses are unac-ceptable North of the border. Other networks target the production and distribution of landmines, sweatshops producing goods for multi-national corporations, and oil refineries (countered by the Oilwatch Network). One such network plays a prominent role in the bio-prospecting/biopiracy issue. The nodes of this network are consti-tuted by aggrieved communities, especially in Third World countries, sympathetic activists in the developed world as well as the Third World, and organizations such as the Research Foundation for Science, Technology and Natural Resources Policy in New Delhi. The network itself is promoted by the Coalition Against Biopiracy (which sponsors the Captain Hook Awards), the Rural Advancement Foundation International (RAFI), and the Indigenous Peoples Biodiversity Information Network (IBIN). RAFI styles itself an 'international civil society organization'. IBIN states that 'IBIN is not itself a policy-making organization or an information publisher, but will act to aid indigenous organizations and networks form their own information-sharing protocols and help make public information on the Convention on Biological Diversity and related processes more accessible to them' (http://www.ibin.org/about.htm).

This anti-biopiracy network is at the forefront of the global discursive struggle with the bioprospectors. But it would be a mistake to see the contest in terms of one homogeneous discourse fighting another—such a contest could be organized centrally. Involving as it does a range of activists and communities around the world, the network brings to bear a variety of local experiences and ecological knowledges which help to construct what biopiracy means in practice, and the variety of ways in which it might be countered. The network form implies that the variety of local interpretations and viewpoints has to be taken into account. Given that the individuals involved come from very different places and cultures, differences and commonalities in their experiences are negotiated by deliberation (often at long distance). There is no shared model concerning what should counter the neo-colonialism of biopiracy. Particular responses might involve defensive legal action, more aggressive legal action to pursue the transfer of private property rights in particular patents to local owners, political protest, organizing a boycott of a corporation, civil disobedience, media publicity, or work on an alternative developmental model to counter the inroads of market capitalism. Some members of the network, for example Vandana Shiva (1997), contextualize biopiracy in the structure and operation of the market liberal economic regime, and so what begins as a critique of biopiracy also questions the normative foundations of global capitalism.

The most appropriate available institutional expression of a dispersed capacity to engage in deliberation that helps determine the terms of discourse in the international system and elsewhere is the network. Empirically, it is straightforward to multiply examples. Nevertheless, one can imagine networks that do not exemplify deliberative virtues of openness, respect, reciprocity, communicative competence, and equality in the ability to raise and question points. So is there anything intrinsic to the network form that requires these virtues? There is indeed such a feature, so long as the network has to negotiate variety in subject positions in the absence of any central organizing authority. Variety may come in terms of nationality, ethnicity, social class, or religion. Now, organizations such as political parties, labour unions or monotheistic religions normally deal with variety from the top down, by organizing individuals and groups on the leadership's terms; but these organizations are not networks. Networks emerge when individuals or groups that are similarly situated in one important respect, but different in most other respects, decide that their common interest would benefit from joint action. When it comes to determination of both the content and process of joint action, the individuals and groups involved have to develop norms of openness, respect, reciprocity, and equality. Sometimes these norms are formalized into network principles. For example, the Southwest Network for Economic and Environmental Justice has adopted guidelines that specify the rights of all members to be heard, respected, and involved in the network (Schlosberg, 1999, p. 128).

Variety within the network means that they can be few taken-for-granted truths immune to discursive scrutiny. For example, the early environmental justice movement in the United States was composed mostly of urban groups for which it was standard to castigate the mainstream environmental groups for emphasizing the protection of nature and wilderness while ignoring urban pollution issues. At the First National People of Color Environmental Leadership Summit in 1991, individuals from these urban groups had to reflect upon and eventually change this perception as a result of encounters with Native American activists for whom the protection of land, nature, and animals was a vital component of environmental justice (Ruffins, 1992). In short: deliberation across variety is a necessary, not a contingent feature of networks, especially transnational networks.

None of this means that the network is the single definitive institutional blueprint for transnational democracy, or the only relevant form (other possibilities include the international discursive designs discussed in Dryzek, 1990*a*, pp. 90–108). Democracy, in the international system no less than elsewhere, is a quintessentially open-ended project, within boundaries defined by a subject matter pertaining to the collective construction, application, distribution, and limitation of political authority (so open-endedness of the project does not mean democracy can mean anything one likes; see Dryzek, 1996, p. 4). In this project, experimentation with what democracy can mean is an essential part of democracy itself.

Inclusion, Exclusion, and Transnational Civil Society

Any invocation of transnational civil society necessitates an examination of the possibilities for, and consequences of, its inclusion in more formally-constituted political authority structures. This analysis will parallel that I developed for domestic politics in Chapter 4. Do such issues arise in the international system, and what is their implication for the vitality of any incipient democracy in the system? The matter is a bit different when it comes to international politics because there is of course no system-level state in which inclusion can be sought or offered. Thus inclusion via political parties and electoral politics is impossible. Nor are there background citizenship rights on which civil society groups can draw, though recent work has pointed to the possibility of transnational citizenship, especially in connection with the European Union (Linklater, 1998; Melchior, 1998). Yet there do exist international governmental organizations (IGOs) which can offer inclusion of a sort to civil society groups and their members. Just as in domestic politics, inclusion can take the form of lobbying, participation in policy development and implementation through negotiations, the acceptance of appointment to offices of the IGO by group representatives, and having the well-being of the group made the target of policy. However, the situation is complicated because IGOs themselves work through states, and their power is largely derived from that of the states which constitute them. Thus IGOs respond mostly to the agendas of their component states, and cannot offer inclusion if it might offend one of these states. The states are themselves unequal in the power they exert in the IGO, so offending the government of the United States is generally a more serious proposition than offending the government of Burkina Faso.

These reservations notwithstanding, one can still think about inclusion in an IGO constituting democratic gain by making the IGO more responsive to a wider variety of group needs. For example, the World Bank, long excoriated for the environmentally abusive projects it financed, did by the 1990s open an environmental department and appoint environmentalists to it.

In Chapter 4 I distinguished between passive and active patterns of interest representation, which can be applied to both inclusion and exclusion. In the international system it is hard to imagine an actively exclusive IGO, one that deliberately tries to undermine the conditions of association in transnational civil society. States sometimes try to attack transnational civil society in this manner: for example, when agents of the French government sank Greenpeace's *Rainbow Warrior* in Auckland harbor. But for states and IGOs alike, it is hard to pursue civil society groups effectively across national boundaries. Indeed, one reason why high-profile groups like the Zapatistas in Mexico and the Ogoni people in Nigeria have sought allies and visibility in transnational civil society is to escape states trying to destroy them.

Actively inclusive representation, in which an IGO would sponsor a civil society group and foster its power within the organization, is possible to imagine, but I can think of no examples in practice, and no discussions of its desirability in theory.

Thus when it comes to both inclusion and exclusion in IGOs, it is the passive form that is at issue. Passive inclusion occurs when the IGO is receptive to lobbying from civil society organizations, welcoming them into negotiations. Agencies of the United Nations with a 'social' mission such as UNESCO, UNICEF, the UN Environment Programme, and the Human Rights Commission are receptive to a variety of inputs. Indeed, former United Nations Secretary-General Boutros Boutros-Ghali spoke in 1996 of the need for 'intergovernmental machinery that is ... more open to civil society' (Boutros-Ghali, 1996, p. 47). Passive exclusion is also common. The United Nations Security Council, the World Trade Organization, the International Monetary Fund and (until recently and partially) the World Bank do not negotiate with or receive lobbyists from civil society groups; but neither do they do anything to undermine the formation and operation of groups.

In Chapter 4 I introduced two questions that should be asked of groups contemplating migration from civil society to the state. First, can the group's defining interest be assimilated to an established or emerging imperative of the state? Because they are not part of a state, most IGOs do not face economic, legitimation, or security imperatives of the kind that constrain states. The exception would be those IGOs that have taken on global economic and security functions—exactly those organizations that I have just listed as having adopted exclusionary patterns of interest representation. If these IGOs do ever open themselves up to more inclusive representation, the first question does come into play. In the case of environmentalists entering the World Bank, the answer was eventually a clear 'no', so the entry proved a poor bargain in instrumental terms, and bad for democracy, because the inclusion proved only symbolic, not substantive. What this suggests is that recent calls to open up the core economic and security IGOs to a wider variety of participants and inputs in the name of cosmopolitan democracy may actually produce bad results for democracy in the international system as a whole. Just as in domestic politics, passively exclusive authority structures can actually benefit the democratic vitality of civil society. NGOs are less beholden to the agendas of states than are IGOs.

The second question introduced in Chapter 4 enters whether or not any imperative is at issue. We should ask whether the group's close association with the IGO would unduly deplete oppositional civil society, leaving the latter less vital and democratic. Just as in the domestic case, such association can constitute an intrinsic democratic loss, even though there may be democratic gain in terms of the IGO's operation. This loss can be additionally severe given that initiatives for further democratization almost always begin in oppositional civil society, no less in international than in domestic politics. Indeed, the very reason that democratization of the international system is now on the agenda is because of the efforts of myriad non-governmental organizations and activists. It is hard to think of an example of a group that has completely forsaken oppositional transnational civil society for close association with an IGO, but that may because the available IGOs are themselves quite weak, so not a good bargain in instrumental terms. The stronger ones remain passively exclusive and so off-limits to inclusion; which, as I have suggested, may not be a bad thing.

Conclusion

The evaporation of the cold war context means that there is a world to create, as well as accommodate, through a politics that can have its own reshaping perpetually in mind. The international system still involves much more in the way of governance than of government. Most of the government that does exist (in the form of organizations such as the UN, WTO, or EU) is not at all democratic, which suggests that transnational democrats might usefully focus their efforts on the governance. Here, the role played by international civil society is crucial; I have argued that the network form in particular can play a key part in establishing deliberative democratic control over the terms of political discourse and so the operation of governance in the international system. More self-conscious political reshaping can come in the form of thinking constitutively about discourses.

Despite these positive prospects, the struggle for transnational democracy also faces some fairly major obstacles. Today we are indeed witnessing the sort of transnationalization of civil society which I have emphasized. But we are also witnessing powerful economic transnationalization. International trade is not of course new, but the discourses and institutions associated with free trade and economic development imperatives are stronger and more confident than ever before. The constraints they impose are both discursive and material. I have already noted that market liberalism is powerful as a discourse. But even if people resist the discourse, they may find themselves unable to resist material economic imperatives. States in particular are heavily constrained: the first concern of any state operating in the international economic system is to maintain and cultivate the confidence of actual and potential investors. Correspondingly, the main fear of any state is disinvestment and capital flight. So even if governments want to (say) introduce a progressive and redistributive social policy, they may find these impersonal economic constraints militating against it. On the one hand, these constraints on the state further justify democratization in civil society rather than the state. On the other hand, the same constraints enable states to resist pressure from transnational civil society.

Thus in addition to discursive contests, the international system also hosts a conflict between material forces and discursive ones (with echoes of the clash between Marxist materialism and Hegelian idealism). The prospects for democracy are positive to the extent that discursive processes involving transnational civil society can make themselves felt in reflexive reconstruction of the international political economy. This is a tall order; the prospects are in many ways more positive than ever before, but a major struggle with market liberalism as a material force as well as a discourse looms.

CHAPTER 6

———

Green Democracy

The extension of discursive democracy's reach beyond the self-governing territory and into the transnational realm is controversial, though, as I argued in the previous chapter, both essential and realistic. In this chapter I argue for an equally essential extension of democracy that presses against, and ultimately transgresses, far more well-guarded frontiers: those between humanity and the non-human world. Even difference democrats, otherwise keen to expand the range of actors that can engage in communication, might balk at such a move. Still, I will argue that discursive democracy is better-placed than any alternative political model to enter into fruitful engagement with natural systems, and so able to cope more effectively with the challenge presented by ecological crisis. The basic reason for my contention here is that authentic deliberation involves reflection upon preferences induced by communication in non-coercive fashion. There is no reason why this communication has to have a human source. Moreover, even when it comes to interchanges between humans, reflection induced in deliberation entails enlarged thinking, as propositions must be cast in terms that are capable of persuading others, rather than simply making personal sense. The interests that become internalized in the processes of enlargement need not be confined within the boundaries of the human world (see also Eckersley, 2000, on the prospects for such enlargement).

Green Structures, Not Just Green Values

Inasmuch as there is a conventional wisdom on the matter of ecology and democracy, it would draw a sharp distinction between procedure and substance. As Robert Goodin (1992*b*, p. 168) puts it, 'To advocate democracy is to advocate procedures, to advocate environmentalism is to advocate substantive outcomes.' The more general case that in a democracy we cannot pre-specify any particular outcome is made by Robert Dahl (1989, p. 191). Thus there can never be any guarantee that democratic procedure will produce ecologically benign substance. This distinction between procedure and substance forms the core of Goodin's (1992*b*) treatment of green political theory. To Goodin, the green theory of value represents a coherent set of ends related to the protection and preservation of nature. This interpretation of green ends is somewhat narrow, as the discussions of environmental justice in the previous two chapters should make clear. For Goodin, the green theory of agency addresses where and how green values might be promoted. He argues that a green theory of agency cannot be derived from the green theory of value. Greens may still want to advocate (say) grassroots participatory democracy; but they should recognize that any such advocacy has to be on grounds separate from basic green values.

This procedure/substance divide arises most graphically in the context of green advocacy of decentralization and community self-control. Such decentralization of political authority would have decidedly anti-ecological substantive consequences in a lot of places with natural-resource-based local economies. Many counties in the Western United States have tried to assert their authority against federal environmental legislation (so far with little success in the courts) in order that mining, grazing on federal lands, and forest clearcutting can proceed unchecked. This is part of the agenda of the ill-named 'Wise Use Movement'. Decentralization will only work to the extent local recipients of authority subscribe to ecological values, or, alternatively, the degree to which they must stay put and depend for their livelihoods solely on what can be produced locally.

On this kind of account, political structure obviously matters far less than the adoption of green values on the part of denizens in that structure, or the occupancy of key positions (such as membership in parliament) in that structure by greens. Along these lines, Eckersley (1992) concludes that the key to green political transformation is the dissemination and adoption of ecocentric culture. In fairness, she also addresses the issue of political structure, though the kind of structure she advocates is pretty close to what already exists in federal liberal democracies. Similarly, to Goodin the key to green politics is participation in electoral politics and coalition with other parties in an effort to ensure that governments in liberal democracies adopt, if only partially and incrementally, those parts of the green political agenda inspired by the green theory of value. As he puts it, 'we can, and probably should, accept green political prescriptions without necessarily adopting green ideas about how to reform political structures and processes' (Goodin, 1992*b*, p. 5). This position resonates with 'Realo' Greens who believe in working through the liberal state rather than pursuing more radical alternatives (see also Barry, 1999). The term 'Realo' comes from a faction within the German Greens pitted against, and eventually overcoming, the radical 'Fundis' (see Wiesenthal, 1993, for advocacy of the Realo position in the German context).

The first problem with Goodin's position here is that it fails to allow that democracy can legitimately protect its own substantive preconditions, such as freedom of speech (Dobson, 1996, p. 136). There are also ecological preconditions for democracy—indeed, for any functioning political system—that democracy must itself protect.

The second problem is that Goodin regards political agency as essentially unproblematical. In other words, all that has to be done is to convince people in positions of political authority that X should be pursued, and X will be pursued. Goodin's 'X' is in fact a rather large one: he considers that the green programme merits adoption on an all-or-nothing basis. But there are good reasons why dominant political mechanisms cannot adopt and implement that programme, or even substantial chunks of it, irrespective of the degree to which green values are adopted by participants in these mechanisms. For any complex system, be it economic, political, ecological, or social, embodies imperatives or emergent properties that take effect regardless of the intentions of the denizens of the system. Such imperatives constitute values that the system will seek. Other values will be downplayed or ignored.

To begin with the currently dominant order of capitalist democracy, all liberal democracies currently operate in the context of a capitalist market system. Any state operating in the context of such a system is highly constrained in terms of the kinds of policies it can pursue. As I observed in Chapter 1 in questioning the assimilation of deliberative democracy to liberal constitutionalism, policies that damage business profitability—or are even perceived as likely to damage that profitability—are automatically punished by the recoil of the market. Disinvestment here means economic downturn. And such downturn is bad for governments because it both reduces the tax revenue for the schemes those governments want to pursue (such as environmental restoration), and reduces the popularity of the government in the eyes of the voters. This effect is not a matter of conspiracy or direct corporate influence on government; it happens automatically, irrespective of anyone's intentions.

The constraints upon governments here are intensified by the increasing mobility of capital across national boundaries. So, for example, anti-pollution regulation in the United States stimulates an exodus of polluting industry across the Rio Grande to Mexico's *maquiladora* sector. Thus irrespective of the ideology of government—and irrespective of the number of green lobbyists, coalition members, or parliamentarians—the first task of any liberal democratic state must always be to secure and maintain profitable conditions for business.

Environmental policy is possible in such states, but only if its damage to business profitability is marginal, or if it can be shown to be good for business. Along these lines, the idea of ecological modernization has recently gained ground in several European states, notably Germany and the Netherlands (Hajer, 1995; Weale, 1992, pp. 66–92). United States Vice-President Albert Gore (1992) once pointed to the degree to which environmental protection can actually enhance business profitability. But if ecological modernization is to move beyond isolated successes on the part of green capitalists, it requires a wholesale reorientation of state structure (Christoff, 1996). If green demands are 'all or nothing' in Goodin's terms, then 'nothing' remains the likely consequence in any clash with economic imperatives.

Even setting aside the economic context of policy determination under capitalist democracy, there remain reasons why the structure of liberal democracy itself is ultimately incapable of responding effectively to ecological problems. To cut a long story short, these problems often feature high degrees of complexity and uncertainty, and substantial collective action problems. Thus any adequate political mechanism for dealing with them must incorporate negative feedback (the ability to generate corrective movement when a natural system's equilibrium is disturbed), co-ordination across different problems (so that solving a problem in one place does not simply create greater problems elsewhere), co-ordination across actors (to supply public goods or prevent the tragedy of the commons), robustness (an ability to perform well across different conditions and contexts), flexibility (an ability to adjust internal structure in response to changing conditions), and resilience (an ability to correct for severe disequilibrium, or environmental crisis) (for greater detail on these requirements, see Dryzek, 1987*b*).

One can debate the degree to which these criteria are met by different political–economic mechanisms, such as markets, administrative hierarchies, and international negotiations, as well as liberal democracies. My own judgement is that liberal democracy does not perform particularly well across these criteria, even when it is organized along the relatively open 'passively inclusive' lines of pluralism, as defined in Chapter 4. Negative feedback under pluralism or polyarchy is mostly achieved as a result of particular actors whose interests are aggrieved giving political vent to their annoyance, be it in voting for green candidates, lobbying, contributing money to environmentalist interest groups, or demonstrating. But such feedback devices are typically dominated by the representation of economic interests, businesses and (perhaps) labour. Co-ordination is often problematical because the currency of interest group pluralism consists of tangible rewards to particular interests. Such particular interests do not add up to the general ecological interest. Further, complex problems are generally disaggregated on the basis of these same particular interests, and piecemeal responses crafted in each of the remaining subsets. The ensuing 'partisan mutual adjustment', to use Lindblom's (1965) term, may produce a politically rational resultant. But there is no reason to expect this resultant to be ecologically rational. In other words, interests may be placated in proportion to their material political influence, and compromises may be achieved across them, but wholesale ecological destruction can still result. Resilience in liberal democracy more generally is inhibited by short time horizons (resulting from electoral cycles) and a general addiction to the 'political solvent' of economic growth (politics is much happier, and choices easier, when the size of the available financial 'pie' is growing).

Despite the ecological inadequacies associated with the interest group pluralism form of liberal democracy, I would argue that among the political mechanisms that have been tried by nation-states from time to time, this form does better than most of the alternatives (see Dryzek, 1987*b*: ch. 9). Only the corporatism associated with ecological modernization may do better (for evidence, see Jänicke, Weidner, and Jorgens, 1997). But even setting aside the issue of the ecological adequacy of liberal democracy, and its relative merits compared to other systems, the fact remains that the way political systems are structured can make an enormous difference when it comes to the likelihood or otherwise of realizing green values. And if this is true, then (to use Goodin's distinction) we should be able to derive an account of politics from the green theory of value, not just the green theory of agency. Let me now attempt such a derivation, which I will link to an extended discursive democracy.

Biocentric and Anthropocentric Models, and their Inadequacies

What, then, might such an account look like? Would it indeed be democratic? If so, in what sense of democracy? Presumably, what we are looking for is some kind of polity that could embed something more than short-term human material interests, and achieve more sustainable equilibria encompassing natural and human systems. Along these lines, Eckersley (1992) uses the term 'ecocentric' to describe her preferred kind of system. The term 'ecocentric' or 'biocentric' implies that intrinsic value is located in nature, and can connote an absence of regard for human interests, essentially shedding one 'centrism' in favour of another. But Eckersley herself is careful to say that she also wants the variety of human interests in nature to be sheltered under her ecocentric umbrella.

Does it make sense for us to speak in terms of ecocentric or biocentric democracy? In perhaps its most widely-used sense, 'ecocentric politics' refers only to a human political system that would give priority to ecological values. To advocate ecocentric politics in such terms is unremarkable, reducing as it does to advocacy of a biocentric ethic—one that accords intrinsic value to natural entities, beyond (though not necessarily excluding) human interest in those entities. Aside from this ethical imperative politics is unchanged, and does not need to stand in any particular *structural* relation to nature. The problem with such a minimalist approach to ecocentric democracy is that it returns us directly to the position I rejected in the previous section, where I tried to establish that we need green political structures as well as green values.

What more can ecocentric politics mean, beyond advocacy of biocentric values? A maximalist view here might emphasize the 'politics' created by and in nature, to which humans could adjust *their* politics. Now, Aristotle suggested long ago that what sets humans apart is that man is *zoon politikon*, the political animal. Primate ethology now suggests that there is something like politics that occurs in animal societies involving, for example, bargaining and trickery in the establishment of dominance hierarchies among males, though even here, one should be wary of anthropomorphizing observed behaviour. Yet even if a quasi-politics can be found among primates or other animals, that kind of politics is one in which we humans cannot participate, just as animals cannot participate in our politics. Moreover, most of what goes on in the natural world (outside animal societies) would still be extremely hard to assimilate to any definition of politics.

The last century and a half has seen the ascription of all kinds of political and social models to nature. Social Darwinists saw in nature a reflection of naked capitalism. Marx and Engels saw evolutionary justification for dialectical materialism. In 1915 the US political scientist Henry Jones Ford saw collectivist justification for an organic state. Nazis saw justification for genocide. Microeconomists see something like market transactions in the maximization of inclusive fitness. Eco-anarchists from Kropotkin to Murray Bookchin see in nature models only of co-operation and mutualism. Roger Masters (1989) has suggested that liberal democracy is 'natural' in its flexibility in responding to changing environments. Ecofeminists see caring and nurturing, at least in female nature. And so forth. In short, just about every human political ideology and political–economic system has at one time or another been justified as consistent with nature, especially nature as revealed by Darwinism.

But this sheer variety should suggest that in nature we will find no single blueprint for human politics. Saward (1993) draws the inference that we should stop looking, that nature has no political lessons to offer. And even if we did locate a single defensible model therein, that model would only prove *ecologically* benign to the extent it could demonstrate that cross-species interactions were universally mutualistic and benign, rather than often hostile and competitive. Following Kropotkin, Murray Bookchin (1982) propounds exactly such a mutualistic, co-operative view of nature, to which he suggests human social, economic, and political life should be assimilated. But Bookchin's position here is, to say the least, selective in its interpretation of nature, and no more persuasive than all the other selective interpretations which have been used to justify all manner of human political arrangements. So a maximalist notion of ecocentric politics of the sort advocated by Bookchin should be rejected.

Yet nature is not devoid of political lessons. What we *will* find in nature, or at least in our interactions with it, is a variety of levels and kinds of communication to which we humans might try to adapt. The key here is to downplay 'centrism' of any kind, and focus instead on the kinds of interactions that might occur across the boundaries between humanity and nature. In this spirit, the search for green democracy can indeed involve looking for progressively less anthropocentric political forms. For democracy can exist not only among humans, but also in human dealings with the natural world—though not *in* that natural world, or in any simple *model* which nature provides for humanity. So the key here is seeking more egalitarian interchange at the human/natural boundary; an interchange that involves progressively less in the way of human autism. In short, ecological democratization here is a matter of more effective integration of political and ecological communication.

On the face of it, this requirement might suggest that the whole history of democratic theory—and democratic practice—should be jettisoned, and that a truly green programme of institutional innovation should be sought under a different rubric than 'democracy'. For democracy, however contested a concept, and in however many varieties it has appeared in the last two and a half thousand years, is, if nothing else, anthropocentric. One way to substantiate this point would be to go through all the major models of democracy (for example, as presented in Held, 1987), and test them for anthropocentrism. Obviously I haven't the space to do that. But let me just note that inasmuch as democratic theory has been taken under the wing of liberalism in the last hundred years (and most of it has been), then its anthropocentrism has been guaranteed. As Freya Mathews (1991*b*, p. 158) notes, 'liberalism as it stands is of course anthropocentric: it takes human interest as the measure of all value.' Liberalism does so because only reasoning entities are accorded political standing. The members of a liberal democracy might of course choose to enact positive measures for environmental protection, for example by granting legal rights to natural objects. Guardians for those objects might then make claims on political and legal systems. But any such status for natural objects might simply *down*grade nature to another set of interests, disaggregating and isolating these interests by assigning them to identifiable natural objects, thus ignoring their intrinsically ecological (interconnected) character.[1]

The Communicative Rationality of Ecological Democracy

Let me suggest that rather than jettison democracy in the search for an ecologically rational political economy, we might better proceed by detaching democracy from liberal anthropocentrism, while retaining an emphasis on deliberation and communication. In Chapters 1 and 2 I argued that a defensible account of deliberative democracy has to be underwritten by a conception of communicative rationality. In Chapter 3 I extended the argument to communication across

[1] Marxism (and so its associated models of democracy) is just as materialistic and anthropocentric as liberalism, seeking human liberation in part through more effective domination and control of nature (see Eckersley, 1992, pp. 75–95). Curiously enough, fascism may do better than either liberalism or Marxism in the anti-anthropocentrism stakes; as Anna Bramwell (1989, pp. 195–208) notes, the first green 'party' in Europe was actually a strand in Hitler's Nazi Party. But fascism obviously takes us quite a long way from democracy, and the arguments of eco-authoritarians such as Robert Heilbroner and Garrett Hardin have been too thoroughly discredited to warrant any attention here.

difference. But what about the difference between human society and non-human nature? Could democracy be made truly green by communicating across this difference?

Eckersley (1992, pp. 109–17) for one argues that it cannot (though later she changes her mind; see Eckersley, 1999). And in the terms in which she argues, she is entirely correct. She points out that for Jürgen Habermas, the leading theorist of communicative rationality, just as for most liberals, the only entities that matter are ones capable of engaging as subjects in dialogue—in other words, human beings. Communicative action is only for those capable of raising, challenging, and redeeming 'validity claims' derived from the presuppositions of truth, sincerity, comprehensibility, and appropriateness that are implicit in all speech. In a belief carried over from his earlier work on the philosophy of science, Habermas considers that the only fruitful human attitude toward the natural world is one of instrumental manipulation and control. Indeed, the whole point of communicative rationalization is to *prevent* human interactions with one another becoming like human interactions with the natural world (see Alford, 1985, p. 77). Human liberation is bought at the expense of the domination of nature, and so Habermas is as anthropocentric as orthodox liberals here. And for this reason Eckersley dismisses Habermas as having no possible relevance to the search for an ecocentric politics.

Let me suggest that a more appropriate move here would try to rescue communicative rationality from Habermas. The key would be to treat communication, and so communicative rationality, as extending to entities that can act as agents, even though they lack the self-awareness which connotes subjectivity. Agency is not the same as subjectivity, and only the former need be sought in nature. Habermas treats nature as though it were brute matter. But nature is not passive, inert, and plastic. Instead, this world is truly alive, and pervaded with meanings.[2]

Minimally, a recognition of agency in nature would underwrite respect for natural objects and ecological processes. Democrats in general, and deliberative democrats in particular, should of course condemn humans who would silence other humans. Silencing in the form of not allowing others to speak is not the issue when it comes to dealing with communication from the non-human world. Nature 'speaks'

---

[2] This point should not be confused with the green spirituality advocated by deep ecologists, goddess worshippers, and others who see divinity in nature. The choice here is not between an inert nature on the one hand and a nature populated by wood nymphs, sprites, and goddesses on the other. Nor does a recognition of agency in the natural world imply thats its entities should be treated like human subjects.

or does not 'speak' irrespective of any attempted human suppression of that ability—indeed, it is not clear what suppression would consist of here, short of destroying nature entirely. But, as Bickford (1996) reminds us, the most effective and insidious way to silence others in politics is a refusal to listen, which is why the practice of effective listening has to be central to any discursive democracy. Recognition of agency in nature therefore means that we should listen to signals emanating from the natural world with the same sort of respect we accord communication emanating from human subjects, and as requiring equally careful interpretation. In other words, our relation to the natural world should not be one of instrumental intervention and observation of results oriented to control. Thus communicative interaction with the natural world can and should be an eminently rational affair (Dryzek, 1990*b*).

Now, it might be argued here that agency as I have defined it is simply the capacity to act instrumentally, in pursuit of some goal, rather than communicatively. However, closer examination shows that communicative capacity too is at issue, even though it is of course not the kind of linguistic communication in which the theory of communicative action is normally grounded. Of course, human *verbal* communication cannot extend into the natural world. But greater continuity is evident in nonverbal communication—body language, facial displays, pheronomes, and so forth (Dryzek, 1990*b*, p. 207). And a lot goes on in human conversation beyond the words, which is why a telephone discussion is not the same as a face-to-face meeting. More important than such continuities here are the ecological processes which transcend the boundaries of species, such as the creation, modification, or destruction of niches; or cycles involving oxygen, nitrogen, carbon, and water. Disruptions in such processes occasionally capture our attention, in the form of (say) climate change, desertification, deforestation, and species extinction.

A sceptic might still maintain that such capturing of our attention is a matter of mere signalling rather than discourse in any meaningful sense, because natural systems cannot challenge *our* interpretations of their needs (Vogel, 1997, pp. 184–6). Thus there can be no reciprocity of the sort commended by deliberative democrats, because there is no possibility of our being able to justify courses of action in terms capable of being accepted by non-human others. The emphasis I have placed (following Bickford) on effective listening as central to discursive democracy helps counter this scepticism. Here we can note that some categories of human beings are not very good at challenging interpretations placed upon their needs: but we should still try to listen to them, and be open to challenges to our interpretations from third parties concerned with these needs. That is at least part of what it means to be a democrat. But the most effective response to the sceptic here is that an ecological democracy would benefit to the degree it is populated by ecological selves (Mathews, 1991*a*). If individual humans can recall their own situation as ecological rather than merely social beings, then they, as ecosystem members, would be in a position to challenge others' intepretations of the needs of ecosystems of which they are component parts. Indigenous peoples can probably do this more effectively than industrial selves long alienated from natural surroundings; but there is no reason why such capacities cannot be recovered.

The idea that there may be agency and communicative capacity in nature might also seem to fly in the face of several hundred years of Western natural science, social science, and political theory. But perhaps the suggestion is not so far-fetched. Accounts of the actual practice of biological science often emphasize not manipulation and control, but rather understanding and communication. Examples here are especially prominent in work on animal thinking (notably by Donald Griffin), ethology (as in the work of Jane Goodall on chimpanzees), ecology (see Worster, 1985), and even genetics (see Keller's, 1983, discussion of the 'feeling for the organism' in the work of Barbara Mclintock).

Agency in nature on a grand scale is proposed in James Lovelock's Gaia hypothesis, which suggests that the biosphere as a whole acts so as to maintain the conditions for life. Lovelock does not suggest that Gaia has awareness, and so it cannot be described as a subject (still less a goddess). Rather, Gaia consists of a complex, self-regulating intelligence. But taking the hypothesis to heart 'implies that the stable state of our planet includes man as a part of, or partner in, a very democratic entity' (Lovelock, 1979, p. 145). Let me suggest that Lovelock's words here may be taken more literally than perhaps he intends, and that his hypothesis can indeed help us conceptualize a non-anthropocentric democracy.[3]

All of these suggestions of agency and communicative capacity in nature have their critics, especially among philosophers, probably less frequently among natural scientists. And it may often be hard to prove these positions scientifically. But that may not be the point. No demo-

---

[3] The Gaia hypothesis bears some resemblance to superorganismic and teleological treatments of ecosystem development, which have long been abandoned by most academic ecologists (except Eugene Odum), who are committed to more reductionist and stochastic models. But the superorganismic view lives on in the pages of *The Ecologist*.

cratic theory has ever been founded on scientific *proof* of anything, and there is no reason to seek an exception here. When it comes to the essence of *human* nature, political theorists can only disagree among themselves. To some, a utility maximizing *homo economicus* captures the essence of human nature; to others (mostly sociologists), it is a plastic, socialized conception of humanity in which there are no choices to be made, let alone utilities to be maximized; to others (such as critical theorists) a communicative and creative self; to others (such as civic republicans) a public-spirited and reflective self. In the present context, the idea of an ecological self (Mathews, 1991*a*) is more appropriate than these established paradigms of personhood. My general point here is that when it comes to an ecological democracy that opens itself toward non-human nature, we should not apply standards of proof which no other democratic theory could possibly meet.

Dobson (1996) argues against this attribution of communicative capacities to the natural world on the grounds that it is too controversial, and so too shaky a foundation for the natural grounding of democracy. However, I believe his criticism misses the point. There are many reasons why democracy in general and deliberative democracy in particular are desirable, only some of which are ecological. Thus the requirement here is not for any proof of the naturalness of democracy—as I argued earlier, no model of politics can be proved natural. Rather, the issue is better approached by showing that an additional argument in favour of deliberative democracy is that it can be extended in an ecological direction, and that the best way to do this is through recognizing the communicative capacities that nature and humanity share. Dobson himself believes that what we share is rather the capacity for autonomy or self-development, such that greens must be democrats—they cannot deny to humanity what they recognize in nature. Here I will set aside the fact that the capacity for autonomy is as controversial as the capacity for communication when applied to non-human entities, and simply thank Dobson for providing an additional argument on behalf of green democracy, and for further eroding the species boundary across which I believe fruitful communication can occur.

I have tried to show that it is conceivable that processes of communicative reason can be extended to cover non-human entities. Now, communicative reason underwrites discursive democracy in human affairs. But of course non-human entities cannot talk, and nor should they be anthropomorphized by giving them rights against us or preferences to be incorporated in utilitarian calculation, still less votes. However, as I have suggested, there are senses in which nature can communicate. So what kind of politics or democracy can be at issue here?

Democracy Across the Boundary with Nature

For most theories of democracy, especially (but not only) those influenced by liberalism, boundaries are important. For any aggregative conception of democracy, the first task is to define the boundaries of the population (society, or citizenry) whose preferences are to be taken into account. In practice, this can be done very precisely, with electoral registers and so forth. This idea of democracy as preference aggregation also presupposes the notion of a self-contained, self-governing community. But, as I argued in Chapter 5, in today's world that notion is becoming increasingly fictional, as political, social, and especially economic transactions transcend national boundaries. In which case, it might be productive to start thinking about models of democracy in which the boundaries of communities are indeterminate. The liberal model of democracy also requires a hard-and-fast boundary between the human and non-human world (not to mention a boundary between public and private realms, now challenged by feminists). For non-human entities cannot have preferences that we could easily recognize, or be at all confident in attributing to them. Thus ecological democracy cannot be sought in the shadow of preference aggregation in liberal democracy. However, it can be sought in the shadow of deliberative democracy.

One such specification is made by Robert Goodin (1996), in a major departure from his previous (1992*b*) scepticism concerning the possibility of deriving structural prescriptions from the green theory of value. Goodin believes that the key to representing nature in politics is via the notion of 'encapsulated interests'. That is, nature's interests are internalized and represented by 'sympathetic humans' (1996, p. 844). Making the connection to deliberation, Goodin argues that 'discursive democracy in the public sphere . . . creates a situation in which interests other than your own are called to mind' (p. 847)—what Eckersley (2000) refers to as 'enlarged thinking'. The latter can, Goodin and Eckersley believe, include those of mute others, such as non-human entities and future generations. Empirical support for these claims can be inferred from Adolf Gundersen's (1995) work on the effects of deliberation. In a series of 'deliberative interviews' about ecological topics with forty-six subjects who at the outset did not label themselves environmentalists, Gundersen finds that in *every* case the individual is more committed to environmental values by the end of the interview.

Goodin's point is a useful one, though democracy is about much more than the representation of interests. In discursive democracy, we look for the essence of democracy not in the aggregation of interests or preferences of a well-defined and well-bounded group of people (such as a nation-state), but rather in the content and style of interactions. Some styles may be judged anti-democratic (for example, the imposition of a decision without possibility for debate or criticism), some relatively democratic (for example, wide dissemination of information about an issue, the holding of hearings open to any interested parties, etc).

In Chapter 3 I argued against critics who claim that deliberation privileges rational argument by showing that deliberation can accommodate other kinds of voices. A similar extension may be in order to accommodate non-human communication (which Goodin, 1996, p. 841 allows). This extension means that we are now well-placed (or at least better-placed than aggregative liberal democrats) to think about dismantling what is perhaps the biggest political boundary of them all: that between the human and the non-human world. This is indeed a big step, and no doubt some people would still believe that it takes us out of the realm of politics and democracy altogether, at least as those terms are conventionally defined. Yet there is a sense in which human relationships to nature are *already* political. As Val Plumwood (1995) points out, politicization is a concomitant of human colonization of nature. Such colonization connotes an authoritarian politics; democratization would imply a more egalitarian politics here.

This sort of egalitarian politics transcending (and helping to dissolve) the boundary between humanity and nature would be consistent with deliberative democracy's stress on political equality, which I endorsed in earlier chapters. But what can equality between humans and non-humans mean, especially in a deliberative context? It cannot mean literal equality in the capacity to speak. But it can and should mean two things. The first is equality in the capacity to be represented. Representation is actually a thorny problem for traditional kinds of democratic theory. As Pitkin (1967, p. 9) points out, the concept of representation involves treating something as present which is 'nevertheless not present literally or in fact'. The same status can be accorded non-human nature. There are plenty of humans who cannot easily speak for themselves: the very young, mentally ill, intellectually disabled, and so forth. Yet democrats should have little trouble in agreeing that such people deserve equal representation. More generally, the ubiquity of representation in democracy means that a 'politics of ideas' is more common than a 'politics of presence' (to use the terminology of Phillips, 1995). So even if nature cannot receive equality in the politics of presence, it can receive such treatment when it comes to the politics of ideas.

Yet democracy, as I have just observed in discussing Goodin's views, is about much more than representation, and this is where a second kind of equality comes into play. Non-human nature can make equal demands on our capacity to listen. As I argued earlier, following Bickford, a capacity for effective and egalitarian listening is an essential component of discursive democracy; it is also helpful in undermining unequal power distributions. When it comes to improvement of our social listening capacity in an environmental context, a number of institutional devices are already at hand—such as mandatory state-of-the-environment reporting, and cumulative regional impact assessment (Eckersley, 2000).

At one level, it is possible to propose green democracy as a regulative ideal. This is, after all, how the basic principles of both liberal and deliberative democracy can be advanced (Miller, 1992, pp. 55–6). For aggregative liberals, the regulative ideal is fairness and efficiency in preference aggregation: the various institutional forms under which preference aggregation might proceed are then a matter for investigation, comparison, and debate. Similarly, for deliberative democrats, the regulative ideal is free discourse about issues and interests; again, various institutional forms might then be scrutinized in the light of this ideal. For green democrats, the regulative ideal is effectiveness in communication that transcends the boundary of the human world. As it enters human systems, then obviously ecological communication needs to be interpreted, and so we move from a politics of presence to a politics of ideas. However, unlike the situation in aggregative liberal democracy, this communication does not have to be mediated by the material interests of particular actors.

The content of such communication might involve attention to feedback signals emanating from natural systems; in which case, the practical challenge when it comes to institutional design becomes one of dismantling barriers to such communication. It is also important to attend to the feedback signals emanating from those closest to environmental damage. Plumwood (1998, p. 579) calls this the capacity to hear 'the bad news from below'. With these principles in mind, it is a straightforward matter to criticize institutions that try to subordinate nature on a large scale, and those that are remote and so incapable of hearing any news from below, be it good or bad. Think, for example, of the development projects sponsored by the World Bank, which until recently did not even pretend to take local environmental factors into account (now they at least pretend to), and which have been widely criticized for the social and ecological devastation left in their wake. Yet it is also possible to criticize approaches to our dealings with the environment that do exactly the reverse, and seek only the removal of human agency. On one of his own interpretations, Lovelock's Gaia can do quite well without people. And a misanthrope such as David Ehrenfeld (1978) would prefer to rely on natural processes left well alone by humans.

With this regulative ideal of green democracy in mind we are, then, in a position both to criticize existing political–economic arrangements and to think about what might work better. The construction of democracy should itself be discursive, democratic, sensitive to ecological signals—and open-ended. Idealist political prescription insensitive to real-world constraints and possibilities for innovation is often of limited value. Further, variation in the social and natural contexts within which political systems operate means that we should be open to institutional experimentation and variety across these contexts (though, as I noted earlier, an ability to operate in different contexts may itself be a highly desirable quality for any political–economic mechanism).

When it comes to criticism of existing political (and economic) mechanisms, it is reasonably easy to use the ecological communicative ideal to expose some gross failings. Perhaps most obviously, to the degree any such mechanism allows internal communication to dominate and distort signals from the outside, then it merits condemnation. So, for example, a bureaucracy with a well-developed internal culture may prove highly inattentive to its environment. And bureaucratic hierarchy pretty much ensures distortion and loss of information across the levels of hierarchy. Indeed, these are standard criticisms of bureaucracy as a problem-solving device, though such criticisms are usually couched in terms of a human environment, not a natural one. Markets can be just as autistic, if in different ways. Obviously, they respond only to *human, consumer* preferences that can be couched in *monetary* terms. Any market actor trying to take non-pecuniary factors into account is going to have its profitability, and so survival chances, damaged (this is not to gainsay the possibility of green consumerism). Conversely, the positive feedback of business growth (and the growth of the capitalist market in general) is guided by processes entirely internal to markets.

Above all, existing mechanisms merit condemnation to the extent their size and scope do not match the size and scope of ecosystems and/or ecological problems. Under such circumstances, communications from or about particular ecological problems or disequilibria will be swamped by communications from other parts of the world. Here, markets that transcend ecological boundaries, which they increasingly do, merit special condemnation. The internationalization and globalization of markets makes it that much easier to engage in local despoliation. It may be quite obvious that a local ecosystem is being degraded and destroyed, but 'international competitiveness' is a good stick with which to beat environmentalist critics of an operation. For example, they can be told that old growth forests must be clearcut, rather than logged selectively. Obviously, some ecological problems are global, as are some markets. This does not of course mean that effective response mechanisms to global ecological problems can be found in global markets. Market autism guarantees that they cannot.

Turning to the desirable scope and shape of institutions suggested by the ideal of ecological democracy, the watchword here is 'appropriate scale'. In other words, the size and scope of institutions should match the size and scope of problems. There may be good reasons for the predispositions toward small scale in ecoanarchism and 'small is beautiful' green political thought. Most notably, feedback processes in natural systems are diffuse and internal (Patten and Odum, 1981), and do not pass through any central control point. Highly centralized human collective choice mechanisms are not well placed to attend to such diffuse feedback. Moroever, the autonomy and self-sufficiency advocated by green decentralizers can force improved perception of the natural world. To the degree a community must rely on local ecological resources, it will have to take care of them. It does not follow that local self-reliance be taken to an extreme of autarchy. Rather, it is a matter of degree: the more the community is politically and economically self-reliant, then the more it must take care of its local ecosystems. Presumably the degree of self-reliance necessary to secure adequate care here depends a great deal on the level of environmental consciousness in the community in question. To the extent environmental consciousness is lacking, then economic consciousness has to do all the work, so there are many places (such as resource-dependent local economies in the American West) where only autarchy would do the trick.

There is no need in this scheme of things to privilege the nation-state, and every reason not to; few, if any, ecological problems coincide with national boundaries. The institutional possibilities associated with bioregionalism merit further exploration (see McGinnis, 1998). Bioregionalism begins with a rejection of ecologically arbitrary political units, such as counties, provinces, states, and nation-states. Bioregional boundaries are defined instead by watershed, topography, or species composition of ecosystems. But bioregionalism is not just a matter of redrawing political boundaries: it is also a matter of living in place. Redesigned political units should promote, and in turn be promoted by, awareness on the part of their human inhabitants of the biological surroundings that sustain them.

While one can argue endlessly about exactly how and where bio-regional boundaries should be drawn, it is easy to see that (say) a bioregional authority for the Colorado River basin makes more eco-political sense than dividing control of the basin between six states and a federal government. Among existing bioregional authorities, one of the most interesting is the Northwest Power Planning Council (NWPPC) celebrated by Kai Lee (1993), which is actively engaged in ecological restoration in the Columbia River Basin in the Pacific Northwest of the United States. The NWPPC relies for its ecological information not just upon the work of biological scientists as trans-mitted to ecological managers, but also on structured opportunities for participation in a variety of forums organized by the Council. These forums welcome the various human users of the ecosystem: Native American tribes, commercial and recreational fishers, other recreational users, wilderness advocates, and those who rely on the river for power, water, and navigation. All these people have material interests of their own to pursue; but many of them are also in day-to-day contact with particular aspects of the ecosystem, and therefore in a much better position than distant managers or politicians to hear news from it. The very existence of these forums in the overtly bio-regional context provided by the NWPPC has helped to cultivate bioregional awareness among participants. This is not a matter of dis-carding material interests in favour of a different set of ecological interests, but rather recognizing how these material interests are aspects of ecological well-being. Such effects are consistent with the capacity of discursive democracy to induce individuals to reflect upon their preferences and so broaden their conception of interests.

Co-ordination Through Spontaneous Order

An ecological democracy could, then, contain numerous loci of polit-ical authority, including bioregions. Obviously not all ecological problems and feedback signals reside at the local level. Some of them are global, and hence demand global institutional response. The obvious question here is: how does one co-ordinate between the various sites of political authority, given that one cannot (for example) resolve air pollution problems while completely ignoring the issue of water pollution, or deal with local sulphur dioxide pollution while ignoring the long-distance diffusion of sulphur dioxide in acid rain? The way this co-ordination is currently accomplished is by privileging one level of political organization. In unitary political systems, this will normally be the national state, though matters can be a bit more complicated in federal systems. The state (national or sub-national) will of course often contain an anti-pollution agency that (nominally, if rarely in practice) coordinates policy in regard to different kinds of pollutants. But, as I have already pointed out, from an ecological point of view this is an entirely arbitrary solution, and no more defensible than privileging the local community, or for that matter the global community.

The state and its environmental problem-solving capacities are likely to be with us for the foreseeable future, so their role in co-ordination should not be ignored. However, an ecological perspective points to kinds of co-ordination that are not organized centrally (as in the state), but arise as emergent properties as the scale of ecological and social organization rises. Such spontaneous orders can achieve coordination where the state does not or cannot—for example, at the system level in international affairs (see the previous chapter).

The best-known such order is the market, explicitly celebrated in these terms by F. A. von Hayek (see Goodin, 1992*b*, p. 154). But markets are not exactly an ecological success story, as I have already noted. Nor are they much good at co-ordinating the activities of *political* authorities. Within decentralized political systems, co-ordination is achieved largely through the spontaneous order of partisan mutual adjustment, which to Lindblom (1965) is at the core of collective decision in pluralistic liberal democracies. Such regimes may contain more formal and consciously-designed constitutions, but partisan mutual adjustment proceeds regardless of the content of such formalisms. This adjustment involves a complex mix of talk, strategy, commitment, and individual action devised in response to the context created by the actions of others. As I argued earlier, this kind of spontaneous order under liberal pluralism leaves much to be desired when scrutinized in an ecological light.

Ecosystems, including the global ecosystem, are also examples of spontaneous order, so one might try to devise an imitation which included humans. Along these lines, Murray Bookchin (1982) attempts to develop a naturalistic justification for human political organization. His eco-anarchist prescriptions might make some sense at the local level. But he can develop no *naturalistic* justification for the kinds of political order that would be needed to transcend localities, beyond relying on the spontaneous generation of structures whose specification is completely indeterminate (which is really no answer at all).

Let me suggest that there are two related kinds of spontaneous order which might perform the requisite co-ordinating functions quite well. The first is that which exists in connection with the organizations of civil society. The environmental movement and its associated networks are now international, and organizations such as Greenpeace or Friends of the Earth International can bring home to particular governments the international dimension of issues, such as (say) the consequences to Third World countries of toxic wastes exported by industrialized countries. Along these lines, Goodin (1992*b*, pp. 176–7) argues that green parties can assist in the 'coordination of international environmental policies', though as a green 'Realo' he appears to have only conventional party political participation in state politics in mind, rather than public spheres. To take another example, international public spheres constituted by indigenous peoples and their advocates can bring home to boycotters of furs in London or Paris the resulting economic devastation such boycotts imply for indigenous communities in the Arctic, which rely for cash income on trapping. A public sphere on a fairly grand scale was constituted by the unofficial Global Forum that proceeded in parallel with the United Nations Conference on Environment and Development in Rio in 1992. The point is that the reach of public spheres is entirely variable and not limited by formal boundaries on jurisdictions, or obsolete notions of national sovereignty. And they can come into existence, grow, and die along with the importance of particular issues. So, for example, it is entirely appropriate that the West European peace movement declined as cold war tensions eased in the 1980s.

A second kind of spontaneous order exists in association with the organizations of civil society, but at the same time transcends them. This second kind of order is discursive. Especially when institutional hardware is weak or absent, discourses as social phenomena can and do co-ordinate the understandings and actions of disparate actors. These discourses need know no geographical boundaries. Of course, it matters a great deal how and by whom their terms are set. A dispersed capacity to determine these terms of discourse is especially conducive to coordination across space and across issue areas. In Chapters 3 and 5 I argued that such dispersed capacity finds expression in the network form of organization, itself at home in civil society and the public sphere. The exemplary network is the environmental justice movement, within the United States and across national boundaries. Networks of this sort seem to be particularly at home in the environmental area.

Such networks and related kinds of spontaneous order should not be construed as operating smoothly, consensually, and in fully rational terms. In practice they feature information asymmetries, conflicts, and misunderstandings. In conflicts with other centres of political power, sometimes they will prevail, sometimes not. But in all of these features they are no different from imposed orders in human affairs, such as state bureaucracies, legal systems, or liberal constitutions. Yet out of the negotiation of difference and conflict order can emerge—and disappear. There is no reason to lament the disappearance of a particular network or discourse. Defensible spontaneous orders are problem-driven and do not outlive their usefulness—unlike, for example, state bureaucracies, which are often near-immortal.

There are many different ways of achieving co-ordination in collective decision-making, some spontaneous, some imposed. Examples are hierarchies, markets, bargaining, law, coercion, violence, discussion, partisan mutual adjustment, and moral persuasion (for an extended evaluation of the co-ordination capacities of these mechanisms in an ecological context, see Dryzek, 1987*b*). I have emphasized here sources of order that are defensible in both ecological and democratic terms. My argument is not that dispersed control over the contestation of discourses and associated networks should completely replace the more familiar sources, but that the world will be a greener and more democratic place to the extent their relative weight increases.

Conclusion

In contemplating the kinds of communication that might ensure more harmonious co-ordination across political and ecological systems, there is an ever-present danger of lapsing into ungrounded idealism and wishful thinking. I have tried to develop an alternative to ungrounded idealism by showing how discursive democracy can be extended in a direction that overcomes anthropocentric arrogance and that can cope more effectively with the ecological challenge. Democracy is, if nothing else, both an open-ended project and an essentially contested concept; indeed, if debates about the meaning of democracy did not occur in a society, we would hesitate to describe that society as truly democratic. What I have tried to do in this chapter is introduce another—major—dimension of contestation. If the sceptic believes that in so doing I have moved beyond the bounds of legitimate democratic theory, then so much the worse for democratic theory.

CHAPTER 7

Discursive Democracy in a Reflexive Modernity

Starting from a distinction between liberal constitutionalist and discursive conceptions of deliberative democracy, I have argued that the promise of democratic authenticity held by the deliberative turn can only be redeemed to the extent of a critical orientation to established power structures. Recall that the authenticity of deliberation requires that communication must induce reflection upon preferences in noncoercive fashion. This means, to begin, an emphasis on the contestation of discourses in the public sphere, rather than exclusive reliance on the deliberative institutions of the liberal state. Sometimes deliberative democracy can find a home in the state, but a vital civil society characterized by the contestation of discourses is always necessary. The authenticity of *democracy* requires in addition that these reflective preferences influence collective outcomes, and so both an orientation to the state and discursive mechanisms for the transmission of public opinion to the state are required, so long as the state is the main (though far from exclusive) locus of collective decision.

Aside from this insurgent aspect in relation to state structures, I have argued that discursive democracy can and should be transnational in relation to state boundaries, and ecological in its orientation to environmental problems. Throughout, I have argued that it is important that contestation be engaged by a broad variety of competent actors. The network form of institutionalization proves especially important, in international no less than domestic society. In this chapter I will first show that the insurgent, transnational and ecological moments of discursive democracy fit together quite tightly, and so summarize the shape I believe the theory of democracy should take in the wake of the deliberative turn. I will also revisit the intramural points of dispute in the theory of deliberative democracy that I listed in the introduction, demonstrating the light that can be shed on all of them by the analysis of the intervening chapters.

An account of democracy grounded in communicative action in the public sphere and civil society highlights the degree to which engagement is possible across the boundaries of different discourses. While discourses do indeed help to condition the way people think, individuals are not necessarily prisoners of the discourses that have helped to create their identities. Instead, the essence of engagement and challenge across discourses is that individuals can be brought to reflect upon the content of discourses in which they move. Thus the balance of discourses is amenable to democratic control; it is the (provisional) outcome of this contest that determines the meaning of 'public opinion' at any given time.

Democracy in Reflexive Modernity

Such engagement across discourses is possible; but is it likely? In contemplating the history of traditions of political thinking, Alasdair MacIntyre, for one, believes that such engagement is possible but rare. It is likely only when a tradition encounters a crisis which its adherents recognize but cannot solve using the resources of their own tradition. Solutions can be proposed by a competing tradition using language intelligible to adherents of the tradition in crisis (MacIntyre, 1988, pp. 364–5). An example would be medieval Christianity's (re)discovery of the Aristotelian tradition.

But that was then, this is now. There are reasons to suppose that the necessary conditions for interchange across what MacIntyre would call traditions or Foucault would call discourses are in today's world increasingly prevalent, and need not wait for the rare crisis. Another way of putting the matter is that crisis is now the normal condition of many traditions. This era may be one where conscious and critical reshaping of politics is more possible than ever before, meaning that individuals and societies need never resign themselves to fate in the form of events and discourses beyond their control. Here it is useful to introduce the related notions of de-traditionalization and reflexive modernization recently developed by, among others, Ulrich Beck, Anthony Giddens and Scott Lash (1994). The reflexive aspect of these ideas refers precisely to the questioning of previously taken-for-granted forces of social control—such as discourses. These notions can be applied to culture and aesthetics, though obviously their political dimension is most important when it comes to democracy.

Reflexive modernization is linked to environmental issues by Beck (1992) via the idea of an emerging 'risk society' which displaces the 'semi-modernity' of industrial society. The defining feature of politics in industrial society was social class, whose importance is now waning with de-industrialization. In industrial society, processes of economic development and technological change were mostly treated as given, and beyond any possibility of democratic questioning and control. The defining feature of politics in risk society is hazard, be it nuclear, chemical, or biotechnological. Issues such as the fallout from the Chernobyl nuclear explosion in 1986, the scare over BSE (mad cow disease) in Britain in the mid-1990s, and ozone layer depletion loom large in risk society. Risks of this sort have of course long accompanied industrial development, but Beck argues that risk society is qualitatively different because these hazards can no longer be dealt with piecemeal, as treatable side-effects to an ever-growing collective well-being. Rather, the perceived serious and cumulative character of risks threatens the legitimacy of the political–economic system. This threat to legitimacy arises because risks are not treated as matters of fate. Europe in the fourteenth century was a much riskier place than today, but the bubonic plague was regarded as beyond collective control.

Beck connects risk society to democracy in arguing that this legitimation problem can be ameliorated by broad participation in the selection, allocation, distribution and amelioration of risks. In this light, it should come as no surprise that since about 1970 the environmental area has led all other issue areas in democratic innovations (see Paehlke, 1988, 1995). These innovations include public inquiries, right-to-know legislation, citizen juries, policy dialogues, impact assessment with public comment, regulatory negotiation, mediation and other kinds of third-party-facilitated conflict resolution. (Even critics of these approaches, such as Amy, 1987, allow their legitimating function.)

Beck himself hopes for something grander out of such reforms than piecemeal institutional innovations. Ultimately he is interested in bringing economic development and technological change as a whole under democratic control, such that they are no longer treated as the province of experts. Reflexive modernization means a future that is chosen, rather than a trajectory to which everyone must adjust. But precisely because this future is chosen, the mere ubiquity of risk will not *cause* it to happen. Very different things could happen too, such as a stronger administrative state reasserting effective control over risks.

But the ubiquity of risk at least makes possible new kinds of democratic politics, where citizens do not accept the authority of states and professional risk apologists working for government or industry. Instead, citizens demand an effective voice in basic decisions about economic and technological development. Beck is a bit vague on the details of how such enhanced democratic control might be sought and implemented.

Beck's position is actually a very Kantian one. Kant defines Enlightenment as mankind's escape from its self-imposed immaturity. A refusal to accept the authority of risk apologists mirrors an earlier refusal to accept religious authority. But Kantians as we have seen favour a restricted view of deliberation that does not admit rhetoric. So does an invocation of reflexive modernization mean that we have to jettison rhetoric? In previous chapters I argued that rhetoric is necessary in deliberative democracy, one of the reasons being that deliberators have to make credibility judgements about alleged authorities and experts. However, distrust of experts does not mean that everyone has to *become* an expert. Instead, it can mean approaching expert testimony with a sceptical attitude, perhaps questioning the credentials of experts, seeking corroboration for any contentious claim, refusing to believe an expert if his or her research is funded by the offending industry, or if his or her record indicates an axe to grind.

Are developed countries indeed moving from industrial society to risk society? Is class politics disappearing along with this transition? Clearly Beck exaggerates the degree to which issues of economic growth and material distribution are vanishing. Indeed, risk issues can reinforce class politics, as the environmental justice movement in the United States has demonstrated. The first concern of all governments is still to maintain the confidence of actual and potential investors—increasingly so, in light of economic globalization. So far, risks such as ozone layer depletion or mad cow disease have not led a large number of citizens to examine capitalist democracy's legitimating principles.

These criticisms of Beck notwithstanding, the salience of risk issues has clearly undergone a secular increase since around 1970, even though particular risks and their associated scares have come and gone. Corresponding to this secular increase is growing distrust of experts and governments; too many have been exposed as liars. In this light, reflexive political action in the presence of risk has increased. Whether or not this bears interpretation as heralding a reflexive *modernity* is more debatable. However, contemplation of the prospects for discursive democracy amid the contestation of discourses in the public sphere requires only that this potential is present in particular cases, not that it is always and inevitably achieved or advanced. The achievement or negation of reflexive modernization depends crucially on the specific choices of political actors, not on any process of ineluctable historical development. (In the terms of Harold Lasswell, 1965, reflexive modernization is therefore a 'developmental construct'.)

The international system too can be approached in these terms. Some of the more prominent issues of risk, such as global warming and ozone layer depletion, arise in the international system, and so Beck's ideas about the prospects for democratization in an environment of risk apply here no less than within national boundaries.

The international system's counterpart to the loss of immutable commitment to economic growth and technological progress is its loss of the stable parameters for action that the cold war once provided. The context of international relations is now much more fluid than before, though just where this might lead remains uncertain. Arguably, the new ordering principles for the system are organized around economics rather than security, introducing new parameters and constraints, indeed a new master-discourse of market liberalism. Still, given fluidity in the system, intelligent actors have to recognize that their actions help to constitute and create contexts. I argued in Chapter 5 that a key—perhaps the key—aspect of the context that can be so created is the prevailing or emerging constellation of discourses in the international system. In this light, acting rationally means not merely identifying and implementing good means to clarified ends, but also thinking about how one's actions help constitute the emerging international order and its balance of discourses.

Whether or not one accepts the grander claims made on behalf of reflexive modernization, it provides further justification for an account of the public sphere and its relation to both the state and international government in terms of the contestation of discourses. This account was initially rooted in a response to the social choice theorists' and difference democrats' critiques of deliberation, and as a corrective to the liberal constitutionalist assimilation of deliberative democracy. The notion of risk society linked to reflexive modernization also helps explain why discursive democratic innovation is especially likely in the vicinity of environmental issues.

The Shape of Deliberative Democracy

In trying to determine the shape that the theory of democracy should take in the wake of the deliberative turn I have been less concerned with intramural disputes among deliberative democrats, except insofar as they are central to the distinction I have drawn between liberal constitutionalist deliberative democracy and discursive democracy. Still, the analysis of the preceding chapters can be deployed to shed light on many of these points of contention. Let me now return explicitly to the points I listed in the Introduction.

Should deliberation be restricted to rational argument, or admit other kinds of communication? An account of deliberative democracy grounded in communicative action in the public sphere requires some means of transmission of public opinion to the state. I argued in Chapter 2 that rhetoric is an important mode of communication here because it entails communication that attempts to reach those subscribing to a different frame of reference, or discourse. Thus rhetoric plays an important role in deliberating across difference, as well as across the boundary between the state and the public sphere. Rhetoric can also involve emotional appeals to an audience, and claims about character that both defend and question the credibility of authorities such as expert witnesses. Other kinds of communication proposed by difference democrats, notably testimony or storytelling and greeting, are readily incorporated into discursive democracy (see Chapter 3). However, we should also be aware of the dangers inherent in rhetoric, testimony/storytelling, and even greeting. Rhetoric can coerce its audience by manipulating their emotions. Storytelling can coerce the storyteller, especially in a group where only a particular kind of story is acceptable. Greeting can be used to intimidate. I argued in Chapter 3 that all forms of communication should be admitted only if they are (*a*) noncoercive, (*b*) capable of connecting the particular to the general. The group representation to which some difference democrats connect alternative kinds of communication is unacceptable if it extends to veto power, because so long as it retains a right to veto the outcome, a group's participation in deliberation is in bad faith.

If deliberation does admit these other kinds of communication, how should their relation to argument be conceptualized; should rational argument remain sovereign, or can these alternatives contribute equally to the outcome of deliberation? As I have just noted, these alternative forms of communication, while valuable, can also be coercive. The standards to which they are held are rational ones. When it comes to rhetoric, emotions must in the end be capable of rational justification, and claims about the character and so credibility of (say) a particular expert must be open to testing (for example, by examining the expert's qualifications, history, and source of employment and funding). Standards of communicative rationality can be applied to the context in which testimony and storytelling proceed, in order to guard against coercion of the storyteller by the group. The other problem with these alternative forms of communication is that they are incomplete, because insufficient to warrant any particular collective decision. They need not necessarily be subordinated to rational argument, but their deployment only makes sense in a context where argument about what is to be done remains central.

Does deliberation's emphasis on reasoned argument constitute a restraining and possibly even anaesthetizing force that neutralizes justified dissent? Contemporary postmodernists are fond of exploding claims to the neutrality of rationality. At an extreme, all forms of knowledge are to postmodernists really only forms of power. In this light, reasoned argument itself might seem to provide the foundations for just another repressive discourse. It is hard to disprove such sceptical claims because one's standards of proof and disproof can be always be questioned by the sceptic. However, I have shown in Chapter 3 that discursive democracy can accommodate difference, and different modes of communication beyond rational argument. It is possible to accommodate some postmodern concerns by allowing a plurality of discourses in deliberation in the public sphere. Such a move will not satisfy the hard-line sceptic, who is more likely to emphasize discontinuity and rupture across discourses, rather than their constructive engagement. Still, an emphasis on the contestation of discourses as central to an account of discursive democracy allows for dissent and for voices from the margins to be heard.

Are there some kinds of communication (perhaps prejudiced, racist, or sectarian) that should be ruled out in advance? Some proponents of deliberative democracy believe that particular kinds of communication and argument should be ruled out in advance; for example, those that deny basic principles of human integrity, or political equality. Racist and sectarian communication would fall into this category. Some discourses by their very nature would seem antithetical to effective deliberation. For example, market liberalism helps to create individuals who are social isolates and rational egoists, therefore capable of wreaking havoc on democratic politics of any sort. However, one cannot abolish prejudice, racism, sectarianism, and rational egoism by forbidding their proponents from public speaking. A model of deliberative democracy that stresses the contestation of discourses in the public sphere allows for challenge of sectarian positions, as it allows for challenge of all kinds of oppressive discourses. Indeed, if there were no such oppressive discourses to challenge, a vital democratic life in the public sphere would be hard to imagine. Deliberative democrats are those who have faith in the powers of deliberation itself to root out bad arguments and sectarianism; to deny their advocates admission into the forum is to reveal a lack of confidence in the efficacy of deliberation. Rather than attach preconditions for entry into deliberation, we should rely as far as possible on mechanisms endogenous to deliberation itself to change views and beliefs in a benign direction—and also, in the language of social choice theory, to restrict domain and so make collective choice more tractable. Discursive democracy is not an exclusive gentlemen's club.

Are there particular process values (such as impartiality, civility, or reciprocity) to which deliberators must be committed before they can be admitted to the forum? As seen in Chapter 1, public reason of the Rawlsian sort specifies a set of commitments that individuals must adopt if they are to be admitted to the public arena. But those with greater faith in the efficacy of deliberation would emphasize instead mechanisms endogenous to deliberation that promote these process values (see Chapter 2). The only way to learn civility and reciprocity is through practice in deliberation itself. Again, deliberative democracy is not an exclusive gentleman's club.

Must acceptable argument be couched in terms of the public interest, common to all, or are more particular and partial interests admissible? Some proponents of 'public reason' believe that the only arguments that should count are those couched impartially in terms of the public interest, to the exclusion of any partial, let alone private interest. But again, there are mechanisms endogenous to deliberation which promote the expression of interests in public interest terms, and the crafting of proposals sensitive to interests so expressed (see Chapter 2). Arguments made in these terms are more likely to be persuasive, and individuals who couch their arguments in this way may come to convince themselves too, and so overcome their own partiality. Though such shifts toward the generation of truly public interests are welcome from the point of view of social problem solving, it should be remembered that partial interests can also be legitimate, so purging partial interests should not be at issue. Again, we should rely on mechanisms endogenous to deliberation to achieve an appropriate and acceptable balance here between private and public interests, partial and impartial concerns.

If particular and partial interests can enter, do we allow deliberation to coexist with bargaining? Many collective choice processes begin in terms of bargaining. The essence of bargaining is strategic action in which each participant tries to maximize his or her own benefits in an environment constituted by other individuals trying to do exactly the same, in which offers and threats can be made. One easy way to dispose of bargaining is by definition: deliberation requires that participants be amenable to reflecting upon and changing their preferences and views. Politics conceived as purely strategic action is an incoherent mess, as rational choice theory has proven so well. But to dispose of bargaining in this fashion is too easy. Deliberative democrats should instead point to those mechanisms endogenous to deliberation which curb strategic action and induce individuals to reflect on the interests of themselves and others, and also upon common interests. But even when the degree of mistrust among participants means that bargaining is decisive in determining a collective outcome, deliberation can still play a useful role by inducing participants to multiply dimensions and options, thus increasing the possibilities for stable and non-arbitrary bargains (see Chapter 2).

Should deliberation be oriented to consensus, or is it just a prelude to voting? Consensus is by definition unanimous agreement not just on a course of action, but also on the reasons for it. As seen in Chapter 1, consensus in this sense orients both Rawlsian public reason and Habermas's ideal speech situation, two roots of contemporary thinking on deliberative democracy. However, those who believe the consensus principle can be applied in the real world set up an easy target for both social choice theorists (Chapter 2) and difference democrats (Chapter 3). In a pluralistic world, consensus is unattainable, unnecessary, and undesirable. More feasible and attractive are workable agreements in which participants agree on a course of action, but for different reasons.

Is the proper location of deliberation the existing representative institutions and legal system of liberal democracy, or should deliberation extend more broadly throughout society? Might existing representative institutions prove inhospitable to effective deliberation, such that alternative locations should be sought? Deliberation can occur within representative institutions and the legal system, but they should not constitute its only homes. Liberal constitutionalist deliberative democrats in particular tend to ignore the fact that these institutions are part of an entity called the state, and so subject to major constraints upon the degree to which authentic democratic control can be exercised within them. Statist 'difference democrats' also ignore this problem. These constraints are mostly related to the economic system within which the state must operate, and are intensified with free trade and capital mobility. As I have argued throughout, the most important alternative location for deliberation is civil society or the public sphere. A vital public sphere is essential for the continued health of democracy because a flourishing civil society provides both a resource for future democratization of the state and a check against reversal of the state's democratic commitments. The democratic vitality of the public sphere can be facilitated by a state that is passively exclusive in the kind of interest representation that it adopts, and so highly constrained in the scope of deliberation that it can itself encompass (see Chapter 4). This emphasis on civil society does not consign deliberative democracy to a powerless realm, because connecting deliberation to the contestation of discourses within the public sphere shows that public opinion so generated can be translated into administrative power. A number of transmission mechanisms are available, including discursive ones. Elections are not the only possible means of transmission of public opinion to the state, or even necessarily the most important ones.

Should deliberation be constrained by constitutional specifications that rule out in advance particular outcomes of deliberation? The longstanding tension between democracy and constitutionalism has been resolved by liberal constitutionalist deliberative democrats in three ways, discussed in Chapter 1. First, deliberative principles can be used to justify liberal rights. Second, the constitution can be devised such as to protect a deliberative domain. Third, constitution-making itself can be a deliberative process. Deliberation can, then, operate within a liberal constitutional context that guarantees the rights of individuals and minorities against state power, be that power constituted through democratic or authoritarian means. I have argued (see especially Chapters 1 and 4) that there are limits to the degree to which the contemporary liberal capitalist state can be democratic, in which case individuals may need rights to protect them against the undemocratic actions that the state might take against them more than they need rights to protect themselves against democracy. Thus protection against what the outcome of deliberation may do to violate the rights of individuals or groups looms less large here than it does for liberal constitutionalist deliberative democrats.

The liberal constitutionalists are correct that deliberative democracy must be allowed to protect its own preconditions, which means that citizens' rights to freedom of speech and association can be upheld through reference to the idea of deliberation itself. Yet there are also mechanisms endogenous to deliberation that can effectively protect those values that liberals enshrine as rights. In particular, deliberative democracy can be made responsive to the interests of all those entering the forum, rendering these entrants less in need of protection in the form of rights. The fact of participation in deliberation generally leads individuals to call to mind interests beyond their own—including the interests of individuals and groups who might without the reflection induced by deliberation be disadvantaged or attacked by public policy. The extension of deliberation to encompass different kinds of communication (such as storytelling and rhetoric) can also help protect minorities against what majorities might do to them.

Is political equality central to the deliberative ideal, and if so how much deviation from that ideal should be tolerated? What if anything is to be done about unequal individual capacities to deliberate? Political equality is the presumption that all participants in a process have an equal chance of affecting the outcome. Any departure from this ideal violates a key principle of deliberative democracy, highlighted if we ground the latter in communicative rationality (as I have argued in Chapter 1 must be the case). Under communicative rationality, the only power exercised is, in Habermas's terminology, 'the forceless force of the better argument'. If we open deliberation to kinds of communication other than argument, then still the only power should be 'the forceless force of better communication'.

Material inequality can produce political inequality, for poverty can inhibit communicative capacity. This is why some deliberative democrats, for example Gutmann and Thompson, see welfare state redistribution as required by the deliberative model. However, if we regard effective redistribution as a necessary prerequisite for deliberation we may be in for a long wait, given growing material inequality within many developed societies, and growing transnational inequality. We should also be wary of the implicit condescension involved in claiming that materially disadvantaged people are necessarily the poorest communicators. Thus deliberative democratization should never wait for material redistribution, though in the long run it would probably benefit from such redistribution.

The capacity to deliberate can never be fully equalized across individuals, and discursive democracy as the contestation of discourses may even require some degree of inequality as grist for the contest. Some individuals may not wish to participate in deliberation, which is why democratic legitimacy needs to be couched in terms of the *right* to participate, not the compulsion to do so. Still, among those who wish to enter the forum, unequal capacity remains. Expanding the range of admissible modes of communication along lines addressed in Chapter 3 will help, though there is no guarantee that inequality in (say) the capacity to tell one's story will not reinforce inequality in the capacity to argue, rather than compensate for the latter. Some people are shy, therefore less able to engage effective verbal discussion. Among deliberative democrats there is some disposition to structurelessness in the forum, but more structured opportunities for communication may help compensate for inequality caused by shyness, in that it requires individuals to speak at well-defined times. But deliberation need not be confined to talk in a public forum. Especially if we think in terms of the contestation of discourses in the public sphere, written communication matters too, as does conversation in small groups.

Is deliberation a means for arriving at decisions that solve social problems more effectively, or is it just an intrinsically desirable procedure, irrespective of the problem-solving substance of its outcomes? In Chapter 4 I argued that the social-democratic corporatist state is comparatively effective in solving social problems, especially those connected to social justice, redistribution, economic stability, and environmental quality. This state is not internally very democratic. But if it is conceptualized as part of a political system that locates discursive democracy in a public sphere defined by its orientation to the state, the combination yields both problem-solving effectiveness and democratic authenticity. In more decentralized settings, such as the international system, discursive networks of the kind emphasized in Chapters 3 and 5 both highlight the dimensions of social problems and co-ordinate responses across them. In Chapter 2 I showed that deliberation can uncover or create additional dimensions in social choice, thus facilitating the negotiation of a complexity that can otherwise render democratic procedures both arbitrary and unstable.

Elsewhere, I have argued that discursive democracy may be the most effective political means currently available to solve complex social problems, because it provides a means for coherent integration of the variety of different perspectives that are the hallmark of complexity (Dryzek, 1990*a*, pp. 57–76). This is why discursive designs have made appearances in many public policy settings in recent years, especially in regard to complex issues featuring deep conflict.

Deliberation can be justified in many ways: for example, in terms of the intrinsic qualities of its process, or its facilitation of the assertion of identity and interchange across difference. A 'proceduralist' position seeks quality only in terms of procedures, such that outcomes produced by good procedures are by definition good outcomes. 'Good procedures' here might be defined as those that are fair, equal, reciprocal, and free from coercion, deception, and manipulation. The contrasting epistemic argument for deliberation has recently been advanced by, among others, David Estlund (1997) and Carlos Niño (1996), who believe that deliberation is justified to the degree it produces more rational outcomes. Rationality here is defined according to some standard external to deliberation (and so should not be equated with any notion of communicative rationality). The epistemic justification hinges on the ability of deliberative democracy to sort good arguments from bad, not just to bring all reasons into play. Any connection of deliberation to collective problem-solving requires this epistemic dimension.

Should we try to subject all decisions to extensive deliberation, or just particular important ones, such as constitutional matters? Deliberation consumes time and energy; sheer reasons of economy suggest that not all decisions, public or private, be subjected to it. On the other hand, there is no need to confine deliberation to rare constitutional occasions, as some American liberal constitutionalists wish. Deliberation is best suited to those decisions which are important, or otherwise intractable, or both. Beyond this there is actually little need for the democratic theorist to specify exactly how important or how intractable a decision needs to be before demanding deliberative resolution. That decision can itself be left to actors in the public sphere. If enough of them feel an issue merits attention, that is enough to put it on the discursive agenda. From a different direction, public officials may feel that democratic legitimacy requires setting up a deliberative process (such as a public inquiry).

Is deliberation to be confined to members of a predefined community, or can it occur effectively across community boundaries, or when no established community is present? A community is by definition composed of direct and many-sided relationships among its members. Communitarian political theorists sometimes apply the idea on a larger scale to those adherents of a common tradition which gives them a shared way of life, within which politics should occur (and people should not in general question those foundations). As such, assimilating deliberative democracy to communitarianism would unnecessarily restrict the scope of deliberation, and make it an altogether conservative enterprise. The danger of the gentlemen's club, in which deliberation is a dull affair among those who agree on basics, is again apparent. I have argued that deliberation can and should occur when no community in this strong sense is present—for example, across national boundaries (Chapter 5), and across difference within national boundaries (Chapter 3). If democracy is silent on issues that transcend community boundaries then democracy is banished from many of the main issues in the contemporary world. In emphasizing the contestation of discourses within the public sphere, I have also shown how deliberation across different traditions can occur.

Conclusion

The deliberative turn in democratic theory promises a renewed focus on the authenticity of democracy, thus deepening democracy. But that promise remains unfulfilled so long as deliberative democracy remains confined to the constitutional surface of political life. The assimilation to liberal constitutionalism needs to be resisted. A more critical project of discursive democracy has to get beneath the surface to reveal and counteract the extra-constitutional factors that can prevent or distort political dialogue and its connection to collective decision making. These factors include imperatives that states (including liberal states) face, as well as the way states choose to pattern interest representation (corporatist or pluralist, inclusive or exclusive, active or passive). While allowing that deliberation can occur within (or sometimes about) the structures of the liberal state, detaching discursive democracy from liberal constitutionalism also opens our eyes to a host of other democratic possibilities: In the contestation of discourses in the public sphere, in the international system (where there is no liberal constituion), even across the boundaries between humanity and nature. Discursive democracy can embrace difference as well as consensus, the public sphere as well as the state, transnational as well as domestic politics, and nature as well as humanity.

BIBLIOGRAPHY

ACKERMAN, BRUCE. 1991. *We the People*, i. *Foundations*. Cambridge, Mass.: Harvard University Press.
—— 1992. *The Future of Liberal Revolution*. New Haven: Yale University Press.

ADORNO, THEODOR W. 1973. *Negative Dialectics*. New York: Continuum.

ALFORD, C. FRED. 1985. *Science and the Revenge of Nature: Marcuse and Habermas*. Gainesville, Fla.: University Press of Florida.

ALMOND, GABRIEL A. 1988. The Return to the State. *American Political Science Review*, 82: 850–74.

AMY, DOUGLAS. 1987. *The Politics of Environmental Mediation*. New York: Columbia University Press.

ARATO, ANDREW. 1993. 'Interpreting 1989', *Social Research*, 60: 609–46.

ARCHIBUGI, DANIELE, and DAVID HELD (eds.), 1995. *Cosmopolitan Democracy: An Agenda for a New World Order*. Cambridge: Polity.
—— —— and Martin Köhler (eds.), 1998. *Re-Imagining Political Community: Studies in Cosmopolitan Democracy*. Cambridge: Polity.

ARENDT, HANNAH. 1958. *The Human Condition*. Chicago: University of Chicago Press.

ARROW, KENNETH J. 1963. Social Choice and Individual Values, 2nd edn. New York: Wiley.

ASH, TIMOTHY GARTON. 1990. *The Uses of Adversity: Essays on the Fate of Central Europe*. New York: Vintage Books.

AUSTEN-SMITH, DAVID. 1990. 'Information Transmission in Debate', *American Journal of Political Science*, 34: 124–52.
—— 1992. 'Strategic Models of Talk in Political Decision-Making', *International Political Science Review*, 13: 45–58.
—— and WILLIAM H. RIKER. 1987. 'Asymmetric Information and the Coherence of Legislation', *American Political Science Review*, 81: 897–918.

BARBER, BENJAMIN. 1984. *Strong Democracy: Participatory Politics for a New Age*. Berkeley, Calif.: University of California Press.

BARBOUR, ROSE, and JENNY KITZINGER (eds.), 1999. *Developing Focus Group Research*. London: Sage.

BARRY, BRIAN, and RUSSELL HARDIN (eds.), 1982. *Rational Man and Irrational Society?* Beverly Hills, Calif.: Sage.

BARRY, JOHN. 1999. *Rethinking Green Politics: Nature, Virtue and Progress*. London: Sage.

BECK, ULRICH. 1992. *Risk Society: Towards a New Modernity*. London: Sage.
——, ANTHONY GIDDENS, and SCOTT LASH. 1994. *Reflexive Modernization: Politics, Tradition and Aesthetics in the Modern Social Order*. Cambridge: Polity.

BENHABIB, SEYLA. 1990. 'Communicative Ethics and Contemporary Controversies in Practical Philosophy', in Seyla Benhabib and Fred Dallmayr (eds.), *The Communicative Ethics Controversy*. Cambridge, Mass.: MIT Press.

—— 1996*a*. 'Introduction: The Democratic Moment and the Problem of Difference', in Seyla Benhabib (ed.), *Democracy and Difference: Contesting the Boundaries of the Political*. Princeton: Princeton University Press, 3–18.

—— 1996*b*. 'Toward a Deliberative Model of Democratic Legitimacy', in Seyla Benhabib (ed.), *Democracy and Difference: Contesting the Boundaries of the Political*. Princeton: Princeton University Press, 67–94.

BERGER, THOMAS. 1985. *Village Journey: The Report of the Alaska Native Review Commission*. New York: Hill and Wang.

BESSETTE, JOSEPH M. 1980. 'Deliberative Democracy: The Majoritarian Principle in Republican Government', in Robert A. Goldwin and William A. Shambra, *How Democratic is the Constitution?* Washington, DC: American Enterprise Institute, 102–16.

—— 1994. *The Mild Voice of Reason: Deliberative Democracy and American National Government*. Chicago: University of Chicago Press.

BICKFORD, SUSAN. 1996. *The Dissonance of Democracy: Listening, Conflict and Citizenship*. Ithaca, NY: Cornell University Press.

—— 1999. 'Reconfiguring Representation: Identity and Institutions in the Inegalitarian Polity', *American Journal of Political Science*, 43: 86–108.

BLAUG, RICARDO. 1996. 'New Theories of Discursive Democracy: A User's Guide', *Philosophy and Social Criticism*, 22: 49–80.

BLOCK, FRED. 1977. 'The Ruling Class Does Not Rule: Notes on the Marxist Theory of the State', *Socialist Revolution*, 7: 6–28.

BOHMAN, JAMES. 1995. 'Public Reason and Cultural Pluralism: Political Liberalism and the Problem of Moral Conflict', *Political Theory*, 23: 253–79.

—— 1996. *Public Deliberation: Pluralism, Complexity and Democracy*. Cambridge, Mass.: MIT Press.

—— 1998*a*. 'The Globalization of the Public Sphere: Cosmopolitan Publicity and the Problem of Cultural Pluralism', *Philosophy and Social Criticism*, 24: 199–216.

—— 1998*b*. 'The Coming of Age of Deliberative Democracy', *Journal of Political Philosophy*, 6: 399–423.

—— and WILLIAM REHG. 1997. *Deliberative Democracy: Essays on Reason and Politics*. Cambridge, Mass.: MIT Press.

BOOKCHIN, MURRAY. 1982. *The Ecology of Freedom: The Emergence and Dissolution of Hierarchy*. Palo Alto, Calif.: Cheshire.

BOUTROS-GHALI, BOUTROS. 1996. *An Agenda for Democratization*. New York: United Nations.

BOWLES, SAMUEL, and HERBERT GINTIS. 1986. *Democracy and Capitalism: Property, Community, and the Contradictions of Modern Social Thought*. London: Routledge and Kegan Paul.

178 Bibliography

BRAMWELL, ANNA. 1989. *Ecology in the Twentieth Century: A History*. New Haven: Yale University Press.

BRENNAN, GEOFFREY. 1989. 'Politics *With* Romance: Towards a Theory of Democratic Socialism', in Alan Hamlin and Philip Pettit (eds.), *The Good Polity: Normative Analysis of the State*. Oxford: Basil Blackwell, 49–66.

—— and LOREN LOMASKY. 1993. *Democracy and Decision: The Pure Theory of Electoral Preference*. Cambridge: Cambridge University Press.

BUCHANAN, JAMES M. 1986. 'Then and Now, 1961–1986: From Delusion to Dystopia'. Paper presented at the Institute for Humane Studies, George Mason University.

BUNCE, VALERIE. 1992. 'Two-Tiered Stalinism: A Case of Self-Destruction', in K. Z. Poznanski (ed.), *Constructing Capitalism: The Re-Emergence of Civil Society and Liberal Economy in the Post-Communist World*. Boulder, Colo.: Westview.

BURCHELL, GRAHAM, COLIN GORDON, and PETER MILLER (eds.), 1991. *The Foucault Effect: Studies in Governmentality*. Chicago: University of Chicago Press.

BURNHEIM, JOHN. 1985. *Is Democracy Possible?* Cambridge: Polity.

CARRUTHERS, DAVID V. 1995. 'The Political Economy of Indigenous Mexico: Social Mobilization and State Reform', Ph.D. dissertation, University of Oregon.

CHAMBERS, SIMONE. 1996. *Reasonable Democracy: Jürgen Habermas and the Politics of Discourse*. Ithaca, NY: Cornell University Press.

CHRISTOFF, PETER. 1996. 'Ecological Modernisation, Ecological Modernities', *Environmental Politics*, 5: 476–500.

COCHRAN, MOLLY. 1998. 'Democracy, Global Governance and Public Spheres in International Relations'. Paper presented at the conference of the American Political Science Association, Boston.

COHEN, JEAN, and ANDREW ARATO. 1992. *Civil Society and Political Theory*. Cambridge, Mass.: MIT Press.

COHEN, JOSHUA. 1989. 'Deliberation and Democratic Legitimacy', in Alan Hamlin and Philip Pettit (eds.), *The Good Polity: Normative Analysis of the State*. Oxford: Basil Blackwell, 17–34.

—— 1996. 'Procedure and Substance in Deliberative Democracy', in Seyla Benhabib (ed.), *Democracy and Difference: Contesting the Boundaries of the Political*. Princeton: Princeton University Press, 95–119.

—— and JOEL ROGERS. 1992. 'Secondary Associations and Democratic Governance', *Politics and Society*, 20: 393–472.

COLEMAN, JULES, and JOHN FEREJOHN. 1986. 'Democracy and Social Choice', *Ethics*, 97: 6–25.

CONNOLLY, WILLIAM E. 1991*a*. *Identity/Difference: Democratic Negotiations of Political Paradox*. Ithaca, NY: Cornell University Press.

—— 1991*b*. 'Democracy and Territoriality', *Millennium*, 20: 463–84.

—— 1995. *The Ethos of Pluralization*. Minneapolis: University of Minnesota Press.

CONNORS, MICHAEL. 2000. 'Democracy and National Ideology in Thailand'. Unpublished Ph.D. thesis, University of Melbourne.

DAHL, ROBERT A. 1956. *A Preface to Democratic Theory*. Chicago: University of Chicago Press.

—— 1985. *Controlling Nuclear Weapons: Democracy versus Guardianship*. Syracuse, NY: Syracuse University Press.

—— 1989. *Democracy and its Critics*. New Haven: Yale University Press.

DEWEY, JOHN. 1927. *The Public and its Problems*. New York: Holt.

DOBSON, ANDREW. 1996. 'Democratizing Green Theory: Preconditions and Principles', in Brian Doherty and Marius de Geus (eds.), *Democracy and Green Political Thought: Sustainability, Rights and Citizenship*. London: Routledge, 132–48.

DOWIE, MARK. 1995. *Losing Ground: American Environmentalism at the Close of the Twentieth Century*. Cambridge, Mass.: MIT Press.

DRYZEK, JOHN S. 1987*a*. 'Discursive Designs: Critical Theory and Political Institutions', *American Journal of Political Science*, 31: 656–79.

—— 1987*b*. *Rational Ecology: Environment and Political Economy*. New York: Basil Blackwell.

—— 1990*a*. *Discursive Democracy: Politics, Policy and Political Science*. New York: Cambridge University Press.

—— 1990*b*. 'Green Reason: Communicative Ethics for the Biosphere', *Environmental Ethics*, 12: 195–210.

—— 1992. 'How Far Is It From Virginia and Rochester to Frankfurt? Public Choice as Critical Theory', *British Journal of Political Science*, 22: 397–417.

—— 1996. *Democracy in Capitalist Times: Ideals, Limits and Struggles*. New York: Oxford University Press.

—— 1997. *The Politics of the Earth: Environmental Discourses*. Oxford: Oxford University Press.

EASTON, DAVID. 1953. *The Political System*. New York: Knopf.

ECKERSLEY, ROBYN. 1992. *Environmentalism and Political Theory: Toward an Ecocentric Approach*. Albany, NY: State University of New York Press.

—— 1999. 'The Discourse Ethic and the Problem of Representing Nature', *Environmental Politics*, 8.

—— 2000. 'Deliberative Democracy, Ecological Risk, and "Communities-of-Fate" ', in Michael Saward (ed.), *Democratic Innovation: Deliberation, Association, and Representation*. London: Routledge.

EHRENFELD, DAVID. 1978. *The Arrogance of Humanism*. New York: Oxford University Press.

ELSTER, JON. 1998. 'Introduction', in Jon Elster (ed.), *Deliberative Democracy*. New York: Cambridge University Press, 1–18.

ERIKSEN, ERIK O. 1994. 'Deliberative Democracy and the Politics of Plural Society'. Paper presented at the Arena Conference on the Europeanisation of Normative Political Theory, Oslo, Norway.

ESTLUND, DAVID. 1993. 'Who's Afraid of Deliberative Democracy? On the Strategic/Deliberative Dichotomy in Recent Constitutional Jurisprudence', *Texas Law Review*, 71: 1437–77.

—— 1997. 'Beyond Fairness of Deliberation: The Epistemic Dimension of Democratic Authority', in James Bohman and William Rehg (eds.), *Deliberative Democracy*. Cambridge, Mass.: MIT Press.

EVANS, PETER B., DIETRICH RUESCHEMEYER, and THEDA SKOCPOL (eds.), 1985. *Bringing the State Back In.* Cambridge: Cambridge University Press.

EVANS, SARAH M. and HARRY C. BOYTE. 1986. *Free Spaces: The Sources of Democratic Change in America*. New York: Harper and Row.

FEARON, JAMES D. 1998. 'Deliberation as Discussion', in Jon Elster (ed.), *Deliberative Democracy*. New York: Cambridge University Press, 44–68.

FEMIA, JOSEPH. 1996. 'Complexity and Deliberative Democracy', *Inquiry*, 39: 359–97.

FISCHER, FRANK. 1993. 'Citizen Participation and the Democratization of Policy Expertise: From Theoretical Inquiry to Practical Cases', *Policy Sciences*, 26: 165–87.

FISHKIN, JAMES. 1991. *Democracy and Deliberation: New Directions for Democratic Reforms.* New Haven: Yale University Press.

—— 1995. *The Voice of the People: Public Opinion and Democracy*. New Haven: Yale University Press.

FISK, MILTON. 1989. *The State and Justice: An Essay in Political Theory*. Cambridge: Cambridge University Press.

FOLLETT, MARY PARKER. 1918. *The New State: Group Organizations—The Solution of Popular Government.* New York: Longmans, Green.

FOUCAULT, MICHEL. 1984. 'On the Genealogy of Ethics: An Overview of Work in Progress', in Paul Rabinow (ed.), *The Foucault Reader*. New York: Pantheon.

FRAAD, HARRIET, STEPHEN RESNICK, and RICHARD WOLFF. 1994. *Bringing It All Back Home: Class, Gender, and Power in the Modern Household*. London: Pluto.

FRASER, NANCY. 1992. 'Rethinking the Public Sphere: A Contribution to the Critique of Actually Existing Democracy', in Craig Calhoun (ed.), *Habermas and the Public Sphere.* Cambridge, Mass.: MIT Press, 109–42.

FREEMAN, JOHN R. 1989. *Democracy and Markets: The Politics of Mixed Economies*. Ithaca, NY: Cornell University Press.

GILBERT, ALAN. 1992. 'Must Global Politics Constrain Democracy? Realism, Regimes, and Democratic Internationalism', *Political Theory*, 20: 8–37.

GOLDGEIER, JAMES M., and MICHAEL MCFAUL. 1992. 'A Tale of Two Worlds: Core and Periphery in the Post-Cold War Era', *International Organization*, 46: 467–91.

GOODIN, ROBERT E. 1980. *Manipulatory Politics*. New Haven: Yale University Press.

—— 1992a. *Motivating Political Morality*. Oxford: Basil Blackwell.

—— 1992b. *Green Political Theory*. Cambridge: Polity.

—— 1996. 'Enfranchising the Earth, and its Alternatives', *Political Studies*, 44: 835–49.

GORE, ALBERT. 1992. *Earth in the Balance: Ecology and the Human Spirit.* Boston: Houghton Mifflin.

GOULD, CAROL C. 1988. *Rethinking Democracy.* Cambridge: Cambridge University Press.

GROFMAN, BERNARD. 1993. 'Public Choice, Civic Republicanism, and American Politics: Perspectives of a "Reasonable Choice" Modeler', *Texas Law Review*, 71: 1541–87.

GUINIER, LANI. 1991. 'The Politics of Tokenism: the Voting Rights Act and the Theory of Black Electoral Success', *Michigan Law Review*, 89: 1077–154.

—— 1994. *The Tyranny of the Majority.* New York: Free Press.

GUNDERSEN, ADOLF. 1995. *The Environmental Promise of Democratic Deliberation.* Madison: University of Wisconsin Press.

GUNNELL, JOHN G. 1986. *Between Philosophy and Politics: The Alienation of Political Theory.* Amherst, Mass.: University of Massachusetts Press.

GUTMANN, AMY, and DENNIS THOMPSON. 1996. *Democracy and Disagreement.* Cambridge, Mass.: Harvard University Press.

HABERMAS, JÜRGEN. 1975. *Legitimation Crisis.* Boston: Beacon Press.

—— 1979. *Communication and the Evolution of Society.* Boston: Beacon Press.

—— 1982. 'A Reply to my Critics', in John Thompson and David Held (eds.), *Habermas: Critical Debates.* Cambridge, Mass.: MIT Press, 219–83.

—— 1984. *The Theory of Communicative Action I: Reason and the Rationalization of Society.* Boston: Beacon Press.

—— 1987. *The Theory of Communicative Action II: Lifeworld and System.* Boston: Beacon Press.

—— 1989. *Structural Transformation of the Public Sphere: An Inquiry into a Category of Bourgeois Society.* Cambridge, Mass.: MIT Press.

—— 1996*a*. *Between Facts and Norms: Contributions to a Discourse Theory of Law and Democracy.* Cambridge, Mass.: MIT Press.

—— 1996*b*. 'Three Normative Models of Democracy', in Seyla Benhabib (ed.), *Democracy and Difference: Contesting the Boundaries of the Political.* Princeton: Princeton University Press, 22–30.

HAJER, MAARTEN A. 1995. *The Politics of Environmental Discourse: Ecological Modernization and the Policy Process.* Oxford: Oxford University Press.

HANSON, RUSSELL L. 1985. *The Democratic Imagination in America: Conversations with our Past.* Princeton: Princeton University Press.

HEALY, PATSY. 1993. 'Planning Through Debate: The Communicative Turn in Planning Theory', in Frank Fischer and John Forester (eds.), *The Argumentative Turn in Policy Analysis and Planning.* Durham, NC: Duke University Press.

HELD, DAVID. 1987. *Models of Democracy.* Cambridge: Polity.

HELD, DAVID. 1995. *Democracy and the Global Order: From the Nation State to Cosmopolitan Governance*. Cambridge: Polity.

HINDESS, BARRY. 2000. 'Representation Ingrafted upon Democracy', *Democratization*, 7 (forthcoming).

HIRST, PAUL. 1994. *Associative Democracy: New Forms of Economic and Social Governance*. Cambridge: Polity.

ISAAC, JEFFREY C. 1993. 'Civil Society and the Spirit of Revolt', *Dissent*, 40: 356–61.

—— 1994. 'Oases in the Desert: Hannah Arendt on Democratic Politics', *American Political Science Review*, 88: 156–68.

JAMES, WILLIAM. 1979 [1896]. *The Will to Believe and Other Essays in Popular Philosophy*. Cambridge, Mass.: Harvard University Press.

JÄNICKE, MARTIN. 1996. 'Democracy as a Condition for Environmental Policy Success: The Importance of Non-Institutional Factors', in William M. Lafferty and James Meadowcroft (eds.), *Democracy and the Environment: Problems and Prospects*. Cheltenham: Edward Elgar, 71–85.

—— HELMUT WEIDNER, and HELGA JORGENS (eds.), 1997. *National Environmental Policies: A Comparative Study of Capacity-Building*. Springer-Verlag.

JOHANSEN, ROBERT C. 1992. 'Military Policies and the State System as Impediments to Democracy', *Political Studies*, 40 (special issue): 99–115.

JOHNSON, JAMES. 1998. 'Arguing for Deliberation: Some Skeptical Considerations', 161–84 in Jon Elster (ed.), *Deliberative Democracy*. New York: Cambridge University Press.

KAVANAGH, DENNIS, and ANTHONY SELDON (eds.), 1989. *The Thatcher Effect*. Oxford: Oxford University Press.

KELLER, EVELYN FOX. 1983. *A Feeling for the Organism: The Life and Work of Barbara McLintock*. San Francisco: W. H. Freeman.

KEMP, RAY. 1985. 'Planning, Public Hearings, and the Politics of Discourse', in John Forester (ed.), *Critical Theory and Public Life*. Cambridge, Mass.: MIT Press, 177–201.

KITSCHELT, HERBERT. 1988. 'Left-Libertarian Parties: Explaining Innovation in Competitive Party Systems', *World Politics*, 40: 194–234.

—— 1994. *The Transformation of European Social Democracy*. Cambridge: Cambridge University Press.

KNIGHT, JACK, and JAMES JOHNSON. 1994. 'Aggregation and Deliberation: On the Possibility of Democratic Legitimacy', *Political Theory*, 22: 277–96.

—— —— 1997. 'What Sort of Equality Does Deliberative Democracy Require?' in James Bohman and William Rehg (eds.), *Deliberative Democracy*. Cambridge, Mass.: MIT Press, 279–320.

KÖHLER, MARTIN. 1998. 'From the National to the Cosmopolitan Public Sphere', in Daniele Archibugi, David Held, and Martin Köhler (eds.), *Re-Imagining Political Community: Studies in Cosmopolitan Democracy*. Cambridge: Polity, 231–51.

KORNHAUSER, WILLIAM. 1959. *The Politics of Mass Society*. New York: Free Press.

KRIESI, HANSPETER. 1995. 'The Political Opportunity Structure of New Social Movements: Its Impact on their mobilization', in Craig J. Jenkins and Bert Klandermans (eds.), *The Politics of Social Protest*. Minneapolis: University of Minnesota Press.

LACLAU, ERNESTO, and CHANTAL MOUFFE. 1985. *Hegemony and Socialist Strategy: Towards a Radical Democratic Politics*. London: Verso.

LAFFERTY, WILLIAM M. 1996. 'The Politics of Sustainable Development: Global Norms for National Implementation', *Environmental Politics*, 5: 185–208.

LASKI, HAROLD J. 1919. *Authority in the Modern State*. New Haven: Yale University Press.

LASSWELL, HAROLD D. 1965. *World Politics and Personal Insecurity*. New York: Free Press.

LEE, KAI N. 1993. *Compass and Gyroscope: Integrating Science and Politics for the Environment*. Washington, DC: Island Press.

LEHMBRUCH, GERHARD. 1984. 'Concertation and the Structure of Corporatist Networks', in John H. Goldthorpe (ed.), *Order and Conflict in Contemporary Capitalism*. Oxford: Clarendon.

LIJPHART, AREND. 1977. *Democracy in Plural Societies: A Comparative Exploration*. New Haven: Yale University Press.

LINDBLOM, CHARLES E. 1965. *The Intelligence of Democracy: Decision Making Through Mutual Adjustment*. New York: Free Press.

—— 1977. *Politics and Markets: The World's Political-Economic Systems*. New York: Basic Books.

—— 1982. 'The Market as Prison', *Journal of Politics*, 44: 324–36.

LINKLATER, ANDREW. 1998. 'Citizenship and Sovereignty in the Post-Westphalian European State', in Daniele Archibugi, David Held, and Martin Köhler (eds.), *Re-Imagining Political Community: Studies in Cosmopolitan Democracy*. Cambridge: Polity, 113–37.

LIPSCHUTZ, RONNIE. 1995. *Global Civil Society and Global Environmental Governance The Politics of Nature from Place to Planet*. Albany, NY: State University of New York Press.

LITFIN, KAREN T. 1994. *Ozone Discourses: Science and Politics in Global Environmental Cooperation*. New York: Columbia University Press.

LOVELOCK, JAMES. 1979. *Gaia: A New Look at Life on Earth*. Oxford: Oxford University Press.

LOWI, THEODORE J. 1969. *The End of Liberalism*. New York: W.W. Norton.

—— 1971. *The Politics of Disorder*. New York: Basic Books.

LYNCH, MARC. 1998. 'International Public Sphere Theory and Rogue States: Insights from the Rationalist-Constructivist Debate'. Paper presented at the annual meeting of the American Political Science association, Boston.

MCCLURE, KIRSTIE. 1992. 'On the Subject of Rights: Pluralism, Plurality, and

Political Identity', in Chantal Mouffe (ed.), *Dimensions of Radical Democracy*. London: Verso, 108–27.

McGINNIS, MICHAEL (ed.), 1998. *Bioregionalism*. London: Routledge.

MacINTYRE, ALASDAIR. 1988. *Whose Justice? Which Rationality?* Notre Dame, Ind.: University of Notre Dame Press.

McKELVEY, RICHARD D. 1976. 'Intransitivities in Multidimensional Voting Models and Some Implications for Agenda Control', *Journal of Economic Theory*, 12: 472–82.

MACKIE, GERRY. 1995. 'Models of Democratic Deliberation'. Paper presented to the Annual Meeting of the American Political Science Association, Chicago.

—— 1996. 'Science Against Democracy: The Aggregation Model'. Unpublished paper, University of Chicago

—— 1998. 'All Men are Liars: Is Deliberation Meaningless?' in Jon Elster (ed.), *Deliberative Democracy*. New York: Cambridge University Press, 97–122.

MANIN, BERNARD. 1987. 'On Legitimacy and Political Deliberation', *Political Theory*, 15: 338–68.

MASTERS, ROGER D. 1989. *The Nature of Politics*. New Haven: Yale University Press.

MATHEWS, FREYA. 1991a. *The Ecological Self*. Savage, Md.: Barnes and Noble.

—— 1991b. 'Democracy and the Ecological Crisis', *Legal Service Bulletin*, 16 (4): 157–9.

MEADOWS, DONELLA H., DENNIS L. MEADOWS, JORGEN RANDERS, and WILLIAM H. BEHRENS III. 1972. *The Limits to Growth*. New York: Universe Books.

MELCHIOR, JOSEPH. 1998. 'Is a Transnational Political Community Possible? Nation-State Legacies and European Perspectives'. Paper presented at the meeting of the American Political Science Association, Boston.

MELUCCI, ALBERTO. 1989. *Nomads of the Present: Social Movements and Individual Needs in Contemporary Society*. Philadelphia: Temple University Press.

MILL, JOHN STUART. 1962 [1835]. 'Tocqueville on Democracy in America', in Gertrude Himmelfarb (ed.), *John Stuart Mill, Essays on Politics and Culture*. New York: Doubleday, 171–213.

MILLER, DAVID. 1992. 'Deliberative Democracy and Social Choice', *Political Studies* 40 (special issue): 54–67.

—— 1995. *On Nationality*. Oxford: Oxford University Press.

—— 1999. 'Is Deliberative Democracy Unfair to Disadvantaged Minorities?' Unpublished paper, Nuffield College, Oxford.

MOUFFE, CHANTAL. 1996. 'Democracy, Power, and the "Political" ' in Seyla Benhabib (ed.), *Democracy and Difference: Contesting the Boundaries of the Political*. Princeton: Princeton University Press, 245–56.

NIÑO, CARLOS. 1996. *The Constitution of Deliberative Democracy*. New Haven: Yale University Press.

NUSSBAUM, MARTHA CRAVEN. 1996. 'Aristotle on Emotions and Rational Persuasion', in Amélie Oksenberg Rorty (ed.), *Essays on Aristotle's Rhetoric.* Berkeley: University of California Press.

O'CONNOR, JAMES. 1973. *The Fiscal Crisis of the State.* New York: St. Martin's.

—— 1984. *Accumulation Crisis.* Oxford: Basil Blackwell.

O'NEILL, JOHN. 1998. 'Deliberation and its Discontents'. Unpublished manuscript, University of Lancaster.

OFFE, CLAUS. 1984. *Contradictions of the Welfare State.* Cambridge, Mass.: MIT Press.

—— 1985. 'New Social Movements: Challenging the Boundaries of Institutional Politics', *Social Research,* 52: 817–68.

—— 1990. 'Reflections on the Institutional Self-Transformation of Movement Politics: A Tentative Stage Model', in Russell J. Dalton and Manfred Kuechler (eds.), *Challenging the Political Order: New Social Movements in Western Democracies.* Cambridge: Polity.

—— 1997. 'Micro-Aspects of Democratic Theory: What Makes for the Deliberative Competence of Citizens?' in Axel Hadenius (ed.), *Democracy's Victory and Crisis.* Cambridge: Cambridge University Press, 81–104.

PAEHLKE, ROBERT. 1988. 'Democracy, Bureaucracy, and Environmentalism', *Environmental Ethics,* 10: 291–308.

—— 1995. 'Environmental Values for a Sustainable Society: The Democratic Challenge', in Frank Fischer and Michael Black (eds.), *Greening Environmental Policy.* New York: St. Martin's, 129–44.

PATAI, DAPHNE, and NORETTA KOERTGE. 1994. *Professing Feminism: Cautionary Tales from the Strange World of Women's Studies.* New York: Basic Books.

PATTEN, BERNARD C., and EUGENE P. ODUM. 1981. 'The Cybernetic Nature of Ecosystems', *American Naturalist,* 118: 886–95.

PEKKARINEN, JUKKA, MATTI POHJOLA, and BOB ROWTHORN. 1992. *Social Corporatism: A Superior Economic System?* Oxford: Oxford University Press.

PHILLIPS, ANNE. 1993. *Democracy and Difference.* University Park: Pennsylvania State University Press.

—— 1995. *The Politics of Presence.* Oxford: Oxford University Press.

PITKIN, HANNAH FENICHEL. 1967. *The Concept of Representation.* Berkeley: University of California Press.

PIVEN, FRANCES FOX, and RICHARD A. CLOWARD. 1971. *Regulating the Poor: The Functions of Public Welfare.* New York: Random House.

PLUMWOOD, VAL. 1995. 'Has Democracy Failed Ecology?' *Environmental Politics,* 4: 134–68.

—— 1998. 'Inequality, Ecojustice, and Ecological Rationality', in John S. Dryzek and David Schlosberg (eds.), *Debating the Earth: The Environmental Politics Reader.* Oxford: Oxford University Press, 559–83.

POGGE, THOMAS W. 1992. 'Cosmopolitanism and Sovereignty', *Ethics*, 103: 48–75.

—— 1997. 'How to Create Supra-National Institutions Democratically: Some Reflections on the European Union's Democratic Deficit', *Journal of Political Philosophy*, 5: 163–82.

PRZEWORSKI, ADAM. 1991. *Democracy and the Market: Political and Economic Reforms in Eastern Europe and Latin America*. Cambridge: Cambridge University Press.

—— 1998. 'Deliberation and Ideological Domination', in Jon Elster (ed.), *Deliberative Democracy*. New York: Cambridge University Press, 140–60.

—— and John Sprague. 1986. *Paper Stones: A History of Electoral Socialism*. Chicago: University of Chicago Press.

RAWLS, JOHN. 1987. 'The Idea of an Overlapping Consensus', *Oxford Journal of Legal Studies*, 7: 1–25.

—— 1989. 'The Domain of the Political and Overlapping Consensus'. *New York University Law Review*, 64: 233–55.

—— 1993. *Political Liberalism*. New York: Columbia University Press.

—— 1997. 'The Idea of Public Reason Revisited', *University of Chicago Law Review*, 94: 765–807.

REHG, WILLIAM. 1997. 'Reason and Rhetoric in Habermas's Theory of Argumentation', in Walter Jost and Michael Hyde (eds.), *Rhetoric and Hermeneutics in Our Time*. New Haven: Yale University Press, 358–77.

REMER, GARY. 1998. 'Deliberative Democracy, Rhetoric, and the Ratification of the Constitution: The Case of the Massachusetts Debates'. Paper presented at the conference of the American Political Science Association, Boston, 3–6 September.

RIKER, WILLIAM H. 1982. *Liberalism Against Populism: A Confrontation Between the Theory of Democracy and the Theory of Social Choice*. San Francisco: Freeman.

RORTY, RICHARD. 1983. 'Post-Modernist Bourgeois Liberalism', *Journal of Philosophy*, 80: 583–9.

—— 1989. *Contingency, Irony, and Solidarity*. Cambridge: Cambridge University Press.

—— 1998. *Achieving Our Country: Leftist Thought in Twentieth Century America*. Cambridge, Mass.: Harvard University Press.

ROSENAU, JAMES N. 1992. 'Governance, Order, and Change in World Politics', in James N. Rosenau and Ernst-Otto Czempiel (eds.), *Governance Without Government: Order and Change in World Politics*. New York: Cambridge University Press, 1–29.

—— 1998. 'Governance and Democracy in a Globalizing World', in Daniele Archibugi, David Held, and Martin Köhler (eds.), *Re-Imagining Political Community: Studies in Cosmopolitan Democracy*. Cambridge: Polity, 28–57.

ROSENBLUM, NANCY L. 1998. *Membership and Morals: The Personal Uses of Pluralism in America*. Princeton: Princeton University Press.

RUCHT, DIETER. 1990. 'The Strategies and Action Repertoires of New Movements', in Russell J. Dalton and Manfred Kuechler (eds.), *Challenging the Political Order: New Social and Political Movements in Western Democracies*. Cambridge: Polity.

RUESCHEMEYER, DIETRICH, EVELYN HUBER STEPHENS, and JOHN D. STEPHENS. 1992. *Capitalist Development and Democracy*. Chicago: University of Chicago Press.

RUFFINS, PAUL. 1992. 'Defining a Movement and Community', *Crossroads/ Forward Motion* 11.

RUGGIE, JOHN. 1992. 'Multilateralism: The Anatomy of an Institution', *International Organization* 46: 561–98.

SALKEVER, STEPHEN. 1998. 'The Deliberative Model of Democracy and Aristotle's Ethics of Natual Questions'. Paper presented at the annual meeting of the American Political Science Association, Boston.

SANDERS, LYNN. 1997. 'Against Deliberation', *Political Theory*, 25: 347–76.

SAWARD, MICHAEL. 1992. *Co-optive Politics and State Legitimacy*. Aldershot: Dartmouth.

—— 1993. 'Green Democracy?' in Andrew Dobson and Paul Lucardie (eds.), *The Politics of Nature: Explorations in Green Political Theory*. London: Routledge.

—— 1998. *The Terms of Democracy*. Cambridge: Polity.

SCHLOSBERG, DAVID. 1995. 'Communicative Action in Practice: Intersubjectivity and New Social Movements', *Political Studies*, 43: 291–311.

—— 1998. 'Resurrecting the Pluralist Universe', *Political Research Quarterly*, 51: 583–615.

—— 1999. *Environmental Justice and the New Pluralism: The Challenge of Difference for Environmentalism*. Oxford: Oxford University Press.

SCHMIDHEINY, STEPHAN. 1992. *Changing Course: A Global Business Perspective on Development and the Environment*. Cambridge, Mass.: MIT Press.

SCHMITTER, PHILIPPE C. 1992. 'The Irony of Modern Democracy and Efforts to Improve its Practice', *Politics and Society*, 20: 505–12.

—— and GERHARD LEHMBRUCH (eds.), 1979. *Trends Toward Corporatist Intermediation*. Beverly Hills, Calif.: Sage.

SCRUGGS, LYLE A. 1999. 'Institutions and Environmental Performance in Seventeen Western Democracies', *British Journal of Political Science*, 29.

SELZNICK, PHILIP. 1966 [1949]. *TVA and the Grass Roots: A Study in the Sociology of Formal Organization*. New York: Harper and Row.

SHAPIRO, IAN, 1996. *Democracy's Place*. Ithaca, NY: Cornell University Press.

SHIVA, VANDANA. 1997. *Biopiracy: The Plunder of Nature and Knowledge*. Boston: South End Press.

SKOCPOL, THEDA. 1979. *States and Social Revolutions*. Cambridge: Cambridge University Press.

—— 1985. 'Bringing the State Back In: Strategies of Analysis in Current Research', in Peter B. Evans, Dietrich Rueschemeyer, and Theda Skocpol (eds.), *Bringing the State Back In*. Cambridge: Cambridge University Press, 3–37.

SMITH, GRAHAM, and CORINNE WALES. 1999. 'Toward Deliberative Institutions: Lessons from Citizens' Juries'. Paper presented at the Workshops of the European Consortium for Political Research, Mannheim, Germany.

SMITH, STEVE. 1986. 'Reasons of State', in David Held and Christopher Pollitt (eds.), *New Forms of Democracy*. London: Sage, 192–217.

SPRAGENS, THOMAS. 1990. *Reason and Democracy*. Durham, NC: Duke University Press.

STROM, Gerald S. 1990. *The Logic of Lawmaking: A Spatial Theory Approach*. Baltimore, Md.: Johns Hopkins University Press.

SUNSTEIN, CASS. 1993*a*. *The Partial Constitution*. Cambridge, Mass.: Harvard University Press.

—— 1993*b*. *Democracy and the Problem of Free Speech*. New York: Free Press.

—— 1997. 'Deliberation, Democracy, Disagreement', in Ron Bontekoe and Marietta Stepaniants (eds.), *Justice and Democracy: Cross-Cultural Perspectives*. Honolulu: University of Hawai'i Press, 93–117.

TARROW, SIDNEY. 1994. *Power in Movement: Social Movements, Collective Action and Politics*. Cambridge: Cambridge University Press.

TESH, SYLVIA N. 1993. 'New Social Movements and New Ideas'. Paper presented at the Annual Meeting of the American Political Science Association, Washington, DC, 2–5 September.

THOMPSON, DENNIS. 1999. 'Democratic Theory and Global Society', *Journal of Political Philosophy*, 7: 111–25.

TILLY, CHARLES, LOUISE TILLY, and RICHARD TILLY. 1975. *The Rebellious Century, 1830–1930*. Cambridge, Mass.: Harvard University Press.

TORGERSON, DOUGLAS. 1990. 'Limits of the Administrative Mind: The Problem of Defining Environmental Problems', in Robert Paehlke and Douglas Torgerson (eds.), *Managing Leviathan: Environmental Politics and the Administrative State*. Peterborough, Ontario: Broadview, 115–61.

—— 1995. 'The Uncertain Quest for Sustainability: Public Discourse and the Politics of Environmentalism', in Frank Fischer and Michael Black (eds.), *Greening Environmental Policy: The Politics of a Sustainable Future*. Liverpool: Paul Chapman, 3–20.

TRUMAN, DAVID B. 1951. *The Governmental Process: Political Interests and Public Opinion*. New York: Knopf.

UHR, JOHN. 1998. *Deliberative Democracy in Australia*. Melbourne: Cambridge University Press.

VANBERG, VIKTOR, and JAMES M. BUCHANAN. 1989. 'Interest and Theories in Constitutional Choice', *Journal of Theoretical Politics*, 1: 49–62.

VAN MILL, DAVID. 1996. 'The Possibility of Rational Outcomes from Democratic Discourse and Procedures', *Journal of Politics*, 58: 734–52.

VOGEL, STEVEN. 1997. 'Habermas and the Ethics of Nature', in Roger Gottlieb (ed.), *The Ecological Community: Environmental Challenges for Philosophy, Politics, and Morality.* New York: Routledge, 175–92.

WAINWRIGHT, HILARY. 1994. *Arguments for a New Left: Answering the Free-Market Right.* Oxford: Basil Blackwell.

WALTZ, KENNETH. 1979. *Theory of International Politics.* Reading, Mass.: Addison-Wesley.

WALZER, MICHAEL. 1991. 'Constitutional Rights and the Shape of Civil Society', in Robert E. Calvert (ed.), *The Constitution of the People: Reflections on Citizens and Civil Society.* Lawrence: University Press of Kansas.

—— 1994. 'Multiculturalism and Individualism', *Dissent*, 41: 185–91.

WAPNER, PAUL. 1996. *Environmental Activism and World Civic Politics.* Albany, NY: State University of New York Press.

WARREN, MARK. 1992. 'Democratic Theory and Self-Transformation', *American Political Science Review*, 86: 8–23.

WEALE, ALBERT. 1992. *The New Politics of Pollution.* Manchester: Manchester University Press.

WELSH, MICHAEL. 2000. 'Towards a Theory of Discursive Environmental Policy Making: The Case of Public Range Management'. Unpublished Ph.D. dissertation, Department of Political Science, University of Oregon.

WENDT, ALEXANDER. 1992. 'Anarchy is What States Make of It: The Social Construction of Power Politics', *International Organization*, 46: 391–425.

WHITE, STEPHEN K. 1988. *The Recent Work of Jürgen Habermas: Reason, Justice and Modernity.* Cambridge: Cambridge University Press.

WIESENTHAL, HELMUT. 1993. *Realism in Green Politics: Social Movements and Ecological Reform in Germany.* New York: St. Martin's.

WORSTER, DONALD. 1985. *Nature's Economy: A History of Ecological Ideas.* Cambridge: Cambridge University Press.

YOUNG, IRIS MARION. 1989. 'Polity and Group Difference: A Critique of the Ideal of Universal Citizenship', *Ethics*, 99: 250–74.

—— 1990. *Justice and the Politics of Difference.* Princeton: Princeton University Press.

—— 1992. 'Social Groups in Associative Democracy', *Politics and Society*, 20: 529–34.

—— 1996. 'Communication and the Other: Beyond Deliberative Democracy', in Seyla Benhabib (ed.), *Democracy and Difference: Contesting the Boundaries of the Political.* Princeton: Princeton University Press, 120–35.

—— 1997. 'Difference as a Resource for Democratic Communication', in James Bohman and William Rehg (eds.), *Deliberative Democracy.* Cambridge, Mass.: MIT Press, 383–406.

—— 1998. 'Inclusive Political Communication: Greeting, Rhetoric and Storytelling in the Context of Political Argument'. Paper presented at the Annual Meeting of the American Political Science Association, Boston.

YOUNG, ORAN R. 1994. *International Governance: Protecting the Environment in a Stateless Society.* Ithaca, NY: Cornell University Press.

ZOLO, DANILO. 1997. *Cosmopolis: Prospects for World Government.* Cambridge: Polity.

INDEX